A FANTASY OF FAR JAPAN

By Viscount Kencho Suematsu
Cover Design by Alex Struik

ISBN-13: 978-1479270392

ISBN-10: 1479270393

LE SAMURAI

C'était un homme à deux sabres.

D'un doigt distrait frôlant la sonore bîva,
A travers les bambous tressés en fine latte,
Elle a vu, par la plage éblouissante et plate,
S'avancer le vainqueur que son amour rêva.

C'est lui. Sabres au flanc, l'éventail haut, il va.
La cordelière rouge et le gland écarlate
Coupent l'armure sombre, et, sur l'épaule, éclate
Le blason de Hizen et de Tokugawa.

Ce beau guerrier vêtu de lames et de plaques
Sous le bronze, la soie et les brillantes laques
Semble un crustacé noir, gigantesque et vermeil.

Il l'a vue. Il sourit dans la barbe du masque,
Et son pas plus hâtif fait reluire au soleil
Les deux antennes d'or qui tremblent à son casque.

JOSÉ-MARIA DE HEREDIA.

PREFACE

In the following pages I have depicted certain Japanese ideals and notions, as well as some historical facts which seemed likely to interest those of the sympathetic Western public who may be inclined to study the mental side of Japan.

The dialogues are founded upon actual conversations, not indeed always in exactly the same phraseology, nor under exactly the same circumstances, but something very like. The questions put into the mouths of the characters in the book are the kind of questions which are being constantly put to me, and my answers are always on the same lines; so that my readers may regard the book as a serious treatise so far as the materials are concerned. This is the reason why I have written this book in a light, conversational style, and not in the form of an ordinary critical or expository treatise. Besides, I thought that more lucidity of exposition and more penetration into the inner views could be achieved by writing in the way I have done.

The period to which these conversations relate is chiefly the summer of the present year, 1905, and the greater part of this book was written before peace was concluded, and therefore there may be occasionally some dicta which sound somewhat polemic. On that point I can request my readers to show leniency.

I have appended to the dialogues a few papers on various subjects. They deal with subjects germane to those treated in the body of the work, and it is hoped that they will afford the reader first aid in acquiring information relative to the analysis of Japanese social life which has here, however imperfectly, been attempted.

I may add a few words. In publishing this volume, I am not in the least degree actuated by a desire to exalt my country unduly,—still less to boast about her achievements. My sole object has been to show Japan as she is, and to claim Occidental sympathy to such a degree as she may deserve.

K.S.

PARIS, November 1905.

Contents

I

It was a cool summer afternoon in a quiet hotel in a quiet part of Paris. I threw myself lazily into an easy-chair on the balcony and began reading Le Journal. I was somewhat tired and soon felt myself drowsily wandering into dreamland as the breeze lulled me soothingly. I felt myself, as it were, wafted through the air. Soon I found myself in the company of a friend of mine and his wife, though I do not know how all that came about. We passed together through the Bois de Boulogne, now amidst tall, green forests, now along the turfy shores of mirror-like lakes. We arrived at last before the entrance of a large house. It was the residence of the Duke of Fairfield. His wife, the Duchess of Fairfield, is a star in Parisian society and a great hostess. Her salon is periodically filled with politicians, savants, great artists, and the most fashionable ladies and belles of the day. Her forte is politics, and indeed she is no mean politician in her way. It was in that lady's drawing-room that we in no time found ourselves.

−'I am so glad that you were able to come here to-day,' said the duchess. 'I was very anxious to make your acquaintance, and so asked your friend to bring you. I have known you long by "interviews" and articles. We all read them with delight. They are read on the Continent far more than you imagine.'

−'Don't mention it, madam,' said I. 'It is a great honour, I feel, to have access here. As to my articles, I am highly flattered to hear they have any interest for you.'

There were already many people in the salon. I was naturally introduced to some of the ladies and gentlemen present. In a few moments I found myself talking with the duchess on some questions of the day.

−She said, 'Some people foresaw, even before the war had began, what the issue would be. General Penetrator, for instance, I learned a good deal from him,—and also from my own observations.'

−'May I add,' said I, 'General Foresight also? I have heard some incidents about him quite lately. But I am glad to see you take so much interest in our affairs.'

−'No!' said the duchess, 'they are not exclusively your affairs. We are also much concerned in the matter, as you know. But let us stop a moment. Baron,—won't you have a cup of tea? Do take one.'

−'If you please.'

The duchess had already risen and was proceeding towards a table where the tea was laid out. I stood up also and followed her, saying, 'Allow me, madam, I will help myself, I'm troubling you too much'; but the duchess taking no notice of my words prepared a cup of tea and gave it to me where I stood; she was assisted by one of her daughters who offered me some cakes. I noticed that the tea was poured out of a pot made in the shape of a beautiful waterfowl, its beak forming the spout.

—'It is very artistic,' I said, pointing to the tea-pot.

—'It is Japanese ware,' said the duchess. 'This kind of ware is, I suppose, only made for the foreign markets, and not used in Japan, and so probably you have not seen it before. We think it rather nice. You see our taste has little depth.'

—'Well! madam, I must apologise to you for carelessly expressing approbation of an article coming from my own country. I would not have done so if I had carefully examined it and had made sure that it was Japanese, but it certainly looks charming.'

We sat down again and resumed our conversation.

—'Do you read our papers much?' said the duchess.

—'Not much, madam, only those parts which interest me particularly—the war, for instance.'

—'Then you speak French, of course,' said she.

—'Only a very, very little, madam, and unless spoken very slowly, I do not understand at all,' I replied. 'People in society generally do not care to take that trouble.'

−'Very true, indeed,' she said, 'one often forgets that one is speaking to a foreigner while actually doing so. But what do you think of our papers?'

−'They seem generally good,' I answered, 'though not perhaps as good as those of England, for there, far more money is spent in obtaining good items of news from all parts of the world. But this is too trite, I think, to speak to you about.'

−'I am sorry for it,' she said, 'but I must say that most of our journals appear not to have done sufficient justice to your country, in regard to the present war.'

−'To be frank, madam, I must say that they generally were not quite fair. I am afraid they have done more harm than good to the country which they meant to befriend, for if they had not given so much encouragement to that country, much misfortune which has overtaken it might have been evaded or at least lessened. It may have been only due to a pacing mistake. The press is much better now, and is beginning to represent more truthfully the sentiment of the people, I think.'

−'It is very true,' she said; 'at the same time, I must say that the aggressive attitude of that country could not have been created by our journals, however partial they may have been. In that respect, there may be another country which is more responsible.'

All the while other guests and members of the house were carrying on conversation in a very lively manner, in twos, threes, or fours.

—'But, baron, what do you think of the present political situation?' she said. 'What is the real sentiment of England?'

—'You must know such things better than I. To me, however, it seems England is perfectly sincere in her good wishes towards France. She has no arrière pensée.'

—'But some people say she wants war with our neighbour,' said she.

—'No! decidedly not,' I said. 'I know there are many people in England who have no confidence in German policy; but "want war," "provoke war," decidedly not!'

—'That's my opinion too,' said she quickly.

Hereupon a few gentlemen joined in our discussion. We went over the international situation of the day from many points, with many hypotheses and conjectures. We thought the discussion both interesting and beneficial; the trend of the conversation naturally turned upon the bearing of the international relationship in the Far East. A rumour recently circulated was mentioned by one of those present, to the effect that German policy was to draw France into some sort of 'combination' similar to that which took place after the Sino-Japanese war. A gentleman who is senator and an ex-minister said that it was, of course, necessary to watch what the Premier was going to do, but that he trusted the Premier would not be so imprudent. If ever, he added, he were to be drawn into such an unjust and imprudent action, he would at once revolt all statesmen, indeed all the French public, and, moreover, the rumour was more likely unfounded than true. To this opinion all present expressed an assent.

At this point some more visitors arrived, and the duchess left us to welcome them. I also rose, and slowly went into the next room, which was the study of the duke, but its sliding door was opened and formed with the drawing-room one long salon. The other daughter—the duchess has two daughters only, and no sons—was there, together with a few young folk. She observed me at once, and we were soon talking together. There was a book lying on a table beside us. Opening it at random, a picture of a warrior appeared before us.

—'It is Condé,' she said.

—'Yes, so I see,' I replied; 'he was a great general. I admire him very much. His splendid career, which I read many years ago in history, is still vividly impressed on my memory!'

—'And Jeanne d'Arc too, I suppose,' she said.

—'Of course, mademoiselle.'

—'Women sometimes do fine things, don't they! but Japan is a country of heroes and heroines.'

—'I dare say, but Jeanne d'Arc especially appeals to one's imagination.'

—'I admire your Bushido so much,' said she.

—'Do you? I am glad to hear you say so.'

Looking up, my eyes caught sight of many pictures hanging on the walls: for the most part they seemed family portraits, and most of them men in military uniform. I was tempted to make some observations, and unconsciously stood up to approach nearer to them. She followed my example and walked by my side. Pointing to them, one after another, she told me this was her grandfather, that her great-grandfather, these were this one's sons or daughters, those that one's, etc. Amongst them, no doubt, there were some who had done noble service for their country; that fact was evident from the pedigree of her family. But, unlike ordinary people, she had neither the necessity nor desire to glorify her ancestors, but for my part I wished she had explained a little more of their history. Finally, she pointed out a picture as that of her mother, saying she did not like it, and that it did not resemble her.

−'Why not? One cannot expect a portrait to be like the original at every stage of life,' I remarked.

−'No! I did not mean exactly in that way,' she answered.

We were now at the end of the room leading on to a balcony. We stepped on to it. I leaned on the railing; she stood not far off from me. The garden was not very large, but neat and clean. Now I looked down at the garden, now I turned towards Lady Modestina, which is her Christian name, exchanging some remarks about flowers and trees. Her sister now joined us coming forth from the drawing-room. Dulciana is her name. Our conversation somehow or other turned on works of fiction.

−'Do you read fiction much, baron?' asked Lady Dulciana.

−'No; not much. But I have read nearly all Beaconsfield.'

−'I understand,' said she, 'his books are always full of spirit and aspiration. Incidents d'amour are only secondary, and that suits your taste, I suppose—I mean, your countrymen in general.'

−'Just so, the majority of our works of fiction are stories of heroic characters—stories of the Alroy type, perhaps, with a little more definite morals, and something more of loyalty or patriotism.'

−'I can understand that, too, from what I have heard and seen of late,' said she.

−'But have you not in your country,' interposed Lady Modestina, 'any works of fiction solely based on romantic incidents? Western fictions are, I am afraid, too full of such.'

−'Well, we also have one kind of literature which may be called "love stories." They are mostly written in an easy style, more for the less educated portion of the public.'

−'Are they read much?' she asked.

−'Not very much,' I answered; 'with us those books do not hold a high position.'

−'And the plots. What are they like?' she asked.

−'Perhaps you know,' I answered, 'we have had certain customs which resembled those of Greece and Rome. Consequently the plots of such books, like the Greek and Roman comedies, are much influenced by those customs and do not suit the tastes of modern refinement.'

14

—'Am I too curious if I ask the nature of those customs and manners?'

—'Oh no! In Greece and Rome there was, perhaps you know, a certain class of females called Hetaira, also a class of males called parasites. They mixed pretty freely with men of good standing, and, of course, are not to be judged by the same standard as the disreputable of modern days. In Japan, also, there existed an almost identical class. I am referring to those females known to the occidental races by the name of Geishas, and the men we call Taiko-Mochi, i.e. 'tam-bour,' though the latter were comparatively few in number. The chief profession of the Geisha was music. Indeed, the books I have just referred to are peopled with this class. Novelists in those days were never recognised as legitimate literati, and were quite content to be associated with the so-called town people, and to write chiefly about their surroundings. The very condition of the higher classes supplied but few subjects for romance, and the altered social conditions of present-day Japan clearly shows the reason why their works do not suit the modern taste.'

—'I suppose that sort of people, I mean the class resembling those of Greece and Rome, exists no more.'

—'Yes, they still exist. The modern Geisha, as a rule, are the same in kind, but not in quality. In the days gone by, that is, during the feudal period, social discipline was very rigid, and the occasional adventures of those people were regarded as good subjects for Romancers, whilst the modern ones are far too degraded—they have either no romance, or too much, to be made the subject of romance. Excuse my telling you such things, I only do so from a sociological point of view.'

−'Science will cry out, if you make use of her name in such a place.'

−'Never mind, but listen! The fiction written in the new era differs, widely differs, in the selection of subjects, from that of the old. Only remember! Even those books, I mean the old love stories, portrayed a great deal of female chivalry and heroism. Indeed, a spirit of chivalry was the forte of the period. I can tell you, if you like, one plot which I recollect.'

−'Do, please.'

−'There was a young Samurai, X., and a maiden, Y., who loved each other. They were not decreed by fate to marry. X., the young Samurai, was the second son of his father, and, therefore, not the heir. He was adopted by another Samurai, and eventually marries Z., the daughter of the house. Now, in Japan adoption is, as it was with the Romans, a common custom; it was more so in days gone by. This was natural enough because, apart from other reasons, every Samurai was a retainer of a feudal lord from whom he received a certain allowance annually for his services, and his family depended upon him. In default of a male heir, the house, in other words the family, lost every privilege and emolument. The succession, however, could be made good by an heir, adopted from a blood relation, or even from a totally strange family. On the other hand, the second or third son of a Samurai had no legal status as a Samurai, and was vulgarly called "Cold Rice Meals" or "Back Room Resident." Personal service of a Samurai house to its lord was only required of its head. Succession of Samurai—the title as well as emolument—was according to primogeniture, and, therefore, a second or third son could scarcely get a livelihood, unless adopted by another Samurai, or unless a totally different kind of profession be adopted, or else he was made, by some lord, head of a new Samurai house, by virtue of some well-merited distinction, which was a matter of rare occurrence. Well, X. was adopted by the family of Z., his future wife according to that custom.

'Misfortune fell upon the family of Y., the maiden, and she became a Geisha, an actress, if you like, not from levity on her part, but from a sense of duty, which caused her to sacrifice herself to the occupation just mentioned—a sentiment which is unintelligible in the West. The story proceeds to narrate how X., the young Samurai, and Y., his former sweetheart, meet each other after a long lapse of time by pure accident, and how their love of days gone by revived in their hearts, especially from the pity which the young Samurai felt for her misfortune and her corresponding responsiveness. Further, how the young Samurai began to neglect his official duties and to incur the displeasure of the councillors of his lord, and was on the brink of becoming a Ronin—a masterless Samurai, the greatest shame of a Samurai, if incurred by his own dishonourable conduct.

'In those days, it must be remembered, the moral discipline of the Samurai was very rigid. The conduct of our young Samurai involved not only the ruin of himself but also the destruction of the family as a Samurai, a matter most lamentable to the house of a knight. At last Z., the despairing wife, takes the matter very seriously to heart, not so much from jealousy as from a sense of duty to her house and a desire to save her lord and husband from disgrace. She forms a bold plan, and personally visits her rival to obtain her confidence. She persuades her, not by any vulgar quarrel, but by serious reasoning and rational appeal, to put a stop to all connection with her husband. The rival assents and gives her promise. Then comes the climax. After a great struggle between love and reason, and hampered by several circumstances which made her unable to fulfil her promise, the rival puts an end to her own life, committing jigai, which is equivalent to Seppuku—vulgarly called Harakiri—in the case of a man, leaving some touching and well-meant letters behind her. What became of the young Samurai and his wife after that I scarcely need to relate here. Such, then, is the kind of plot we find in that class of books.'

While discoursing in this strain, a young lady—an English maiden—joined us.

−'Your plot seems not altogether like ours,' said the English lady. 'I dare say you have read some of our everyday novels?'

−'Well, I have read some, but it is now so many years ago that I do not remember them, with one exception, and that is Jane Eyre. Years ago I read some chapters of it, and those are enough. The general contents of those chapters remained ever in my memory. A little time ago I was staying at Folkestone. One gloomy afternoon, when I was intent over many things, that memory recurred to me all of a sudden. I went to a bookseller and bought a copy of the book: I read through once more some of the earlier chapters, and it created a great impression on me.'

−'What caused that impression, I should like to know?' interposed Lady Modestina.

−'Well, I cannot explain the reason very well,' I answered.

—'I can see it very well,' said the English lady; 'you are too proud to explain the reason,' Turning to the Ladies Modestina and Dulciana, she continued. 'Perhaps you have not read, or do not remember well, the story of our English novel. The story is this: Jane Eyre, a young girl, suffers every torture in the house of her uncle at the hands of young John Reed and his sisters, and indeed of Mrs. Reed also. You know Jane Eyre was the orphan child of a sister of Mr. Reed. He had taken her into his family in order to bring her up with his own children. He died some time after, enjoining his wife on his deathbed to look after her kindly. You see, therefore, though Jane Eyre was not properly a member of the family, some of the same blood ran in her veins as in theirs. In spite of that fact, and in spite of the injunction of Mr. Reed, her uncle, and, above all, in spite of all the modesty and good behaviour she showed, Jane was tormented by every member of the family. That is no doubt the point which has impressed the baron so much to think of——'

—'Perhaps,' I said smilingly.

—'Never mind, baron, Jane was of strong enough character to emerge from the trouble, and so will Japan, in spite of all the calumnies, if indeed she has not done so already.'

At this point a bustle was heard in another part of the room. Lady Modestina cast her eyes in that direction and said: 'Here comes a lady, a friend of ours, a star in our society, we think much of her—I must go to her.' And as she was moving away slowly, remarked to me, 'I will introduce you to her.' To which I replied, 'I shall be delighted.'

We went together towards the lady mentioned, to whom I was duly introduced. She was the Marchioness de

Vivastine, and was extremely beautiful, looking far younger than her age must be, for I afterwards heard that she is the mother of a married daughter.

Her face was covered by a veil, but her round and brilliant eyes sparkled through it. Her beauty, however, was not the point of my appreciation, but her vivacity and frankness. I soon entered into conversation with her. She spoke fluently and unhesitatingly. We commenced to speak on art.

—'I admire Japanese art very highly: it is so natural and vivid, flowers and animals and what-not.'

—'May be, but our human figures are very bad,' said I.

—'Perhaps so,' said she, 'in the later productions, but not in antique works. I think there has been no nation which has produced such striking representation of nature as your country. Curiously enough, one sometimes notices very close representations of nature in the carvings or the inscriptions of very primitive tribes. Don't misunderstand me. I do not mean that yours are of that kind.'

—'You must be, madam, very well acquainted with our arts. Whence have you acquired that taste?'

—'From the time of the last Great Exhibition here, when your country sent so many valuable specimens of art.'

—'You must yourself be an artist. I can see it from your observations.'

—'Yes, she is an artist, although an amateur,' interposed Lady Modestina.

−'No, don't say that,' interrupted the marchioness.

−'I dare say you paint much,' said I.

−'No, not at all,' replied the marchioness, and continued as she laughed slightly, 'except, perhaps, that I used to paint occasionally my own portrait, of course after the style of the chef-d'œuvre of your "literary picture" in the faintest and lightest colours. By the way, I also like Japanese methods of gardening. I once had a Japanese gardener for three years at my country seat.'

−'Really,' said I, 'you interest me very much.'

−'He was very clever; far more so than any European, any Frenchman, in the same calling of life could ever possibly be.'

−'With us,' said I, 'it is very common. Every gardener understands the ordinary art of "garden-making," though, of course, there are only a few real experts. But let me tell you that it comes more from the general atmosphere and surroundings in which they grow up. There is nothing surprising in it to our eyes.'

−'May be. But to us it seems extraordinary. After three years, during which he served me very faithfully, I transferred him to a Frenchman, Mr. Canny by name.'

−'Is that so? I have seen his Japanese gardens.'

−'Then you know him?'

−'Yes, I first came to know him when he visited my country some years ago. The other day I made a great circuit round Paris in his motor: we left Paris by the Bois, then St. Cloud, Versailles, on to Fontainebleau, making a large circuit through Cagny, Surveilliers, Beaumont, Pointoise, thus reaching St. Germain, thence on to St Cloud and back to Paris by the same route. We must have travelled three or four hundred kilometres.'

−'Then you must have passed through the forests of Fontainebleau. Are not the trees and rocks there splendid?'

−'Yes, that is just what struck me very much, but I am most interested to hear that you appreciate the value of natural rocks. They are very important elements in our Japanese gardens.'

−'I cannot understand how so great a number of rocks could have been heaped up there in that peculiar way. Some people imagine that at one time they formed the bottom of the sea.'

−'Oh! but if so, it must have been a very long time ago. At all events, before we came into existence,' said I, laughing, and added, 'I should like to get a concession from the government to take those rocks, because the time will certainly come when they will be wanted for French gardens, and perhaps I could then become a millionaire.'

Thereupon we all broke out into laughter. The marchioness still continued to talk on different subjects. She had no affectation: she said boldly just what she thought with all the sparkle of her intelligence. I tried not to be overwhelmed by her eloquence, and the consequence was

22

that we had a very heated discussion on the customs and manners of different countries. Reverting to Japan she said:

−'I hear one can marry for two months in Japan. Is that true?'

−'I beg your pardon?'
−'Well, that is what I have heard,' she said, 'from an acquaintance. He said that he himself had married when he was staying in Japan, having gone through the requisite wedding ceremony—partaking of saké cups with the bride.'

−'Well, madam,' I said, 'I must say it is possible. Nay, more than possible. I can go further and tell you that such things may occur even for much shorter times than that. But similar customs! Is it not the same all over the world?— even in Paris itself, I am afraid. However, I must say the nuptials of that particular kind are far less in number in my country than in most of the civilised countries.'

Thereupon she burst into great laughter, as also did the others, and she said:

−'I should like to hear something of your marriage ceremony. Is it a civil or religious one?'

−'Entirely civil, madam,' I replied. 'We hear now and then of people celebrating a religious marriage after the fashion of the West, but it is very rare, as rare as one or two stars in a cloudy sky.'

−'You seem to imitate the West in everything,' said she; 'but what I would like to know of is your national ceremony.'

−'Our marriage ceremony is a time-honoured one and entirely civil,' I said. 'There is always an officiating person or a witness or an assistant, if you like. He is the person who is responsible for the completion of a marriage. Generally he is the person who arranges the matter from the very beginning—I mean, from the time when the engagement is formally made between the parties and, therefore, he is called a Nakaodo, a middle-man, or a go-between, as you like. Even when all the preliminary arrangements have been made by a second person, and another person, for some reason, is preferred to officiate, the latter is called theoretically, or, as it were, officially, a Nakaodo, and he is considered as being responsible for all. A middle-man must be married, for his function must be shared by his wife, especially when the essential part of the ceremony is performed; besides, a bachelor or widower would never be considered a fit person for such an occasion. But do you mean to make me give you the whole history of a wedding?'

−'Of course! Your story is just beginning to be most interesting,' said she.

−'Very well! The ceremony is very elaborate and solemn, though the scale differs, or rather is magnified or simplified, according to circumstances. To begin with, when the engagement is formally made, certain presents called "Yuino" are at once exchanged simultaneously between the families of the bride and bridegroom elect— there are certain usages in the selection of these presents.'

−'What kind of things, for instance?' she asked.

−'A staff for ceremonial "onna-obi" (a sort of a broad sash for women) for the bride, and a staff for a ceremonial

24

"hakama" (a sort of long kilt) and an "otoko-obi" (a sort of sash for men) for the bridegroom. They are invariably accompanied by "noshi" and "katsuo."'

−'What are they?'

−'They are things which you have not got in Europe. One made of seaweed and the other of dried fish meat, but it is waste of time to describe them, for you would hardly realise them if I did so. Suffice it to say that they are of little value intrinsically, but they are used in Japan to signify felicity. Remember, practical people sometimes substitute cash and a list of presents: the conventionality of the world is apt to take this form. These presents correspond to your giving an engagement ring, only ours are more solemn and, moreover, not one-sided.'

−'And what next?'

−'Pray be patient. There is no fixed usage as to the length of the interval between the engagement and wedding, but some months usually intervene. Nevertheless, we are not so patient, like many Occidentals, as to let it stand over for many years. When the time which is convenient for both parties approaches, the date is fixed, a selection being made of a day of happy omen, as is also the case when the engagement presents are made. You see, there exists more or less a sort of superstition in every country.'

−'Let us suppose that day arrived. What takes place then?'

−'Wedding ceremonies are generally performed in the evening and at the house of the bridegroom. But remember, here again a restaurant or some other place is sometimes substituted for the residence, if the latter is not suitable for the occasion.'

—'Naturally.'

—'All the paraphernalia and suchlike of the bride are sent to her future home some days previously. They are generally packed up in boxes in such a way that each box can be carried on the shoulders of two persons by poles. They are not packed and sent by carts, as when moving the place of one's residence. The escort and carriers receive good tips on arriving at their destination, so that those who happen to perform that duty are only too glad to do so. The quantity and quality of the articles thus sent, of course, vary according to the conditions and positions of the parties.'

—'As ours do, I presume.'

—'But there are certain articles which are most usually prepared for the bride.'

—'As ours are also.'

—'Previously to the departure of the bride from her home, some entertainments are generally given to her near relations, intimate friends, and also to the servants for a farewell, or at least all the members of the family gather together and make some merriment. This generally takes place on the previous evening. On the day of her departure, the officiating person and his wife go to her parents' home and accompany her to her future home. Her parents, brothers, and sisters also accompany, nay more, all her near relations and those of the bridegroom also are invited, in order to be formally introduced to each other and be present at the wedding banquet. In China the character which means "to return" is generally used also to signify the act of a bride leaving her home and going to the home of her future husband to be married to him. The idea is that her future home, to which she is now going, is imagined to be her real home, where she is now going back, and she is not expected to return to her previous home for good, or rather for any permanent purpose, for such a thing is considered out of the question altogether. This notion is also the same with us Japanese; consequently in Samurai families the same formality as that of the departure of the dead is generally performed at the departure of the bride. I wonder if the Western custom of throwing slippers has any similar origin!'

−'Very likely!' the marchioness interposed.

−'And yet,' interrupted Lady Modestina, 'girls, and indeed young men, too, are compelled to marry without knowing and seeing each other at all before the wedding, as people say. Poor girls! Poor young men, too!'

'Not exactly,' I answered; 'remember, Napoleon and the Archduchess of Austria had never seen each other before her state entry into the French territory. The duchess, it is said, heaved deep sighs of relief at the first sight of Napoleon, who was not after all a monstrous creature, as she had fancied from the stories she had heard of the sanguinary battles he had fought everywhere. Such things—at least, similar things—often take place even in Europe. So with us, too, in former days, marriages of great feudal lords were generally not unlike Napoleon's second marriage. But with the people in general the matter was different. In these cases Miai, which literally means to see each other, was essential and almost the formal part of the ceremony. When "preliminary inquiries," so to say, had turned out satisfactory, the so-called seeing each other took

27

place, that is to say, a rendezvous was arranged in one way or the other, say, at a flower garden or a theatre, in such a manner that neither of the parties felt any discomfort, and it did not become an obligation to either of them. Remember there was nothing indiscreet in the affair, as both of the parties were always accompanied by some near relatives or trustworthy friends. In nuptial affairs, parental authority was much exercised, as in this country, it is true; but the power of vetoing was always reserved by the would-be bride, and still more by the bridegroom, especially after the rendezvous. It was, however, thought advisable that as full preliminary inquiries as possible should be made before the rendezvous, in order that one side might not inconsiderately disappoint the other.'

−'But what do you mean by preliminary inquiries?'

−'It means obtaining as much information as possible with regard to family affairs, family traditions, the character and attainments, even habits and tastes of the would-be bride or bridegroom as the case may be, and I dare say the faces also, even the number of the black spots on it.'

−'Please be serious.'

−'I don't think private detectives were employed, as in the Slater case.'

−'No joking, please.'

−'But nearly similar things used to be done. Friends and schoolmates, servants, ex-servants, teachers of music, jewellers, fishmongers, grocers, tailors, dress-makers, or anybody who had any connection with the family whatever, were one and all an object from whom as much information as possible was extracted directly or indirectly; above all, Mrs. Hairdresser, who knows such matters best. You know, our ladies arrange their hair in all sorts of very complicated forms, and hairdressers make it a regular profession, paying professional visits constantly to ladies' homes, and our ladies do not mind wasting time in such matters any more than their sisters of other countries.'

−'Please to the point.'

−'I am to the point. It was only after these inquiries that, to use a diplomatic phrase, pourparler for negotiations began. Of course all the inquiries were done by some one else on behalf of the would-be bride or bridegroom. They would certainly be too delicate for a girl of, say, "sweet seventeen," to carry them out for herself. Don't you agree with me on that point?'

−'Life is short. Please don't spin out webs too long. But how do matters stand nowadays?'

−'Much the same,' I replied. 'But in our own days society gives much more facility for young people to see and know each other. And I may add that nowadays photos play a great part in the first stage of the inquiries. They say photos are for studying physiognomy in order to discern the character and intellectual capabilities, but I am afraid it is also to study the looks as well, or rather chiefly. Human nature is weak after all.'

−'Still spinning out.'

−'Oh no! I am only giving out the essence.'

−'Let us then proceed with the ceremony.'

29

−'Very well, the essential part of the ceremony consists in the bride and bridegroom partaking saké cups, as you know, but perhaps not exactly as your acquaintance did,' said I teasingly. 'The room wherein that part of the ceremony is performed is kept sacred for the occasion. The bridegroom is led to that room by the officiating person, and the bride by his wife. In our rooms there is a small part, a little elevated, called Toko-no-ma (alcove): it is the place of honour in the room, and it is there that the Kakemono (hanging picture or writing) is hung—sometimes a single one, sometimes a pair, or a series of three. We do not hang up pictures all over the walls like a picture exhibition; and it is also there that we arrange flowers and plants in vases. The Kakemono would be the chosen ones having some signification of felicity. There are many subjects for such purposes, for instance, the landscape of the mythological island of Mount Horai, where immortals are said to reside, or cranes and long hair-tailed mythical tortoises, or the three twin plants of pine, plum, and bamboo. All of these objects are popularly viewed as emblems of longevity. The flowers or plants arranged in the vase for the occasion would also be of the same nature.'

−'And you have a special art in the arrangement of flowers, I understand, not as we do in the West by simply putting bunches into the vase without any discrimination.'

−'Just so!' I answered, 'and there would be a Shimadai on Toko-no-ma.'

−'What's that?'

−'Shimadai is a representation of the Mount Horai which I have just mentioned. In later days Jo-tom-ba, more correctly Jo-to-uba, that is, the old couple of Takasago,

30

came to be usually to be represented with it as well Jo-tom-ba were mythical man and wife who lived very long and happy lives. They are supposed to have dwelt in the beautiful pine forests on the lovely seashore of Takasago, where they spent their days in gathering pine needles. Small artificial mounts and pine forests and figures of the aged couple are tastefully arranged on a clean tray of white wood, the edges of the tray being indented in order to represent an idea of the sea-coast, with some cranes on the branches of the pine, generally with a nest and young ones, as well as the hair-tailed tortoise on the seashore. Cranes and tortoises play their part in our ceremonies so often, you see. I will here tell you the gist of a common song. Once a crane married a tortoise. Now, cranes are supposed to live one thousand years and tortoises ten thousand years. In the course of a duet pouring forth their touching sentiments, the wife gives vent to her thought to this effect: she feels sad at the idea that after a happy life of nigh a thousand years she would have to lead a young widow's life for nine thousand years.'

−'For us mankind a thousand years is long enough. But please proceed with the main story.'

−'Very well,' said I: 'the bridegroom and bride are seated vis-à-vis before the Toko-no-ma at a distance, with the officiating person next the bridegroom, and his wife next the bride, each giving assistance to the bridegroom and bride respectively. The me-cho (she-butterfly) and o-cho (he-butterfly) enter.'

−'What's that?'

−'Well, you see, butterflies are very beautiful, and when in couples are very amiable to each other. If you see them

31

flying about in the fields, now touching the flowers, now playing with each other, you can well imagine what happy lives they lead. At the wedding two virgins are chosen to represent a male and a female butterfly. They each hold a 'choshi,' a vessel with a long handle for holding saké. To one of the vessels a male butterfly made of paper is fastened, and to the other a female. They both, simultaneously, pour out a few drops for the bride and bridegroom successively, the idea being that two butterflies help the rites.'

−'Your idea of butterflies seems to be different from ours.'

−'Well, we do not attach to them the sense of frivolity. At all events, in case of wedding the point taken into consideration is different. They are also pictured as a symbol of Dream based upon a discourse of an ancient Chinese philosopher, who said that when he became a butterfly in a dream he had no other notion than being a real butterfly, and therefore he could not vouchsafe that his present ego was not similarly a phenomenon of a greater Dream.'

−'But you haven't yet explained where and how the cups are brought in.'

−'The cups generally consist of a set of three, usually of plain, clean earthenware. They are put on a tray of pure white wood with legs called Sambo—a dumb waiter, if you like. They are generally placed together with the saké vase at the Toko-no-ma before the ceremony begins, and are taken out at the bidding of the officiating person by the butterflies. The exchanging of cups between the bride and bridegroom is rather complicated. Each time the bride or bridegroom holds up the cup, three drops of saké are poured into it by each butterfly, and this is repeated three times, and therefore this part is called San-san-kudo, that is, three threes making nine, and that phrase is commonly used to signify a marriage ceremony. This part of the ceremony requires much formality. People concerned have to take some lessons beforehand. But remember people generally do not indulge on such occasions in swallowing too great a quantity, whatever their capacities may be.'

−'No joking, please.'

−'Very well. When this part of the ceremony is over, the officiating person, or a special person who is called into the next room for the purpose, sings a short song called Takasago (one of the classical Japanese songs called "utai"). The song is founded upon the story of the aged couple of whom I spoke, and is regarded as a contribution of good presage. But remember, officiating persons are often indifferent singers, consequently they often merely utter in tone a few words of the song. I remember a very amusing incident. It was told me by the Marchioness Ito. At the wedding of Isaburo Yamagata, son of Marquis Yamagata, Marquis Ito was the officiating person. He was unable to sing, so he said when the moment for singing came, "Isa, let us suppose I have sung. If father asks you what I have done, tell him I have sung all right." The marchioness restrained herself with great difficulty from bursting into laughter. That kind of incident sometimes occurs in reality.'

−'No wonder: people are not always singers. But pray proceed.'

−'The banquet now begins: bride and bridegroom now appear as a married couple, ceremonial cups are exchanged as a token of the cementing of the new relationship of those present, and after a good deal of merriment the couple retire and the guests disperse. On that day the bride and bridegroom wear ceremonial dress as a matter of course. It being a grand day for a woman, it is natural enough that the bride should get herself up as well as she can. I dare say the Western bride does the same, is it not so, madam?'

−'I hear, but please proceed,' said the marchioness.

−'The bride generally wears a dress with bright designs and very long sleeves. But it would be somewhat different if the bride were an old maid or an aged widow, don't you think so?'

−'Please really no more joking. What elderly widow could dress like a young bride?'

−'Very well. The bride often keeps on her head a white headgear called "boshi" until the end of the first part of the ceremony. It answers the purpose of your veil. I think it is used for hiding the blushes. Is it also so here in the West?'

−'I don't remember.'

−'Then also the bride changes her dress several times, twice, thrice, or even four times in the course of the evening, which is quietly made an opportunity for displaying female vanity. Oh, I beg your pardon.'

−'Never mind, but continue.'

−'Very well. After a few days the newly married couple, together with the near relations of the husband, go to the bride's former home and are there entertained at a banquet. It is called a "Satobiraki." At the wedding some suitable presents to each member of the husband's family are made by the bride as a token of the new affection arising between them, so also does the husband on the day of Satobiraki. After a suitable lapse of time all the relatives and friends are invited to a banquet, or some sort of entertainment, at a convenient place, at which the formal announcement of the marriage is personally given to the guests. The invitations are generally issued in common by the fathers of the bride and bridegroom, and thus is concluded the whole wedding ceremony.'

—'And the wedding presents?'

—'Yes, we also make wedding presents, but perhaps there is a slight difference. In the West the presents are on account of individual friendship, but in Japan more on account of family intercourse, that is to say, in Japan such presents would be made by a family if the family of the bride or bridegroom, as the case may be, were in intimate intercourse, even though no particular friendship exists between any particular member of that family and the bride or bridegroom.'

—'I see the ceremony is really very elaborate, but when does the legality of marriage begin?'

—'The ceremony is elaborate, as you see, but it counts for nothing in the eyes of the law: the heart of the law is cold in every country. The legality of a marriage begins in the eyes of the law only when a proper form of it is filled at the office of the registry of "l'état civil." It is desirable that a marriage should be reported in the form thus filed and duly registered as soon as possible after the ceremony.

35

Otherwise, whatever ceremony you may have undergone, the marriage is not recognised in the eyes of the law. But mind! if you ask me what a marriage is, I don't think I can explain it to you. From the Athenian republic down to the twentieth century all philosophers and jurists have been trying to define the exact signification of that word marriage; none of them have ever succeeded. On hearing that fact a peasant exclaimed: "What fools are these mountain-dwellers; every one on earth knows what a marriage is!"'

−'No joking, please,' said the marchioness.

−'But it is a tale I was taught by my teacher when I was studying the law at Cambridge,' said I.

−'Anyhow, I now see very well that all that I was told about the two months' marriage must have been a joke,' said the marchioness. 'There are some more points I should like to ask you, but I will let them stand over until some future occasion.'

The marchioness was originally born of a very high noble family of a neighbouring country, and France is her adopted home by marriage. Her sister, Countess de Daisyland, who had been staying at her sister's, as is her custom from time to time, was also present. I noticed some difference of character between them. While I was speaking with the marchioness, the countess was chiefly talking with Madame Matoni, wife of my friend, though she turned to us occasionally and interposed some laconic remarks. Monsieur Matoni was then engaged in a conversation with the duchess. By shifting seats, so to say, almost unconsciously to one another, the duchess and Madame Matoni now began to converse, and Monsieur

Matoni and the marchioness, who turned towards him without moving, did the same. The countess, who spoke less than her sister, and whose eloquence was of a totally different style, now began to put several questions to me.

−'There is one thing,' said she, 'which has been puzzling me very much of late, and that is, some people speak of the Spartan character of the Japanese women in general, basing their observations upon deeds displayed during the present war. But on the other hand there are many writers who tell us that Japanese women are mere domestic servants. Of course I do not believe that, but there seems too much margin between these observations. If I am not too curious, will you give me your opinion.'

−'With pleasure, countess,' said I. 'Without giving excessive credit to our women, which I do not dare, I can assure you that the Western estimation of our women is generally incorrect. It is perhaps beyond your conception how great an influence a Japanese mother or wife has over her family. I will give you an instance of a mother illustrated in a well-known drama. The scene is a summer evening. The aged mother of Miura Yoshimura (a hero having a real existence in history) lay on her deathbed within a mosquito netting, depending from the four corners of the room. Our mosquito nettings are very large and spacious. A young lady, the hero's fiancée, is waiting upon her as nurse. Here the hero suddenly returns home from the battlefield clad in full armour. He makes inquiry of the young lady about his mother's condition. She tells him that the aged lady's condition has not presented any marked difference, that she often falls into a drowsy state, and is calmly sleeping at that moment. A cough is heard from the room which is separated by paper screens and where the aged mother lay; in fact she had just awoke. She perceives the hero has returned, and with a few terse and killing sentences she

37

admonishes him from where she lay for his conduct. To her it was cowardly to leave the battlefield at that juncture. It was contrary to a warrior's honour and an infringement of loyalty. She will not see him face to face. Her last words are, "If thou darest to approach me, dare to break this net. It is an iron castle of mine." Having thus denounced her beloved son, she falls into a calm slumber again. As a matter of fact, the hero's mind is already made up to sacrifice his life in battle to the cause he was supporting. He merely returned home to bid his last farewell to his dying mother, and to intrust her to the care of his fiancée. His helmet is perfumed with the best kind of incense—an act common to a warrior of distinguished position—the idea being that a hero's head should not be exposed to odious odour after death. The young lady discovers it, and, as is natural in a drama, a bit of love-scene follows. She would not stop him, but at least he might wait until his aged mother awakes again and spend a single night by her bedside. The stay of a single eve, she says, would make no material difference to chivalry and loyalty. He does not listen to her, and shaking her off dashes back to the field, where he meets with an honourable death. The point I wish to lay stress upon is not the last part, but the part where the aged mother speaks of the "iron castle." Does that not show you the kind of authority a Japanese mother wields over her children? Is it any way inferior to that of Coriolanus's mother, before whom that brave Roman warrior had to cry out, "O mother! you have prevailed." It is, of course, a scene in fiction, but with us it is an incident quite imaginable in real life. Indeed, there are several instances of similar nature recorded in history. A Japanese wife has an influence far greater than any outsider can imagine. I can only say, so far as domestic affairs are concerned, she is far more a master of the house than her husband. Think for a moment! If the wife were a mere servant of the house, as is represented by many Western writers, how could it possibly happen that, as a mother, she exercises such austere authority, as the mother of the hero just mentioned did, over her son after her husband's death?'

The countess listened to me very attentively; my long explanation did not appear to weary her. When I had finished it she smiled and said:

−'Then in your country also mothers play a great rôle in the family. Would you also say like Napoleon, "Women are the mothers of the nation"? But won't tell us a dramatic illustration of a wife?'

−'"Too many dishes spoil the appetite," as our saying goes,' I answered, 'so I must not go on endlessly,—but àpropos to the Roman matron, I will tell you an incident which will illustrate that Japanese women, too, do not limit their activity to indoor affairs. You have, no doubt, heard something about Commandant Hirosé, one of our great heroes of Port Arthur. It was in the summer of last year that an eminent English admiral, whom I know very well, wished me to forward to the hero's family a copy of Macaulay's Lays of Ancient Rome as a token of his admiration. He said he thought that Japanese warriors bore a great resemblance to Roman warriors, even to Horatius himself, and Hirosé was the most conspicuous among them. Now Hirosé was a bachelor; his brother, who was his senior, is married, and was also at the front. When I forwarded the book to Tokio, Mrs. Hirosé, in the absence of her husband, took the matter in her own hands and wrote a letter of thanks in English to the admiral, accompanying it with a likeness and facsimile of the last poem of the deceased, all of which she forwarded to me, asking me to send on to the admiral. People might think she was audacious, but the fact was she did not shrink from taking the entire responsibility of the matter. I approve of it. The letter ran thus.'

So saying, I recited the letter. It is strange, but in dreamland one often remembers by heart that which it is impossible to do when awake.

'I tender my sincere thanks to you for your very kind present of a beautiful edition of Macaulay's Lays of Ancient Rome, forwarded to me by Baron Suyematsu.

'The book is so much esteemed in Japan that it is used as a text-book in some schools where English is taught, and part of it was annotated in Japanese in a magazine devoted to the study of English.

'I beg to assure you how much I feel the honour done to my deceased brother-in-law by a renowned admiral of a great and glorious nation, in comparing him with a Roman hero, who is said to have defended the Sublician Bridge against the whole Etruscan army under Porsena, while the Romans broke down the bridge behind him.

'I am happy to say that as a reward for the deed of the late Commander Hirosé, the people of Japan are going to erect his bronze statue to his memory in Tokio, as the Romans did in Comitium.

'May I be permitted to make you a present of the deceased's latest photograph and a facsimile of his autograph poem, which was composed by him just before his departure for the second blocking attempt.

'The poem was intended by him to be the final expression of his desires, and it is sad it proved to be such.

'Literally translated, it runs as follows:

"Would that I could be born seven times
And sacrifice my life for my country!
Resolved to die, my mind is firm,
And again expecting to win success,
Smiling I go on board!"

'I will take the earliest opportunity to refer to your inestimable present in my letter to my husband, the elder brother of the deceased, who is now in the front, commanding the gunboat Chokai, by whom, needless to say, your kindness will be most highly appreciated.'

−'I do not see,' observed the countess, 'much in the mere act of writing a letter, but the letter itself is interesting enough, and, besides, I must say I am much amused at the manner in which you manage to bring out things to suit your purpose, just indeed as though you are writing a novel and would make us serve you as materials.'

−'Not at all, but just a little bit of a Summer Dream,' I said.

−'What!'

−'Nothing, I beg your pardon.'

−'But, baron, I should like to ask you another question. With us, pardon, or an act of forgiving, is considered a great virtue. It is an act of courage, and, at the same time, it contains in it delicacy and tenderness; especially when the subject is a woman, that virtue sometimes amounts to nobleness, or even sublimity. It is, therefore, regarded in the West as one of the greatest elements of ethics; but some

41

people I hear say that that idea is wanting in oriental ethics, though the notion of pity exists. Is that correct?'

−'No, not exactly,' I answered, 'but you interest me by putting such a question. However, it requires some explanation. I am afraid I weary you.'

−'No, not at all; go on, if you please.'

−'Perhaps you know that the fundamental idea in Buddhism is mercy and forbearance. These attributes would already suggest an idea of forgiving and of not taking offence. Then, again, in Japan there are several new Buddhist sects, which are very much like Protestantism in Europe. In fact, some of them go so far as to allow priests to marry. I say new sects, but not so new as you may imagine, because they are as old as eight hundred years. The essence of the tenets held by them is that the great Budha Amida is the very embodiment of mercy and forgiveness, and therefore, if one devoutly throws oneself upon him and asks his salvation, all sins committed by the suppliant would be at once forgiven and salvation granted. Theologically speaking, there is much room for discussion about this, but it is not the point which I have in view. I only mean to say that this theory is nothing else than a great example of pardon. In Confucian ethics there are more names given to different kinds of virtues than in the West. The word "Jen" is the name of a virtue most comprehensive. There is no word corresponding to it in the West. There are some who translate it as "humanity," others "benevolence," some even as "charity" in its broadest sense, but all these only represent a part of the original meaning. In that word the idea of pardoning and forgiving is amply implied. A lord who pardons an offender magnanimously is a lord rich in the virtue of "Jen," There is also one classification of virtues, comprised in two words, "chung," "shu." The first word is generally translated as loyalty, but in this instance it is not necessarily loyalty to a master, but faithfulness and truthfulness in general. The second word, "shu," has no equivalent in the Western language. It means this: We should put ourselves in the position of any one who has done wrong against us or otherwise committed some error, and we view the matter with the greatest leniency, and thus give the most favourable consideration. The Chinese ideograph of it is composed of two other ideographs, "like" and "mind," that is to say, "like one's own mind," meaning—consider the matter as your own, and act toward him in such a way as your own mind would like him to act toward you under the same circumstances if he were in your place. This ideograph is often used for the very purpose of an action which cannot be any other than the equivalent of pardoning and forgiving. Are you not becoming a little wearied?'

−'Oh, no! Go on.'

−'Very well! In our Bushido, that is the teaching of chivalry, of which you must have heard, "pardoning" and "forgiving" is the important element. We have a proverb saying, "When the helpless bird takes refuge in the breast of the hunter, he would not kill it." This proverb is very well known and is considered as the embodiment of a warrior's magnanimity. From all that I have just said you will understand that the criticism which says oriental ethics lack notions of pardon and forgiving is incorrect.'

−'Thank you very much,' said the countess. 'In such matters one requires much study of and penetration into the very depths of thought and reasoning of a people. One certainly ought not to come to a hasty conclusion. Japan is a country which I am so anxious to see.'

−'Go, or rather, come, by all means, you will be most welcome,' I said.

−'But it is so far off and travelling will take such a long time,' said she.

−'No, it will not take so long a time as you imagine. Means of communication are so quick nowadays. The quickest route is through America by the Canadian Pacific via Vancouver. Another route is via San Francisco, which takes a few days longer. If you go by the Canadian Pacific, like a letter in a postbag, it takes only a few days over three weeks. When I came to Europe last year I left Yokohama on the 10th of February. Having arrived at Victoria, in the island of Vancouver, I made my way to Seattle, where I disembarked. I took thence the Great Northern Railway down to St. Paul and Chicago, a route which runs between the Canadian and San Francisco lines, and on to New York. I spent a day at Seattle. I had to stop at the summit of the Rockies for five hours, on account of an accident which happened to a train in front of ours. It made me miss the junction, so that I lost more than one day on the way. I spent two days in New York, and one in Washington. The mail steamer in which I crossed the Atlantic was not the quickest one. And yet on the morning of the 13th March I was quietly taking tea at an hotel in Liverpool. Last year was a leap year, but counting by days, inclusive one extra, the whole journey took thirty-two days in all. You see the globe is like an egg—the higher the latitude, the shorter the distance.'

−'That looks long enough.'

−'Well, but one cannot jump over from one side of the world to the other in one leap.'

−'Supposing the Trans-Siberian Railway free again, what do you think of it?'

−'Well, a friend of mine who took that route took twenty days from Petersburg to the Pacific Coast. It is, of course, shorter; but you see travelling continuously by train is not very agreeable. I believe that the railway services in those quarters will be much improved and made quicker, but at present, that is to say, judging from experience before the war, the service is said to be very irregular and long. I should prefer a sea-voyage. The direct service between Europe and Japan on board the German or French mail ships through the Indian Ocean seems to be most agreeable. Of course it takes a longer time: it takes from forty-four to forty-seven days from Marseilles or Genoa to Yokohama. I have twice taken that route on a French mail ship and liked the voyage very much.'

−'But one would be killed by sea-sickness.'

−'Not at all. The sea is not always calm in the Mediterranean, so also between Hong Kong and Japan. But all the other parts are usually very calm. Besides, one soon gets accustomed to the sea, after two or three days, excepting some few persons who are by nature averse to the sea altogether.'

−'I cannot believe it.'

−'You must believe it, it is a fact, and moreover, on mail steamers there is much fun and pleasure; dances and concerts are given on board from time to time. The meals are splendid and plentiful. Passengers soon become friendly.'

−'Ah! that's too good to hear, but I wonder if it is always so,' she said.

A lady, who had travelled in the Far East, joined us a few minutes since. She spent two months in Japan, she said, and supported my views about the voyage, and talked of the pleasure of the trips somewhat in opposition to the observations of the countess.

The marchioness now turned to me and said, 'I have just been talking to your friend Monsieur Matoni about the new invention of Monsieur Blanry. A long account of it was given in Le Matin the other day. It is an improvement on the wireless telegraphy. Guns may be fired, wheels may be turned by electricity produced by wireless apparatus. He is going to give a lecture illustrated by practical experiments. Would you like to go? If so, I would send you a ticket for a box for yourself and friends.'

−'I shall be delighted,' I answered.

−'Marchioness patronises science,' said Monsieur Matoni to me, as though he only meant me to hear him, and in a further subdued voice whispered, 'Her tastes differ from the ordinary tastes of ladies.'

The visitors were now gradually dispersing. The marchioness and her sister also rose to take their leave, asking us, as they did so, to visit them on the marchioness's next reception day. We had stopped for longer than we anticipated, despite an appointment I had at my hotel. Soon after the departure of those ladies, however, we also said our goodbyes to the duchess and her daughters, and to the few people who had still remained.

We were again wafted through the air, and were once more moving over the tops of countless houses on the way. On reaching my hotel, I shook hands with my friend and his wife on the tops of the beautiful avenue-trees in front of the hotel.

II

Greek inspiration—Semitic sympathy—Religion—Difference between Japanese and European chivalry—What is the Bushi?—The weakest point of a hereditary military organisation—Introduction of the new system—New commoners and the history of their emancipation—Combination of democratic ideas and conservative traditions—Old bottles and new wine—The Great Change of 1867—Napoleon—Negligence of a proper estimation—Scenery of Japan—-History of Tokio—European and Japanese method of dwelling—President Roosevelt and jiujitsu

It seems my young secretary, noticing I was asleep, and fearing that I might catch cold, brought a rug and covered me, which action roused me for a moment, but I soon returned to the same dreamland again.

Once more I was wafted through the air, and found myself in a large entrance-hall with gilded ceiling and walls painted with pictures. It was brilliantly lighted, and in one corner a band was playing. A broad staircase, the upper part of which branched off into two, led to the upper part of the house, numerous men in livery lined both sides of the passage, displaying the sure sign of aristocracy. There were balconies, or rather corridors all round overlooking the hall. I ascended the staircase, and, passing along one side of the corridors, entered a large chamber which was evidently the reception-room. But seeing but few people there, proceeded to an open window at the end of the room and looked down into the garden, which was brilliantly illuminated. In a few moments I moved, almost unconsciously, into a further room. It was the study of the host, who with his wife was showing the room to a group of guests. The host, noticing me, made me welcome, and introduced me to one of the guests in particular. It was the Prince Royal of Greece. I exchanged some words with him, in the course of which I remarked that Greece was the country which I was most anxious to see, inasmuch as it teemed with historical interest. As I did so, the scene of many heroic actions, above all, those of Salamis and Marathon, together with the glory which Byron sung for her freedom in the recent century vividly arose before my mental eyes.

It was then announced that the music was about to commence, and the party moved on. I was with a charming lady. She was of Semitic blood. Her complexion was snow white, her eyes were dark, as also her hair, which was surmounted by a coronet of pearls, and round her throat was a necklace of the same. She happened to know me already by name, through her relatives whom I met in England. This naturally afforded us a subject of conversation as we proceeded. On arriving at one end of the corridors we stood, still conversing, and looking down into the hall, while the other people moved on the further end of the corridor where many more guests gradually arrived. While thus conversing, a nobleman passing us was introduced to me.

−'All the generals are gone to the Front,' he said, rather suddenly.

At first I thought he was referring to the war in the Far East, though I soon realised what he meant. He appeared a little excited.

−'There is more exaggeration than fact,' said I. 'I am quite confident that there will be no rupture.'

At that moment some one persuaded my fair companion to go over to where the prince was sitting. I followed at a distance, and took my seat in an obscure place in the corridor. From the corridor of the other side, an operatic singer, accompanied by a pianist, rendered the choicest of his songs, and the bands played in the intervals.

I listened to the songs and the music and watched the people. Sitting alone I am sure I must have looked awkward and stupid; which, however, is a thing I do not much mind. Now and then the host came and exchanged some words with me. He was busy looking after his guests generally, but managed to tell me he would invite me to a special dinner very soon to which also the Duchess Fairfield would be asked. The hostess was similarly occupied, and I did not converse much with her, except to pass a few remarks about music. She said she preferred vocal music to instrumental. The music over, all went down to the garden. It was delightful: the open air on a summer's night is always so. Light but choice refreshments were served there. The guests, partaking of them as they wished, chatted here and there in groups of two and three.

The night was far advanced and the guests began to disperse one after another. I also left, but without bidding adieu either to the host or hostess lest I might disturb them. On my way out I saw the lady with whom I had talked in the corridor still sitting on a bench chatting with a few gentlemen. She seemed to notice me, but I merely bowed and passed on, though I fancied she had some sympathy for us Japanese. She did not, neither does any member of her community, say anything about the hard fate of her race or the countless hardships which they are suffering, especially of late, in certain quarters of the globe. In this world, we know there are many matters in which silence speaks more than words.

Time and space, and indeed, sequence of events, are incongruous in Dreamland. One flits from place to place. I now found myself in a large mansion. It was the residence of the Marchioness Vivastine. I was of the few early arrivals. The salon was rather dark, but cool and spacious. The marchioness was not yet down, but the valet told me she would soon appear. In a minute or two she entered accompanied by her sister, asking as they greeted us our pardon for keeping us waiting. More people now arrived one after the other. The marchioness proceeded to make tea and distributed it, assisted by her sister, much in the same way as did the Duchess of Fairfield and her daughters. I was naturally introduced to many of the visitors, Princess A., Countess B., Baron C., Monsieur D., etc., but for me, a foreigner, it is impossible to remember their names. The Duchess of Fairfield and the Lady Dulciana were among the new arrivals.

−'Baron and I had a very heated discussion the other day,' remarked the marchioness. Then turning to me, she said, 'Did we not?' To which I replied, 'If you please, it was indeed interesting.'

−'Did you go to the Trocadero the other evening?' said the marchioness.

−'Yes! we did. Thank you very much for sending the box. And the duchess and her party were there too,—in a box close by ours,' I added.

−'Did the lecture interest you?' asked the marchioness.

−'Oh yes! the experiments were all very interesting, but I hardly understood a single sentence of the lecture,' I answered.

51

−'No wonder! for no one else understood it, at least, I did not. It was so scientific,' interposed Baron C.

'Ah! you were there too, of course,' said I. 'And the best fun of the evening was that there was a man distributing hand-bills. At first we all thought it was a kind of syllabus of the lecture, but in reality it was the advertisement of a competitor stating that he was an earlier inventor.'

The marchioness and her sister, being the hostesses, were unable to talk long to each guest. I soon found myself sitting next to the duchess on a sofa, with Baron C. in front of us on a chair. Our conversation having turned upon the question of the separation of state and religion, Baron C., who was keen on the subject, being a Deputy, said:

−'With us it is a very interesting question. There are many points to be thought of and discussed, but I think it interests outsiders very little, especially a person like yourself, a Japanese, for I understand the Japanese gentry have very little religion.'

−'And yet,' said the duchess, 'in my opinion there is scarcely a single people who have no religion at all. Bushido is the creed of the Japanese gentry, as I understand, and in truth it is nothing else than a religion. The Latin religio, from which the term religion is derived, comes from the verb religere to hold tight. In that sense, at least, Bushido must also be taken for a religion. I know something about it, especially through your writings. But, baron, will you please explain to me something about the points of resemblance and difference between our ancient chivalry and your Bushido?'

−'I am not, madam, well acquainted with your chivalry, and, therefore, I cannot pretend to hit the mark. But I know that one of the ideals of your chivalry was "bravery" to the point of being fearless of death; in that there is certainly a great resemblance. Another of your ideals was loyalty and truthfulness. Always ready to render assistance to one weaker; in that also there is a great resemblance. The third ideal was: a great devotion to religion. On this point I must admit there is some difference. I do not say our Bushi despised the idea of supernatural beings, but you see our Bushi had more faith in their own spirit of self-reliance, therefore religion governed their thoughts to no such degree as it did in the West. Then comes a great difference between them,—I mean their attitudes as regards the fair sex. But have you no objection to my proceeding further?'

−'Not at all,' said the duchess.

−'Very well,' said I. 'With your chivalry the custom of rendering respect to the fair sex had been carried to such a high pitch that it was nothing less than adoration or worship. I do not say the motive was originally bad, because it came no doubt from the idea of helping the weaker. But, remember, it often happened that too much prominence was given to keeping faithfulness to women, even where one had some higher duty which ought to have claimed the whole loyalty of his heart. The subject is rather too delicate for me to describe minutely, but you can see what I mean. In the days of your chivalry faithfulness in love-affairs was looked upon in general as gallantry, no matter whether the affair was honourable or otherwise, but with the Japanese Bushido it was very different. It was not because a Bushi was heartless toward the weaker sex, but effeminacy was a thing which he despised most. In the days gone by in Japan, if a Bushi had been found paying too much attention to a lady, and making himself a slave to her, to the neglect of his duty, he would have been hooted out of society. With European chivalry, therefore, the tendency of desire was to be noticed by others for his actions performed in homage to a lady, whilst with our chivalry one would try to do his utmost to conceal his emotion and even to look cold. In the West, therefore, the word "gallantry," which was originally used more for "dashing and noble bravery" came in common parlance to have quite a different meaning, as you know. Nothing of the sort has ever taken place with us.'

−'But I thought your Samurai also had love-affairs—I was at least made to understand so from your story of the other day about a young Samurai,' interrupted Lady Dulciana.

−'Yes, that is true, but our Samurai is not "trees and stones" as we say, and you must know there are exceptions to every rule,' I replied and continued.

−'There was also another great difference. In the West chivalry had grown and decayed, traversing always pretty much the same line; I mean it had undergone no great transformation. But in Japan the case was somewhat different. There it became united with the art of intellectual learning, and has made Bushido, that is, the ways of Bushi, more systematic and ethical.'

−'What you have just told us,' said Baron C., 'seems to explain some difference which is said to exist in the attitudes of men towards women in your country and ours.'

−'Perhaps so,' I answered, 'where a gentleman approaches a lady and kisses her hand, as one sees commonly in the best Parisian society, a Japanese would stand at a distance and make a respectful bow. There is no doubt, it seems to me, that a great many of the customs which prevailed in the feudal period are still influencing your modern society, and ours also in Japan; hence the difference which still exists between the customs of Japan and Western nations. Broadly speaking, I can say that in the West friendship or affection moved more towards intimacy, whilst in the East it moved more towards respect.'

−'Ah, I remember one thing. Some years ago there was a smart American who was a keen observer of different customs and manners. He said, "the Japanese hit their wives before strangers, and caress them in private, whilst the Occidentals worship their wives before strangers, and beat them in private." I beg your pardon, I must not tell you such a thing, I withdraw it at once; but I can say this, it is dangerous to gauge the customs and manners of other countries only by the measure of one's own country. The position of our women is not so low as represented by those who look through the colour of their own glass.'

−'Very true,' said Baron C. 'Such things often occur. One ought always to be on guard, lest one commit unaccountable errors quite inadvertently. But what do you mean by saying your Bushido has become systematic and ethical. Let us have a little more light on the subject.'

−'Quite so,' said the duchess. 'I should also like to be more informed on that subject. One never gets tired of things Japanese, especially in these days.'

−'I am afraid I shall appear somewhat dogmatic, but if you have enough patience I will explain. In the Far East, Bun and Bu, that is to say matters pertaining to Intellectual culture and matters pertaining to military training, were always regarded, at least in theory, as co-existent and of equal importance. They were compared to the wings of a bird, or to the two wheels of a cart. The generals who were held in the highest esteem were those who were efficient in both. The same esteem was held for all warriors, no matter their degree or rank; though, of course, the higher the rank the greater the excellence expected. They all became imbued with a desire for literary and ethical education, and thus civil elements were introduced into military training. The best ideas and notions of chivalry were ethically systematised, and these ideas and notions came to be nurtured and developed according to the normal roots of ethics. We were fortunate in arriving at this solution, for the country had enjoyed a long peaceful epoch, and the Bushi had therefore sufficient time to give their attention to both subjects. Besides the policy of the country had been directed to that end. Moreover, four hundred thousand families of Bushi, having enjoyed their position by hereditary succession, and having no need to labour for existence, all that they had to do was to make themselves as much "a gentleman" as possible. Of course, there were some who became outcasts and some who were newly enrolled, and some who were degraded, and some who were promoted from various causes, but these were exceptions. As a general rule they succeeded to their father's position and handed it down to their own successors. Colleges were established by their lords where they received intellectual education side by side with fencing, riding, the use of spears or the art of jiujitsu.'

−'You mentioned just now,' said the duchess, 'four hundred thousand families of Bushi, and of the heredity of their service. That seems to be somewhat different from our knighthood, which was more of the nature of personal distinction, and its ranks were filled by personal enlistment, although naturally they came from the same class of people.'

−'Well,' said I, 'our term Bushi, otherwise called Samurai, is a comprehensive one. It comprised all the retainers of the feudal lords. They generally lived, with their families, in the capital town of the lords under whom they served. There was generally a quarter in these towns where the Samurai lived quite apart from other people. Under some lords, there were Samurai who lived in the country, but they were exceptions. By Bushi then we understand those retainers in general, and as I said the service usually became hereditary. It was the strong point of our military men and also their weakest point, or at least it became so in the course of time.'

−'What do you mean by weak point? Tell me, please,' said Baron C.

−'I say "weak point," because that system as an organisation for fighting purposes became inefficient: the reason is almost plain without saying. You see the hereditary system has one advantage: respect and affection increase from generation to generation. Personal intelligence was also acquired under that system so long as the training and instruction were well attended to, but the descendant of a warrior who had led, for instance, one thousand or one hundred men with great ability, could not always be expected to do as well as his ancestor. This is so from the very fact that ability and skill for qualifying one for a higher position is not a thing which is hereditary. This is the weakest point of an hereditary military organisation. "Ministership and generalship are no inherited stocks" is our old saying. Napoleon's eighteen marshals were, one and all, children of the time. Even before the restoration of the present Imperial régime we perceived this weak point, and that was one of the reasons we made a radical change in our military system and adopted the system of universal service. One might think that, by doing so, the spirit of respect and affection, in other words, loyalty and patriotism, might be lessened in the ranks of the troops; but that is not so, for with us the spirit of loyalty to and patriotism for the Emperor and country is very strong among all the people. And because the feudal system had been abolished and the whole nation came to owe no other allegiance than that which is direct to the Emperor, there is no necessity of making any difference among the different classes of the people in regard to those services. As to intelligence, we do not leave the children without education, whatever class they may belong to, I mean to say, we have adopted a system of universal education which gives sufficient knowledge and therefore intelligence to the men enlisted in the ranks from all classes. As to the officers, we take in any candidates who are willing to be suitably educated as such, provided they show sufficient capacity, without any distinction of class or family. It seems to us the only way to procure the most efficient officers. We are very radical in these matters. One can see in the Japanese army or navy sons of noblemen or rich merchants being commanded and led by an officer who has risen from the lowest class of the people. There may even be officers whose origin, if scrutinised minutely, belonged to a class vulgarly called "New Commoners."'

−'I think I understand now,' said Baron C. 'But do you mean to say Bushido is a thing of the past? We are made to understand that the whole Japanese army and navy, indeed the whole nation, are animated with the spirit of Bushido at this very moment.'

—'No, I did not say Bushido was a thing of the past. Bushi exists no more, it is true, except that those who belonged to that class still enjoy the privilege of being called Shizoku (knight family), which, however, has no legal signification, and therefore is only an empty title. There may be a Shizoku driving a carriage or earning a living by selling trifles. It is sad to think of the fact, as far as personal consideration is concerned, but they have given their benefits and privileges for the general good of the country, and I am glad to say that the spirit of Bushido is now made the common property of the whole nation. It has been spread throughout every rank of the Japanese.'

—'It seems sad when we think about Bushi, as you say, from a personal point of view,' said the duchess; 'but when a country makes such a great change as your country has done, some great sacrifice on the part of some portion of the community is inevitable.'

—'And especially so with our Bushi,' said I, 'because they were in fact the chief instruments by which the present great change has been brought about. When we view things in this way, we can say that our Bushi fought and sacrificed their lives in order to destroy their own order.'

—'But what do you mean by the "New Commoners," which you mentioned just a minute ago?' asked Baron C.

—'By "New Commoners" is meant those who have been newly made ordinary commoners by emancipation. There was in Japan a class of people below the class of the common subjects of the empire; they neither enjoyed the rights of ordinary Japanese nor owed any duty similar to others. I mean to say, they enjoyed no citizenship, but, on the other hand, they had in most cases not to pay taxes for the lands they tilled or dwelt on. Their position may be in one way compared with the slavery which existed in the West from the Roman period onward. But there were two points of a great difference. In the West the slaves had their masters whom they served, and it seems that no personal pollution in our sense was attached to them. In Japan, those people had no masters to serve, and earned their living by their own labour. At the same time, however, they were regarded as having personal pollution, so much so indeed, that they were not allowed, nor did they themselves dare, to enter within the door of an ordinary Japanese, still less could they intermarry or indeed hold any social intercourse with them. A love-affair like that of Aïda, a slave girl, and Ardamès in the opera "Aïda," which I had the pleasure of seeing in your company the other evening, is a thing almost unimaginable in Japan between a girl belonging to the class I have just spoken of, and a man of any other class. The number of these people was only a very small minority of the whole population. But they were to be found in all parts of Japan. In the country they formed here and there small villages. They were also to be found in the vicinity of towns, but always having separate communities. They were the only people who dealt with dead oxen and horses, and even dogs, and also were the only people who dressed the skins of those animals. In former days in Japan no beef was eaten but by those people. Horse flesh was not eaten even by them. The common notion was that horse flesh was sour and inedible, but I am sorry to say that, of late years, it is eaten by the poorer classes to some extent. The dealers in it insist on continuing the trade on the ground that the same business is carried on in the midst of the most enlightened nations in the West. I do not like the idea at all. However, to proceed with my story. When a cow, a horse, or a bullock belonging to a commoner died, it was notified to a community of those people, who in a group came and carried the carcase to a convenient place, where they skinned it and buried the rest; and in the case of a cow or a bullock, if it had not died from any infectious disease, they took away its flesh to their homes, as well as the skin and horns. It was the occupation of those communities who lived in the vicinity of a town to prepare the skins sent to them from all parts of the country. Their lot was not, therefore, an enviable one, as you may perceive. This class of people was called "Yeta," which is represented, though by corruption, by the Chinese ideographs meaning "much pollution." No one knows exactly what their origin was; some say they were the remnants of Mongolian troops who remained in the land after the total destruction of Mongolian armada, while some say they might have been prisoners from Corea; but all these conjectures are not satisfactory. There was another portion of the people very much akin to those just described. They were known by the name of "Hinin," a term which is represented by two Chinese ideographs, meaning "not-man," which suggests a similarity of notion to the European term "outlaw." This class was in number even less than the former. Their occupation was also very different. They chiefly lived by fishing or by making some trifling articles, and, therefore, no such deep stigma of personal pollution was attached to them as to the other ones. In fact, it was supposed that among this class of men there were sometimes to be found a Samurai declassed from one cause or another. In Yedo, now Tokio, homeless destitutes were known by that name. One must not suppose, however, that either class was unprotected by law, for their lives and properties were respected just as those of ordinary people; and, moreover, they were not necessarily poor people, because some of them, especially those who lived near towns, were very well off. A characteristic of these people was that they had a certain sentiment of community throughout their own class without distinction of locality. They had no privilege of attending a "Shinto" or Buddhist temple belonging to the citizen classes, but they had here and there their own Buddhist temple and priests. I have never seen any instance of their possessing any Shinto temples; this fact arises from the very nature of Shintoism, which is most sensitive of anything unclean, in other words, most opposed to any pollution. The Imperial régime was inaugurated with most enlightened notions, especially in the matter of personal freedom. At the very beginning of the Imperial régime, the present Marquis Ito was governor of the prefecture of Hiogo-Kobe, and he emancipated, on his own initiative, the Yeta and Hinin under his government, and made them ordinary commoners. There was little formality in such matters in those days. A governor of a province sometimes took such measures on his own responsibility. In the course of a few years the Imperial Government emancipated all of those people throughout the whole empire, and the people thus emancipated came to be vulgarly called "New Commoners." That term, however, is fast losing its significance, inasmuch as those people are daily acquiring common intercourse with the ordinary people; this is especially the case with those who transfer their abodes to other parts of the country, where their identity is not known. I am even told there are one or two deputies in the House of Representatives who originally belonged to that class.'

—'It shows a very bold and enlightened policy on the part of your Government,' said the duchess. 'From all that you have said, it appears that the success of the great changes in your country is due to the combination of democratic ideas with conservative traditions; in other words, you seem to have well succeeded in "putting new wine into old bottles."'

—'If you please, you may think so,' I said; 'that phrase describes our situation very aptly. You see, the present régime of our Imperial Government is, after all, a restoration to its ancient form, animated by modern spirits. Our change has not taken place through any uprising of the people at large. Before the Restoration, European notions of "Liberty, Equality, and Fraternity" had not been much developed, it is true, but then the people had not been labouring under any great oppression and destitution. They were not rich, as a rule, but they were mostly happy, and not in an extreme condition of misery, as was the case in Europe when the popular movements based on those notions commenced, or as is the case in a certain country now before our eyes. The movements which caused our great change were due almost entirely to aspirations of a political nature, that is to say, for the bettering of the political organism of the country. The matter was taken up by the upper classes, and was fought out chiefly by them, and, therefore, when the strife came to an end there existed no more class animosity, and the people, both high and low, devoted their energy to the common good which they held in view. It is true that at one time their views of the right methods to attain the end were not altogether unanimous. Some of the feudal lords and their retainers fought against other feudal lords and retainers. One side espoused the Imperial cause, and the other opposed, but those who opposed bore no opposition to the Imperial house itself. It was more an opposition to the lords and their clansmen who stood on the other side. You know that, after the submission of the Shogun himself to the emperor, the great majority of the feudal lords in the north and the east of Japan effected a combination among themselves and opposed the troops on the Imperial side. What I said just now was chiefly in reference to that occurrence. The nature of our civil war being such, it was not a matter of surprise that the country should be reconciled and conciliated under the new régime. I may here mention an instance, trifling as it is, to show how it has operated even in ordinary social matters. Marshal Oyama, who is now commanding our armies in Manchuria, is a Satsuma man, and he fought as a young officer of the Imperialists in the east. His wife is a daughter of a Samurai of an eastern feudal lord, one of the staunchest opponents to the Imperial troops, I mean the Lord of Aizu, whose castle was besieged and taken after a long resistance. A sister of Madame Oyama is a lady in our Imperial courts, and her brother, who had been a leader of the troops of his clan, was afterwards a general of the Imperial army, and died in that capacity recently. We have a nobility of five grades, almost identical with the European system. The origin of our noble families is various, but their broad distinctions are: Noblemen who were formerly feudal lords; noblemen who were formerly court nobles attached direct to the Imperial courts before the Restoration, and those who have been newly made nobles by virtue of their meritorious services rendered to the new Government. But in the eyes of the law, or rather in the treatment of them by the Imperial court, there is no difference, nor is there any confliction of interest or sentiment existing between them. Napoleon was a great ruler, there is no doubt, but his one misfortune was that the very nature of his origin was not sufficiently potent to reconcile and harmonise all the difference of this kind in which sentiments go a long way. Supposing he had been a direct scion of the Bourbons, and supposing the general condition of the French people of those days had not been such as it was, and supposing that the great Revolution had been effected by the movements of the aristocracy itself with Napoleon at its head, the course of the history of France might have been very different, although, in spite of that, France has always been a remarkable nation.'

The marchioness seems to have noticed that our conversation was becoming animated and stepped towards us, evidently to take part in it. At this juncture, an elderly gentleman and his wife were ushered into the room. They were duly introduced to us. He was an astronomer. He said that he and his wife had been in Japan years ago when a transit of Venus across the sun was taking place. But their observation of the transit was a failure owing to bad weather. They stayed eight years, and waited for another transit, but again he was disappointed; because a sudden change in the weather obscured the heavens.

−'That must have been a great disappointment,' I said. 'As to myself, I have seen one such transit very well at a temporary observatory erected at Yokohama. It was very interesting to me, unscientific as I am, to see the sun reflected in white on the prepared ground, and the planet, a small black spot, traversing slowly across the white surface. Of course, one could also see the actual sun and planet through a smoked glass. The transit I refer to might have been a different one, or else the locality where I saw it from was not the same. I will tell you a stupid experience of mine,' said I, turning to others present. 'There was a total eclipse of the sun, some eighteen years ago. I was on a trip, and had to cross over a high mountain pass. I, and a few companions, thought it would be great fun to see an eclipse from the summit of the mountain and observe all the changing phenomena of nature from there. So we hurried on our way, but by the time we reached the summit the sky was very cloudy, it even showered, and the consequence was that we did not see much and regretted that we had not stayed a little longer on the lower grounds, from where the people saw the eclipse very well. Fancy the height of a mountain,—however high it may be, it is only an infinitesimal part of the distance between the earth and the sun. To think that we would be nearer to the sun if we climbed to the summit of the mountain was an act of great stupidity; but such things often occur in actual life. We often forget to think about the relative situation between ourselves and others, and make our calculations according

65

to fancy. Thus great errors are often committed. Such is the case when we play at games, say at chess. We make our moves, thinking that our opponent would make his move just as we ourselves would do, but the probability is that he makes a move totally different to our anticipation, much to our chagrin and surprise. All this arises from our negligence of making a proper estimate of the relative position occupied by both sides.'

−'You seem to have some special reference in what you say,' said the marchioness. 'By the bye, Madame P. says she likes Japan very much.'

−'Yes, I do,' said the professor's wife. 'I can never forget it. Miyanoshita, Nikko, Chiuzenzi, and above all, the scenery of the inland sea, are superb.'

−'Yes, those are the places which foreign travellers are fond of and talk about the most. The accommodation of the warm spring of Miyanoshita and the sights of the artistic buildings of the Nikko temples seem to be thought much of. Chiuzenzi, with its calm, mirror-like lake, is certainly an excellent summer resort,—no wonder most of the corps diplomatic in Japan betake themselves thereto every summer. But from our own point of view the Nikko temples are new and consequently the arts displayed there are only of modern type, elaborate but not deep. They are not quite three hundred years old. In fact,—Tokio itself is only a new town, being scarcely three hundred years old. One must go to Kioto and Nara if one wishes to see the real classical Japan. Those are places where there are so many spots of historical and artistic interest, not only in the towns themselves, but also in the surrounding localities.'

−'Yes, my husband and I had opportunities of visiting those places, and we made very pleasant and interesting trips.'

−'But how is it that Tokio is such an important town in these days, as I understand?' asked the marchioness.

−'I will explain,' said I. 'Tokio is situated on both banks of the mouth of a river called Sumida, about the same size as the Seine, running through the middle of a large flat land and flowing into the bay of Tokio. That flat land was formerly called "Musashi-no," that is to say, plain of "Musashi,"—from the fact that the greater parts of it belong to the province of Musashi (we call it a large plain because Japan is so mountainous and flat plains are so rare). It is the plain which was sung of by a poet as one where the moon rises and sinks from grass to grass, there being no mountain for her to seek shelter. When Tokugawa, that is to say, the family of the last Shogunate, became a powerful feudal lord about three hundred years ago, it made the site of the present Tokio its seat and built its castle on the spot where a small old castle had stood some time before. Towns had arisen around the castle, which came to be known as Yedo until it was changed into Tokio thirty-eight years ago. The town, and, indeed, the castle itself, had been gradually enlarged from time to time. It is well known that, not long after Yedo was made the seat of Tokugawa, the house of Tokugawa became the Shogunate, that is to say, the military and administrative government of the empire which used to be called by foreigners the temporary chief of Japan. For nearly three hundred years the Shogunate exercised great power. All the feudal lords were obliged to reside in Yedo every other year. Their families, I mean wives and children, had to live permanently in their mansions at Yedo all the year round as a kind of hostage. Great lords usually had three mansions, the upper, the middle, and the lower ones as they were called; even small lords had two. It was almost necessary for them to have several mansions because Yedo was so famous for fire—

67

fire was called the flowers of Yedo—and they had to move their residence from one to the other in case of fire. Of course, the magnitude of these mansions differed according to the rank and position of the owners, but were mostly very large, and a large number of retainers also resided in surrounding buildings, though the exact number of the retainers also varied according to the ranks of the lords. You may well imagine how expensive such establishments must have been. Hence also the flourishing condition of the town itself, and thus Yedo had become the largest town of the Empire. When the Shogunate came to an end, the emperor removed his residence to Yedo and re-named it Tokio, that is to say, the eastern capital in contrast to Kioto, which is also known as Saikio, i.e. the western capital. It was a masterstroke of the bold policy of the new Government. The removal went a long way in facilitating the renovation of Japan, for it helped the getting rid of old notions and introducing new ideas. Besides, by assuming a commanding position over the whole country, and having been thus made the new Imperial capital, Tokio continues to maintain, even advances in, its prosperity. Voila! the answer to your question.'

−'I suppose Tokio is much changed, as people say?' asked the marchioness.

−'Yes, it is so,' I answered. 'One can no longer see the Tokio of thirty years ago. The residences of the feudal lords in former days were very grand, especially the parts just beyond the inner moats surrounding the castle, where stood the residential mansions of great lords, called Daimio-Koji, i.e. broad way of the Grand Seigneurs. The premises of these mansions generally formed a square, the main building stood in the middle, the four sides of the square were generally occupied by long lines of buildings in which the retainers lived. There were several gateways, the main entrance, of course, being the largest. Some great lords spent a good deal more money than necessary in making their mansions appear grand in order to efface any suspicion of their unfaithfulness to the Shogunate—in other words, they showed by so doing that they had no idea of accumulating wealth for secret designs. I well remember those buildings, but nothing is left of them now. The very centre of the place where those houses stood is now a park. The gates, which were constructed of wood, were very elaborate and imposing. There are only three or four of them left in Tokio, but not on their old sites. They are but reminiscences of old ones, and reconstructed elsewhere by private persons as curiosities. The streets where the great lords once marched in grand state are now crossed in all directions by electric tramways. But we are not sorry for all that.'

−'People say there will soon be no more old Japan to be seen in Japan,' said Lady Dulciana, 'unless one visits her without delay.'

−'That is not likely,' I said. 'A nation cannot completely metamorphosise itself at a moment's notice. Despite all those changes, Japan is still Japan, especially in the interior. The old Japan will not disappear during the lifetime of either you or me. However, we have a saying, "For good things let us hurry." If you have any idea of going to see Japan, which I consider a good thing, hurry by all means.'

−'I suppose the style of residence in Japan differed, and still differs, from ours?' asked the duchess.

−'Yes, very much; and not only the grand residences, but also the houses of all classes. If you allow me to be candid, I will tell you a conversation I had with a Frenchman a little time ago on the very subject. He asked me what I thought of the appearance of Paris, and if I did not think the rows of grand, lofty houses which form the avenues and streets magnificent. "They are magnificent for sights," I answered. The last part of my remark made him a little suspicious, and he pressed me to explain my meaning, and I did so. Can you guess my answer?'

−'No, I cannot.'

−'My answer was to the following effect. You see, here in Paris, people who dwell in a building generally occupy only one part of it. They share a house and live in different flats and corners of the same building; and yet the people, who meet every day at their very door, do not know each other. Their rooms are generally dark, because the buildings overshadow each other. They cannot move out of their rooms without putting on hat and jacket, and generally have no spare ground attached to the house where they can rest or promenade. They seldom see the moon or the beautiful morning and evening sun, being buried in deep valleys of houses. For practical purposes, therefore, my preference is for the style of my country—I mean houses detached, though not grand and lofty, so that one can use every part of the building, from the basement to the roof, with some ground, around the building, be it large or small, tastefully laid out into a garden. I say, therefore, people who live in magnificent, high buildings may not necessarily be happier than those who live in smaller and humbler dwellings. This is what I said to that French friend of mine. Please excuse my making such remarks: I have no thought of running down your style of living, but have only been tempted to say what little good I can of my country.'

−'When spaces are available,' said Baron C, 'we also attach gardens to our houses. Apropos, you were at the matinée dance at the Palais Elysée, were you not?'

−'Yes, I had the pleasure of being invited by Monsieur le President and Madame Loubet.'

−'The trees there are fine, are they not?' said Baron C.

−'Yes, they are very fine, and the gathering was fine also. An incident which I experienced there was rather unique. I was walking with Madame Matoni in the crowd. We encountered two gentlemen clad in fashionable attire. Somehow or other, Madame Matoni began conversing with one of them. At the same time I heard a female voice echoing in my ears—I could not imagine where it came from, except from the gentleman with whom madame was talking. I thought it very queer, but presently I was introduced to them: they were announced as Monsieur and Madame Ecrivan. Then it occurred to me that the person whom I thought a gentleman was in reality a lady of whom I had heard something before. She was an author attired like a man.'

−'Yes, she is an author, and a clever one too,' said the duchess. 'But what did you think of the whole reception?'

−'Simplicity was, I thought, its features as compared with similar occasions in monarchical countries, but it was in unison with the constitution of the country. Then, too, although somehow or other I missed entering into the dancing pavilion, I understood the matinée dance there was customarily given chiefly for the entertainment of the orphan daughters of army and naval officers. The idea is pleasant.'

71

−'And what of the President?' inquired one young lady.

−'A fine old gentleman, I thought, and kind-hearted too. I was specially introduced to him, in the garden, after the formal reception. He repeatedly pressed me to put my hat on while talking with him, because the sun's rays glanced on my head through the foliage.'

−'You met with many fashionable belles there, too, I suppose,' remarked another.

−'There were Madame Riviera, who is so very vivacious, and several other ladies; I mean the wives of cabinet ministers and other high personages. But on the whole, I did not think the gathering was particularly unique for Paris, with regard to beauty.'

−'By the bye, have you ever seen Mr. Roosevelt?' asked the duchess.

−'Yes, I have. He impresses one at first sight with his enormous energy and intellectual power. He likes Japan. He was taking lessons in jiujitsu under a Japanese master when I was at Washington early last year. He told me he had been practising it three times a week.'

−'Yes,' said the duchess, 'I understand jiujitsu is much in vogue in England and America just at present.'

−'It seems so. In New York and Washington some ladies are also taking lessons, I am told; so also in England, as you know.'

−'But I suppose even in Japan it is only studied something like fencing is in our fencing schools, not as a part of the universal education.'

−'Just so,' I answered. 'It does not form a part of the general education, though it is very extensively studied in the higher colleges and schools.'

−'It looks certainly like an art worth paying attention to,' said the duchess.

−'Here, too, some time ago,' said Baron C., 'a Japanese jiujitsu master once came to Paris and gave an exhibition at a theatre, challenging, with the offer of a prize, any Frenchman who would combat with him. No Frenchman won. They were beaten one after the other. The people did not like so much humiliation, and the audience decreased, so the master had to go back to London; such is the Frenchman.'

−'Well,' said I, 'it might have been only a momentary caprice, perhaps because Japan is not your ally, but the audience could not have been diminished for such a cause as you say. There can be no notion of humiliation, because it is a question of art. However, if the Occidentals, with their natural strength and physique, become well equipped with that art, we the small Japs shall never be a match for them; so I would rather wish you Occidentals do not learn the art.'

All present broke into laughter, and in a minute or two I was once more wafted through the air and making my way elsewhere.

III

Japanese art and the West—Night-fêtes—Sale of flowers and plants—Singing Insects—A discussion on the moon, flowers, snow, etc.—Music of snow and rain—Lines on hailstones—A particular evening for lunar perspective—A blind scholar and his wife—The deaf, dumb, and blind of Japan—The calendar and its radical change in Japan—Calumnies on Japan, and an anonymous letter—Japanese ways of counting ages—The question of women and a lady's opinion on Japanese women—Lafcadio Hearn—Japanese names—Difficulty of distinguishing between 'L' and 'R'—Discussion on pronunciation—London and Tokio patois—Japanese nobility and the method of addressing nobility—Books on Japan—Once more on Lafcadio Hearn—Discussion on women's education—The Risen Sun

Time and space in dreamland have become more inconsecutive, and events have crowded rapidly one on another. In dreamland, moreover, one frequently sees in an incongruous group people who in ordinary life seldom come into contact with one another. Such is my experience.

Now I found myself guest at a reception given by a lady whose residence was in the neighbourhood of the Grand Opera, where I met a number of authors and critics of both sexes. Then at our Legation, near the l'Arc de Triomphe, where I was spending the evening in a large company, which included several ladies of my own country. Again at the soirée of an association interested in things Japanese, where also were members of both sexes, and then, hey presto! all these events and places would transform themselves into one single scene, as though they had been but one and the same gathering.

74

I remember well that at the meeting of the association a special toast was proposed after dinner by the president in my honour, to which I responded, saying how much I thanked its members for their sympathy for Japan. The little which Japan had been made known to France, or perhaps to Europe, was largely due to the appreciation of the Japanese arts by those present, and some others who had preceded them, such as MM. Bing and Guimet. I also said that a nation having an art such as ours, though perhaps not equal to the best arts of Europe, could not be so savage and wild as many calumniators represent, and further, that I wished Frenchmen, and indeed Europeans generally, would study and examine Japan a little more, and cast away their prejudices. I also remarked en passant that the oriental section of the Louvre was anything but strong in Japanese objets d'art, Japanese painting was scarcely represented at all. Other conversations that I had were an agglomeration, so that I cannot remember where and with whom they were held.

−'By the bye, have you seen the fêtes of Neuilly?' asked a lady.

−'Yes, I have seen them,' I answered; 'but the place was so crowded, I could scarcely stand. It was interesting to watch the common people enjoy themselves. One thing which struck me most in the fête was that there were so many ménage aux chevaux (roundabouts) without any horses at all. All the objects on which people were riding were other animals—even pigs, the dirtiest animal on earth.'

−'But pigs are considered objects of luck.'

—'Ah! that's an ideal notion of the civilised people, I presume.'

—'Have you any similar fêtes in your country?'

—'Yes, we have. In Tokio, especially, we have fêtes very similar almost all the year round, though not on so large a scale as your night-fêtes of Neuilly. In Tokio there are one or two fêtes in the same night in some quarters of the town. There are many small shrines in different parts of Tokio, and the fêtes are nominally in their honour. I say nominally, because most people who go there, go to see the sights or the pretty things rather than to do homage to the shrines. Each of these shrines has a certain day which is kept in its honour. In our fêtes the things most sold are small plants and flowers with their roots, so that they may be planted as they are! They are taken to the fêtes by gardeners living in the suburbs, who make this kind of business their regular occupation, and therefore the occasion is more properly considered as the gardeners' evening. Sweets, toys, and small light objects for domestic use are sold, and there are different kinds of entertainments as well. The nature of your evening fêtes seems very different. In fact, I have not seen any plants or flowers sold there.'

—'The difference seems remarkable; but what do you do with those plants and flowers?'

—'There is a difference between our common people and yours. You see the bulk of those who frequent the fête in Tokio are ordinary townspeople. They buy the plants or flowers for a small sum of money; when first offered for sale a high price is asked, but it is quite an understood thing to bargain and at last to buy at a very low price. The more advanced the evening, the cheaper one can get them. The bargaining at these fêtes is so lively that it has become

76

proverbial, and people often say, this or that is not like buying night-fête plants. It is, however, a mistake if one were to suppose bargaining is a common thing at every shop in Japan, as in Italy or Egypt. Well, these people, however moderate their means, purchase one or other of the plants or flowers and take them home, and plant them either in their small gardens or in pots and vessels, and place them in their rooms. Some plants or flowers are already planted in a tasteful manner in pots or vessels of different shapes, so that they may be used as they are. The people are very happy with these objects. In summer and autumn all sorts of singing insects[1] are sold in pretty little cages. In the Orient, unlike in the Occident, the term insect itself is very poetic, and conveys more of the significance of the singing than of the object itself.'

—'I have always heard that your people in general are very artistic,' said she. 'I should like to follow their sentiments in regard to nature. For instance, when we look at the moon we sometimes become very sentimental.'

—'You mean in such cases as the night-scene where sweet Jessica and her lover Lorenzo sang "In such a night, in such a night as this."'

—'Exactly.'

—'Well, in that respect,' I answered, 'we are perhaps more developed than other peoples. Even the etymology of our language proves it. We have such terms as Hanami, that is a flower-seeing; Tsukimi, that is moon-seeing; and Yukimi, that is, snow-seeing. You have phrases such as "to see the flowers," "to see the moon," and "to see the snow," but these are hardly an equivalent. Our phrases imply a deeper feeling, both poetical and artistic; may even imply an act of

77

seeing those objects in the company of congenial friends. The snow is, as I indicated, one of these sights. Apropos of snow, I went to Richmond once in company with a few compatriots, to see the snow-scene in the park there, whence one commands a beautiful view of the river Thames. Many years afterwards I was asked if we had snow in my country (you know this kind of question is asked of us very often). I answered "Yes." Thereupon a lady, who happened to remember that I had gone to Richmond to see the snow there years ago, abruptly remarked, "Oh! I thought you had no snow in your country." When I replied, "What makes you think so," she said, "Because you went to Richmond on purpose to see the snow." I had then to explain that our excursion to Richmond was not because we did not know what snow was, but because we liked to see the sight. We do not get tired of seeing such scenes any more than you Europeans get tired of going to the opera, to see, or rather to hear the same opera over and over again, as for instance Faust.'

−'But at the opera we can satisfy our sense of sight as well as that of hearing,' said a young lady, 'but what of the snow! It has no colour, being white,—it has no sound: besides, the season must be cold and the very sight of it must be chilling.'

−'You are partly right, I admit, but is not white the very ideal of purity? Are you not very fond of it? Do not you ladies like wearing pure white dresses? Are you not wearing one at this very moment? We Japanese are very fond of white. The ideal colour of Shintoism is white. According to that creed, even for mourning, white is preferred to black. It suggests a notion of cleanliness, which is the essence of the creed. Besides, you cannot surely say opera boxes are ideally comfortable. They are not cold, it is true, but certainly they are generally stifling.

One sees there scenery, but what is it compared with the grandeur of nature. Then again, you cannot exactly say snow has no sound. We, in our poetry, speak of the music of falling snow, or the music of dropping rain. Those sounds are considered especially musical in the depth of night: we even poetise the sounds of falling hailstones. There is a well-known poem on a hailstorm composed some seven centuries ago. It is a short poem, as ours usually are, but to us it gives a deep impression, and animates a martial spirit. It is difficult to translate, but it runs somewhat like this:

"Oh see in this wilderness of vast Nasu
How the hailstones dash on the frozen ground!
And ring on the gauntlets of hunters bold
As they draw their arrows from leathern fold!"

—'Many hundred years after this poem was composed, when our country was enjoying a perfect peace, a well-known statesman, reflecting on that poem, gave his own bent of thought, as follows:

"Not knowing the age when hailstones rang
On the gauntlets of warriors' hands;
Warmly enveloped I lay me down,
Listening all night to their dropping sound."

—'Apropos of hailstones, what a strange occurrence it was the other day, when hailstones ravaged the vicinity of Paris, and that too in the height of summer. I met a compatriot and his wife, now staying near St. Germain, at a small gathering on the evening of the same day, and they described the size of the stones and the damage done to the glass of the different houses. At first no one present believed them, but my friends did their best to explain that some of the stones they picked up and put on a tray were still large when they had left their home several hours afterwards. What they said was perfectly true, for I read in the papers next morning that in some places the hailstones were like eggs and weighed on an average from twenty to forty grammes; some even two hundred grammes. But ah! how silly I am to tell you all this, as you must all be well aware of it.'

−'Never mind,' said those present, 'but please proceed with your discourse.'

−'Well, there is a particular night of the year which is considered the best for the moon-scene; the 15th of August by the Lunar Calendar. The people generally get up a small social gathering to celebrate that evening. It was on one of those occasions that Hanawa, the celebrated blind scholar of Japan, gently sang as he sighed:

"If it were a flower, I might touch it."

'The line does not sound very sympathetic when translated into a foreign language, but in the original Japanese it is full of poetry, and the meaning is understood that he could not even console himself by the sense of touch. The remark was overheard by his wife, who pathetically joined him by singing:

"This Moon! 'tis the night that makes blind men's wives weep."

−'Very fine and pathetic; but you said just now "celebrated blind scholar,"' remarked a lady. 'What do you mean by that? Do you mean to say he was a blind poet like Homer?'

−'No, he was not exactly a poet, but a great scholar. In England there was a celebrated blind scholar, Fawcett, and Hanawa was our Fawcett. He was a Professor under the Shogunate Government, and one of the best and largest collections of rare old Japanese books made by him was his crowning achievement, and we are all much indebted to him.'

−'I suppose there are as many blind, deaf, and dumb in your country as in any other?' asked another; 'and what do they do, or rather, what do you do with them?'

−'There are some deaf, dumb, and blind schools at present, and those, among them, who are fortunate, are educated there as in Europe. There was no such school in former days, but much care was taken of the blind, even more than at present.'

−'In what way?' asked she.

−'In former days the blind had several privileges. In the first place, there was a special order consisting of several degrees, which was bestowed on meritorious blind people; next, there was a law which protected blind men when lending money, so that they had great facility in getting their dues paid, inasmuch as a lay debtor was summarily ordered to pay any claim raised by a blind man. Then the musical profession was generally assigned to them, thus, the professors of the Koto, a stringed instrument, were generally blind men, and they had the privilege of giving out diplomas to their pupils. In the country parts, blind men

81

were allowed to make a round of visits to the different houses of the gentry, singing a particular kind of war-song, called "Heike," to the accompaniment of the Biwa, another kind of stringed instrument. Then again, the Amma, the Japanese "massage" was mostly the profession of blind men.'

'You say "blind men," but what of blind women?' asked another.

−'Ah! I was wrong, for I have only spoken of blind men, but blind women were accounted much the same. But that Japanese Amma, I can never forget it, especially after hard work when one's muscles have become stiffened. It is such a soothing remedy. In Europe massage is used only for people who have some ailment, but in Japan ordinary people very commonly make use of it, and consequently a large number of blind people follow that occupation. The protection of the blind under the old régime was, of course, good in its aim, but it produced some abuse, and, besides, the great change of all methods of administration also affected the privileges given them. There is no longer any order bestowed on them, nor any special protection given to blind money-lenders, but in other respects their occupations remain pretty much the same.'

−'You have just spoken of lunar months of August,' said another: 'here in Paris the Russian Embassy and the Chinese Legation celebrate their New Year each differently from ours. Russia still sticks to the old style of calendar though solar; and China seems to hold to the lunar. How is it with you? Your calendar does not seem to differ from ours.'

—'Yes, our calendar at present is exactly the same as yours,' I answered. 'It used to be lunar, as is the Chinese, but it is now thirty-four years since we adopted the solar by a stroke of the pen, that is to say, by an edict of the Emperor. We thought in this world of cosmopolitanism that it was rather inconvenient for the different nations to have different calendars, and that it would be expedient to follow the example of the majority of the nations. We considered it a bold stroke of policy, but you see all such changes are made subjects of ridicule, and the Japanese are called mere imitators.'

—'Oh no, you go too far,' said another. 'No one ridicules Japan for that kind of change. It was excellent.'

—'And yet,' said I, 'all other changes are exactly the same in our eyes as that one.'

—'People are now beginning to understand Japan,' said she.

—'May be,' I said. 'I am very glad of it, but, you see, our calumniators even now make very unjust accusations against us, and still speak of us as monkeys. Since my arrival in Europe, not only have I noticed that these things have been written in newspapers, but I have myself received many letters of that kind. I cannot think what good they can do by sending me such letters and wasting stamps. I suppose they are but an infinitesimal part of the money spent for such purposes by our opponents. This very day, when I was coming out of the hotel, I received one of those letters: the postmark is Paris. I read it through on the way, and I have it still here. It is this: you may read it.'

So saying, I handed the letter to the lady, and she read it out as follows:

'MON CHER SINGE JAUNE,—Vous singes jaunes, voulez avoir beaucoup de pièces jaunes—travaillez—vous les aurez; mais avec votre tuerie—vous n'arriverez pas à les avoir—je vous assure. Fichez le camp—allez habiter aux Philipines. L'Europe et l'Amérique sont fermées aux singes jaunes sauvages. Vous martirisez chez vous les femmes! Votre meilleur homme Yoma (sic)—en a tué plusieurs. Vous êtes singes jaunes très méprisables—oh, bientôt l'or aura raison de vos hordes ... Souvenez-vous de mes singes. Singes jaunes sauvages dégoutants.

MISS NELLY.

'Qui ne vous aime pas: oh du tout....'

Finishing the reading, the lady exclaimed, 'What a shame!' in which all those listening joined.

Said I,—'The letter evidently refers to the question of indemnity. You see, it is written on a telegraph-form, and the article and the song, both equally disgusting, pasted purposely for me to read, are cuttings from Russophile papers: you can pretty well surmise from what source it came; the signature is also amusing!'

−'Shame!' they all exclaimed once more, but we all soon burst into laughter. When the laughter, whereby the peace of my dreamland had been a trifle disturbed, subsided, a lady present said:

−'You have a peculiar way of counting one's age, have you not? Has that anything to do with the calendar? Don't you say, for instance, a baby born the year before the last, three years old?'

–'Yes,' I answered, 'we still do so in ordinary conversation. But it has nothing to do with the calendar; it is only a matter of usage. You see the year in which one is born is counted as one year, and the year in which one is counting is counted as another, and therefore, a child born the year before last is reckoned as three years old. In the case of a dead person, the year in which he died is counted as one year; therefore, when you read of the age of our heroes or statesmen in history, you have always to take that into account. In former days, young ladies born late in the year used to complain to their mothers that they had a disadvantage in point of age. Young ladies like to minimise their age all over the world. Don't they?'

–'No joking, please.'

–'Very well! since the alteration of the calendar we have adopted your mode of reckoning for legal purposes, and we say in that case, "full so many years." It is therefore rather strange in actual society to hear people often speaking of so many years of age according to the new style, and so many years according to the old style.'

–'It must sound very odd. Apropos of ladies, I adore Japanese ladies,' said a lady.

–'Ah! that's too much: surely you do not think so,' I remarked.

The lady just referred to was an American by birth, who came to France when a mere child, and having grown up in this country had married a Frenchman. The couple were out in Japan for many years. They had several children, the majority of whom were born there. She had resided in one of the most populous towns, her husband having been attached to a certain public function. She seemed not entirely to approve of the social condition of France.

−'France will be ruined by her women. Look, for instance, at the condition of Paris,' she said.

−'You jest. I imagine your ideal of women must be very different from ours,' I said.
−'No! Not at all,' she answered.

−'And yet,' said I, 'the question of the status of women is becoming more keen, far more keen in America than in this country. I have observed it in many writings.'

−'That's true, I dare say,' she said.

−'A little time ago,' I continued, 'I read an article describing the influence of American wives and daughters over their husbands and parents. I remember one instance mentioned in that article. The daughter of a well-to-do business man took a fancy to live in a town where she had been on a visit for a little time. She prevailed on her father to remove their home to that town. He did so, and the result was his total ruin in consequence of losing old customers and not obtaining new. The story may be a little exaggerated.'

−'No, it is quite possible,' she said. 'I like Japanese ladies and their children. The Japanese ladies I met with were so sweet and gentle and real models of women. I came to know them very intimately in this way. You see, in the town where I lived there is an association for the promotion of the mutual interests of France and Japan, the members being mostly Frenchmen. No lady was admitted into membership at first. I insisted on having it done. I was the first lady member. I induced many Japanese ladies to become members. The views I held were that mutual understanding could only be promoted by both sexes associating with each other. We found the innovation work very satisfactory. I often invited Japanese ladies to my home to spend an afternoon or evening. I usually caused them to bring their children, and made them play with mine. I did all this with as little ceremony as possible, because only by doing so can real friendship be brought about. I, of course, returned the visits and took my children with me. During that intercourse I naturally came to know a great deal about the Japanese ladies, and for that reason I think so much of them. They are real ideals of women. Perhaps a little more freedom for them might be good, but on the whole nothing more could be desired. Don't let them get spoilt by the evil influence of the West.'

−'I think I must reserve my remarks, either pro or con,' I said, 'but it is curious to notice what divergence of opinion there is relating to the condition of Japanese women. Perusing casually a book by Lafcadio Hearn a little time ago, I came across a passage where he speaks of Japanese women as being the most artistic objects, as it were, of the most artistic nation of the world, and laments that this perfection will be deteriorated by the influence of time. There is a lady of good birth in London whom I know very well, who admires Japanese ladies very much, though I am not quite sure that she herself would like to live like a Japanese lady. She told me that when the time came for her two boys to marry she would send them to Japan in order to be married out there. Her words may not have been mere passing compliments, for she has contributed to a monthly an article under the title of the "True Chrysanthemum," which pays a very high tribute to the Japanese women. On the other hand, however, few Occidentals know what the Japanese women are, and writers are not wanting who cast upon them sweeping condemnation. They even say that Japanese women know not what is chastity, and even that no such word exists in the Jananese language.'

—'What nonsense!'

—'Excuse me for pushing my remarks to such a point as this,' I continued, 'but you see I am so blunt in expression, and I cannot make my meaning plain unless I use such cut-and-dry phrases. In my own opinion, without any partiality for my own country, I think I can confidently say that chastity is far more practised in Japan than in any other nation.'

—'Hearn's books, which you have just mentioned, are charming,' said another lady. 'I have read some of them. They go, I think, a long way in contradicting those unfair charges.'

—'Yes, I think so too,' said I. 'But, you know, one tongue is nothing against a hundred, as we say. However that may be, he was a fine writer. It is sad that he died last year. He made, as he said, the study of the Japanese heart and thought his special subject. All his books, therefore, are concerned with some sort of Japanese psychology. They are generally so full of pathos and feeling that even Japanese readers are often moved to tears.'

—'Then you have read all his books. I should like you to give me the outline of them at your leisure,' she said.

—'I don't think that would be possible, because I don't know them all.'

−'But you have just now said "all his books," as though you knew all,' she said.

−'No!' I answered, 'I have not read all. I have seen most of the titles, and some pages here and there, and guessed all the rest. You see, nowadays, printing is comparatively so cheap and people are so fond of writing, and further, nine-tenths of the writers have their books printed at their own expense, so that the publishers run no, risk. If, therefore, one tries to read all books, one would become a mere bookworm and a good-for-nothing fellow. Once a compatriot of mine, when in Germany, was admitted into the study of a great professor. The four walls were covered with nothing but shelves of books. The professor said that all those books were sent to him by writers of all nations who were engaged in the same pursuits as himself. As a matter of fact he was a jurist, and all those books were on law. The visitor asked if he had read all of them, to which the professor answered "Yes." Thereupon he observed, "Impossible, you could not have had time to read them all." The professor then explained that the essential points of any book were all known to experts, so that a few pages on those points, which could easily be found by index, were sufficient to know all that was contained in a book. In that way, he said, "he read all the books which had come to him."'

−'What a joke!' said the lady. 'But what kind of man was he? I mean Mr. Hearn. His life seems to have been much in the clouds.'

−'So far as I am aware of,' said I, 'he was born in Lafcadi, one of the Ionian Islands, when it was under English occupation, having an Irish father, I believe, and a Greek mother. He passed his early years in England until he became a youth, when he went to America, where he remained until after the prime of life. He then went to Japan, and in course of time married a Japanese lady and became a naturalised subject there. So he was a regular cosmopolitan. He always occupied some position as teacher, and was much liked by his numerous pupils. His Japanese name was Koizumi Yakumo. Technically speaking, he caused himself to be adopted by the family of his wife, and so took their family name "Koizumi" for his surname, and Yakumo for his personal name, or, as you call it, Christian name.'

−'What you have just said somewhat strikes me,' remarked the lady. 'You have put the Christian name after the surname.'

−'Ah!' said I, that's a reasonable question. Perhaps you don't know that in Japan we put our family name first. That is to say Gambetta Léon instead of Léon Gambetta, if he were a Japanese. It is so with the Chinese; it is also so with the Hungarians. It is one of the proofs which the Hungarians produce as being descendants of the same stock as the Orientals. When, however, we are in Europe, or write with European letters, we generally reverse the order and make it agree with the European method. Well, unless we do that, we are liable to be called wrongly by having our names reversed, in such a fashio as Monsieur Léon, or Monsieur G. Léon, instead of Monsieur Gambetta, or Monsieur L. Gambetta. Such absurdities often occur in reality, and it is very inconvenient.

−'I see: that accounts for many discrepancies which exist in writing som well-known Japanese names, as I occasionally notice in books or papers written in a foreign language; but it is no use to refer to the Japanese by name, their names are too difficult for us to remember—it took me weeks to remember your name correctly.'

—'Just so,' I answered, 'It is equally difficult for us to remember European names. It is the reason why I do not recollect many people to whom I am continually introduced; to confess, I do not remember your name correctly. Russian names are particularly difficult to remember, not only to us Orientals, but to Anglo-Saxons, even to you, the French. Do you know that in England Rodjestvensky, before he became famous and well known, was called simply "Roj" very often, and aliens sometimes called him "Rotten-cheese-sky." Poor admiral! Witte is simple enough to remember. We Japanese remember and often write General Kuropatkin as Kurobato, that is to say, "black pigeon."

Of course, association is the best means of remembrance. We remember your words "Salle-à-manger" by Sara-mongi, that is, a "plate and written characters," and the English word "Minister" as me-no-shita, that is, "below the eyes." In fact, me-no-shita is used very commonly in corrupt English at the open ports of Japan. Frans-Me-no-shita is "French Minister," and Igiris-Me-no-Shita is "English Minister." A dozen years ago there was in Japan an enterprising man who advertised that he had invented a good system of memory, and even opened a school. It was no other than remembering things by association, and I think there is a good deal in it. A little time ago, as you know, their Highnesses Prince and Princess Arisugawa were on a visit to Europe. Lord Lansdowne had great difficulty in remembering the name. Our Me-no-shita in London asked him if there were not a Princess Alice in England, to which his Lordship replied "Yes." He then asked if there were not a street called "Gower Street," to which his Lordship similarly answered "Yes." Thereupon

91

our minister said: "Very well, Princess Alice and Gower Street, that makes Arisugawa." After that his lordship, the Foreign Secretary of Great Britain, remembered the name of our Prince and Princess very well.'

−'That's all very well,' said she: 'but you mix up r and l altogether.'

−'That's true,' I answered, 'it is the weakest point for us in speaking European tongues. We cannot, or at least without the greatest difficulty, make any difference in pronouncing r and l. Thus "right" and "light" become alike when we speak. It is very necessary to think of that fact when you talk with a Japanese. All this arises from the fact that in the Chinese and Japanese tongues there are not two different sounds of r and l; those sounds in Japanese are more like your ra, ri, ru, re, ro, whilst they are la, li, lu, le, lo in Chinese.'

−'I have noticed it very often,' she said, 'even while you talk you do the same. Your allusion to remembering things by association is very true; we do the same very often. But it often produces curious errors.'

−'True,' I said, 'I know a few instances. In Japan there is a kind of cloth, mostly used for négligées, called Yukata, a bath-cloth, so called because it was originally used after the bath. We call the "evening" Yiukata, the only difference being the "u" in one case being pronounced longer than in the other. We call "shower" Yiudachi. A European lady married to a Japanese appears to have tried to remember the bath-cloth by association. She went to a draper's and asked for a Yiudachi (shower) in place of Yiukata (evening). No one understood it. She was speaking of "shower" instead of "evening," the result of trying to speak by association. We have two ways of counting, and we call the number "ten" either jiu or to. We have a certain kind of boxes which are made to fit one on top of the other, and only the topmost box has a lid. They are called jiu-bako, which means piling boxes. They are used in households very commonly. The same lady appears to have remembered that name by jiu, that is, ten of the number according to one of two ways, and Hako, a box. One day she called her servant to bring to-bako instead of jiu-bako. The servants, of, course, did not understand her. The lady misused the association of counting ten in one way instead of the other.'

–'You said you had no difference between r and l, but I suppose you have almost all sounds of our tongue.'

–'No,' I answered, 'we have not. We have, for instance, no sound of f or v. In some parts of the country people pronounce ha, hi, he, ho like fa, fi, fe, fo, but it is considered bad dialect. The want of v and f in our letters is a point of great difficulty in transcribing foreign words into our writing, but we employ a new method for doing so. On the other hand, our h is pronounced very acutely. You say you have h mute and h aspirate, but in practice I never see, or rather hear, any aspiration at all. Hence, Count "Hisamatsu," our actual military attaché, is always called by the French, as he complains, "Isamatsu," which is not his Japanese name at all. This fact reminds me of a similar matter concerning our own Tokio. The genuine Tokio people generally pronounce Hi as shi. It is curious, but it is a fact. This often causes comical mistakes to be made by servant-girls who are told by their mistresses to pronounce it correctly, for they often mix up and use hi in place of shi and vice versa. Mind! Tokio is the capital of Japan, but its language is not the purest of the Japanese language. The same holds good in London. It is rather strange for us to notice that in London the h is so commonly misused. I once went to a master, or rather mistress, as she was a woman, of elocution, or at least she advertised herself as such, and she told me that one must be very careful not to be corrupted by the London patois, and that one must not say "am and hegg" for "ham and egg," but while she was telling me those things she herself was making an awful mangling of the h. No wonder! She was a pure Londoner. I went to her no more.'

−'That's too awful! She could not have been a well-educated woman, or you are telling us an exaggerated story.'

−'Maybe she was not well educated,' said I, 'but my story is a plain, naked fact. It is very difficult, I think, to get rid of colloquial corruption when once thoroughly imbued with it, even with all the aids of education. I can relate an incident bearing on the point. There is, in Japan, far away from Tokio, a district where people in common parlance can make no difference between shi and su. Once I went to that district and gave a lecture to a large gathering of students belonging to the higher schools of the district. Seven or eight of the most capable students took down my speech, and a complete draft of it was made by them, the defective parts having been supplied by one from the other. It was published in the local papers. It was most perfect, as though taken by shorthand, except in one respect, and it was that shi and su had been intermingled, as though I had spoken in the local dialect. It seems that not only are they unable to distinguish the difference when they themselves speak, but also when they hear other people speak. It is a great drawback to the development of the district. The local authorities hire teachers from other districts and try to correct this defect, but with little success. The function of our ears is strange. Sounds which are quite distinct to some people are quite indistinct to others. Our music has not so high a variation of tune as the Western music, but it has sufficient variation to please our ears; but the Occidentals compare our music to the beating of a drum by a child—no tune and no variation, the reason being, I think, because our tunes and variations are quite inaudible to the Western ear. From the same point of view, crows or cows, and, indeed, all living animals have their own language, only our ears cannot distinguish the difference of their words one from another.'

−'Another pleasantry, I perceive,' remarked a lady. 'But tell me, baron, how do you pronounce the name of your great statesman, "Ito"? Is it pronounced like a-i-t-o-, that is to say, i in the English way of pronouncing Ireland?'

−'No,' I said, 'like a-i-t-o- without a, that is to say, i in your own French way of pronouncing Ireland. I will once for all give you a good clue how to pronounce Japanese names, which you must come across very often nowadays in the newspapers. I is pronounced always like i in your il or English ill. Our E is always like e in French "état" or "été." G is always hard gutteral, that is to say, ga like g in "Gambetta," ge like ge in English "get," and ge in German, and your gue. Gi like gi in the English "gift," and your gui in "Guillaume," and, therefore, you must pronounce General "Nogi" like General "Nogui" in the French way, and not like "Noji" or "Nozi" as you generally do. Our go is always go, in English "got," unless the o is a long one as in Tôgô, and our gu is always like a simple g in Gladstone and Grant.'

−'But how do you then account for u?' interposed she.

−'Our u preceded by a consonant,' I answered, 'is generally sounded very, very slightly—almost inaudibly, in fact—so much so that you need take no notice of it. Therefore ku,

95

su, mu, etc., are like simple k, s, m, etc. There is another secret in pronouncing our names, and it is this: when a consonant is followed by a vowel, pronounce it always together with the vowel. Thus yoritomo should be pronounced yo-ri-to-mo, and not yor-i-tom-o, and pronounce it without putting any accent: if you follow this rule, you will get nearer to the right pronunciation.'

There was among those present the daughter of Prince Ichijo, naval attaché to the Japanese Legation. She was addressed by a person present as Miss Ichijo. This appears to have struck a lady present, who was at a little distance from her. She said to me:

−'Is not that young lady of very high birth?'
−'Yes, she is. Her parentage is very high, though not of the Imperial blood.'

−'Is she not a daughter of Prince Ichijo?'

−'Yes, she is the daughter by his first wife, who is no more; the present princess is his second wife, also of high birth, being a daughter of one of our former great feudal lords.'

−'How is it, then, that the young lady is addressed as "Miss." If she were a European, she would certainly be addressed as princess, or by some other title?'

−'You are right in thinking so,' I answered; 'but in Japan the titles of nobility are only borne personally by the chief of the family and his wife. All the other members of the family differ in no way from ordinary people, except that they share the membership of the family. In this respect our system totally differs from that of Continental Europe. The English system is like ours as far as law goes, but there also the younger members of noble families enjoy some distinction by courtesy. This is the reason why one hears of a marquis, an earl, or a viscount speaking in the House of Commons as an M.P.'

−'I suppose your system of nobility is pretty much the same as the Western ones in other respects,' said she.

−'Yes, our titles of nobility are divided into five grades, corresponding, for example, to the English duke, marquis, earl, viscount, and baron. The first grade, which corresponds to the English duke, is generally translated as prince; I don't know who began it but it is so. In Germany the highest title of nobility is "Fürst," as you know, and it is translated as "prince" in English or French. I believe the analogy is taken from that fact. It must not, however, be confounded with the princes of Imperial blood, for in Japanese the two titles in question are absolutely distinct, though, translated into the European languages, they sound very much alike.'

−'What books written in English on Japan would you recommend me to read?' asked one lady.

−'I cannot say with much authority, because naturally I have not spent much time over those books, but began it from what I have observed and from what I have heard from other people Lafcadio Hearn's are the best to study the Japanese character, but his books are generally collections of different essays, so that they do not give a panoramic survey of Japan. In that respect Advance Japan, by J. Morris, is said to be very handy and good. Concerning that book, I may mention a rather commendable incident which took place last year. A Russian lady, a lover of her own country, I presume, lamented the great lack of knowledge of Japan among her country people, which was, as she thought, the cause of the many misfortunes to her country. She wrote to an English friend of hers asking what book written in English on Japan she would recommend her to translate into Russian. The English lady recommended the book just mentioned, and it was translated and published in Russia. I have myself seen the Russian edition of it, neatly printed and beautifully illustrated. The Rev. William E. Griffis, of America, has written several books on Japan. His Mikado's Empire gives a most excellent generalisation of Japanese history. A new book on Japan, entitled Imperial Japan by Knox, another American, is very good. I have read it through. The only chapter in it which I think very unfair is one relating to Japanese women. Of course, even in the best books there are some points which are not quite exact, and they contain many amusing mistakes when scrutinised from our point of view.'

−'What is then your opinion about Lafcadio Hearn's books, for instance? I would like to know your opinion,' said another lady.

−'You make me traverse almost the same field over again,' I said.

−'Never mind! The points are different,' she said.

−'Well, I need not speak of his occasional mistranslations of Japanese words or some small technical errors, but I can say that, in my opinion, he sometimes goes a little too far in giving reasons to matters concerning feeling and sentiment. For instance, he raises the question, if a soul be something concrete and suppose it is gone somewhere—heaven or Paradise, as one may term it—how would it be possible to be present simultaneously at the place where it is enshrined, or where offerings are made, and he tries to solve the difficulty philosophically and logically. He seems to place too much stress on our notions of ancestral worship. We practise it, we like it, and we think it fine and noble, and yet we do so from a spirit of feeling and sentiment. Many things in connection therewith are done by us, not always with conclusive, logical reasoning. In this respect many Europeans often misjudge us, forgetting that they themselves do the same at home. They canonise meritorious persons, sometimes only legendary; they have their wayside shrines of Madonna; they celebrate All Souls' Day, when the whole town or village flocks to the cemetery; they set up statues of great men,—a statesman, a warrior, a writer, a philanthropist, a musical composer, a sculptor, a scientist, and what not. They construct a grand pantheon or cathedral and consecrate the remains of their distinguished dead therein. They even erect colossal figures of an ideal personification, such as "Liberty" standing on high at the Place de la République, and other figures representing great cities, as at the Place de la Concorde. They sometimes decorate such figures on certain days with flowers, as is the case with the statue of Beaconsfield, which is covered with primroses on Primrose League Day, nay, sometimes a figure is decorated with wreaths all the year round, like Strasbourg at the Place de la Concorde. Mind, with regard to this last, I am not speaking of any political aspect of the matter. All this to my mind is very fine in idea. All this, I think, is not done for mere play, nor are those objects set up for mere ornament. The notion contained therein is, I think, intended to perpetuate and sanctify the memory of the person, or of an idea in the minds of the people. If any stranger, for instance, approach any of these objects and insult it in any gross manner, he would be sure to be much hissed, or even punished. From this, it is certain that these matters belong to the sphere of feeling and sentiment and are not exactly within the limits of strict philosophical and logical reasoning. Our ancestral worship and things connected with it are of the same kind. And yet those Occidentals who have themselves very similar things look upon such institutions in Japan with amazement or curiosity, or even with contempt, or else like Lafcadio Hearn, try to reason out some points which are not altogether soluable by ordinary reasoning. A Confucian saying has this: "When you perform a commemoration in honour of your dead parents, do it as though their spirit is present before you." And I think it quite right; it is no honour to the dead if one make an offering and reasons in his mind at the same time that the dead is nothing more than dust, or that its spirit could not be in existence, or at all events, far away from us in an unknown region. When a foreigner sees the shrine erected in Tokio where men, generals and soldiers alike, who died for their country, are consecrated as a sort of deity, he is apt to think it a peculiar custom. But what difference is there between our observance of the illustrious dead and that of burying a distinguished statesman or soldier in the Pantheon or Westminster Abbey? The only difference in all such matters seems to me to amount to this: the feeling and sentiment of the preservation of the memory of the deserving men is more intent and more general in one case than in the other.'

−'I cannot agree with you altogether in your philosophy,' said a young lady.

−'That may be,' said I. 'You shut your eyes to things near; we have a saying, "A lighthouse does not see its own base." Oh! I beg your pardon. I must not make such remarks; you see, too great a freedom of speech is apt to produce an abuse; nay, that very freedom sometimes even wrecks a grand army on an expedition.'

−'I see. That is the reason why you muzzled all the newspaper correspondents who purposely went out to the Far East, and, by doing so, you have nearly wrecked your own country.'

−'Yes, nearly,' I answered, 'but we happily managed to escape their vindictiveness, and won our battles. No one in the world knew that Togo was quietly waiting with his fleets for the ever-memorable Armada behind the islands of Tsushima, almost on the same spot where the great Mongolian Armada was annihilated some six hundred years ago.'

−'And yet you yourself are rather voluble. You are always talking about something: you talk a good deal more than any ordinary person.'

−'Excuse me,' I retorted, 'I don't think I am voluble at all. By nature I prefer listening to others than talking to them, for in listening to others one can learn something, but nothing when talking to them. I prefer still more to be alone, than either to be listening or talking, for then the waste of time is still less. I only talk when it is absolutely necessary. You know, of course, that from Pythagoras down to Spencer and Huxley, extending, over some four or five thousand years, thousands of philosophers have written books, millions of books, spinning out their thoughts or rather conjectures, like spiders webs, but the essence of it all is summed up in only these few words, "I don't know."'

−'Ah! I see,' cried she, 'you talk nowadays so much, because you think it necessary for the good of your country. Do you know you are generally called the "Japanese Mentor," or the "Missionary of things Japanese."'

−'I don't mind by what name they call me. Don't you remember: "That which we call a rose, by any other name would smell as sweet."'

−'And yet you must not monopolise the time; I must now have my turn of freedom of speech.'

The lady thus claiming her turn of speech was a lively, vigorous, energetic young lady, capable of talking and writing in several languages, confident of herself and of her sex, as confident as though she were carrying on her shoulders the responsibility of half mankind, that is, the whole of womankind. She takes, of course, great interest in women's education and the promotion of women's rights in all matters. She began by saying, with her face turned towards me:

−'In the letter you have just read—'

−'I did not read it,' I interposed; 'it was that lady.'

−'Well, then,' she said, 'in the letter you have brought in your pocket and have made one of the ladies read to us. In that letter mention is made of Japanese ladies—'

−'Oh, no more of the ladies,' I interrupted; 'I have spoken so much of them, that if I repeat too often, I shall weary my readers of A Summer Dream.'

−'What!' she said, 'I do not mind if you read or copy the Midsummer Night's Dream, or the Winters Tale, but I must have my turn of speech. In that letter, the writer speaks of the Japanese killing their mothers, wives, and sisters: by that the writer, no doubt, means the affliction which is put upon them by the death of so many men on the battlefields.

102

But in my opinion, it is not only in Japan that women are killed, but in all countries, in England, in France, in America and everywhere else! Man everywhere despises women's education and deprives women of their lives.'

−'Of course, you take great interest in women's education,' I interposed.

−'Not only,' she continued, 'they despise women's education, but they employ every machination to hinder women from developing brain power, which is their only life.'

−'You are too harsh,' I remarked.

−'No, not at all,' she continued. 'People talk about American girls getting the upper hand of their elders, as though they were not capable of giving advice to their somewhat belated relatives. The younger we are, the older and wiser we deem ourselves: such are the real facts of the world, don't you think so, baron?'

−'Well, not exactly,' I replied.

−'I don't think you take much interest in women's education. You are intelligent, but you are, all the same, a man. You men have all one trait in common, and that is, a desire to exclude women from every sphere of action politically and socially.'

−'No, far from it,' I answered. 'I am a great advocate of the mental and physical development of women. My only desire as man is that the time should soon arrive when we could elect women as deputies to the Chamber; send them to the barracks and ships as soldiers and sailors, and to the field of campaign in time of emergency; select the most beautiful as our ambassadors and ministers to the courts of different countries and win over the hearts of the nation to which they are sent, while all this time we men might stay at home and calmly nurse the babies or indulge in a quiet smoke, of which I am very fond.'

−'Let's have some more serious talk,' remarked another lady. 'You have not yet told us of the foundation of Bushido and its ethics. Let us hear something of that.'

−'It is rather complicated. It will take much time. It won't do for my Summer Dream.'
−'What?' she asked.

−'Nothing. I mean it is too complicated and serious to tell you in this place. On those points, I must refer you to my book entitled The Risen Sun, published by Archibald Constable, the best publisher in London. It is one of the most important books published in the twentieth century; otherwise Archibald Constable would never have published it.'

−'I see a Japanese gentleman is sometimes capable of indulging in a little bluff.'

−'But the twentieth century has only just begun: besides, this kind of bluff is quite harmless. It is very different from that which some people are fond of indulging in, and, above all, it cannot bring about a national catastrophe.'

−'Enough, we all see what you mean. "Their rising senses," as the poet says, will soon "begin to chase the ignorant fumes that mantle their clearer reason." Let us go now,' said one of them, and they all dispersed.

104

Thereupon I also having left the room, sprang into the air, and once more floated away like a sprite, humming as I did so:—

'... I do fly
After summer, merrily:
Merrily, merrily, shall I live now,
Under the blossom that hangs on the bough.'

[1] For these 'singing insects,' which are a distinctive feature in the Far East, see Lafcadio Hearn on 'Insect-Musicians' in his Exotics and Retrospectives (1898), pp. 39-80. The practice of caging them dates at least from 1095 A.D. Insects are now bred for this purpose in enormous numbers.

IV

A talk on brackens—Eating of fruits without peeling—A pet tortoise—Remarks on languages—Discourses on jiujitsu—Comparison of jiujitsu and wrestling—Japanese art and the Kokkwa—Pictures in the Gospel—Discourse on Bushido, its history and the origin of the term—Explanation of the terms Daimio, Samurai, and Bushi—Its literature—Japanese revenge and European duel—Japanese sword—Soul of Samurai—General Stoessel and a broken sword—Discussion on Japanese social morality—Japan far cleaner than any other nation—The condition at the time of the transition—General view of the westernised Japan—Occidental vulgarity

I was at the luncheon table of the Duke and Duchess of Fairfield: quite en famille, there being present only a young nobleman of Italian descent besides the duke and duchess and their two daughters.

In the course of luncheon, casual mention was made by one of the young ladies of the fronds of bracken, called warabi in Japan, regarding which I had made some remarks in England as to its edible properties.

−'I have read in some English papers all that you said about it,' said the young nobleman; 'and, indeed, most of the French journals have also reported it since.'

−'Yes, after I had initiated the matter, almost all the English papers, both in town and country, made some comments. I have even read that a philanthropic gentleman had reproduced the necessary information in leaflet form, for distribution amongst the needy people in some parts of

Wales, where there is often a scarcity of food. The starch made from the roots of bracken is considered in Japan the best, and is used very widely. There is a similar vegetable called jemmai; it is larger than bracken and used in a dried form. It is very soft and palatable, and is very extensively used in Japanese cookery. I do not know for certain if the latter kind exists in Europe, though I believe it does. As to bracken, it grows everywhere. I am, however, but little sanguine that my recommendation will be utilised in England, though the method of preparation is very simple. The secret of the preliminary preparation lies in soaking it, from ten to fifteen hours in water with soda. I revealed it from a philanthropic motive. But, you see, the British are so conservative in such matters. I even noticed, in a newspaper, a letter wherein the writer stated that he had cooked some bracken, but it turned out unpalatable, although quite tender. He did not wait to find out if there might not be room for improvement in his method of cooking: people are so apt to discredit others before they make sure of a fact.'

−'That is generally the case in this world,' said the duchess; 'but I wonder if French bracken is equally good.'

−'Surely it is,' I replied, 'even that in the neighbourhood of Paris: the bracken in Fontainebleau forests is said to be very fine. Only in May last, a number of Japanese ladies in Paris made a special excursion there, and brought back bunches of it. I was one of those who enjoyed the dishes resulting.'

−'You may be sure it is a subject that will be taken up, when the semi-famine days come, and then, perhaps, your name will be remembered,' remarked one of the young ladies.

−'No, I think not,' I replied. 'I believe, I shall be buried long before that, and my name too.'

−'Oh, don't say that,' broke in another of the young ladies.

Dessert was now served, in the course of which I remarked:

−'I will tell you an incident which will probably interest you. I was spending a week-end with the Dake and Duchess of Hamilton, who have always been very courteous to me. One morning, at the breakfast table, I noticed the duchess cut an apple, and gave it to her young son without peeling. This rather struck me, so I asked her reason, when she told me that her medical adviser had instructed her to do so, because the essence of the nourishing part of the fruit was contained just under the skin, so that it was better not to remove the skin. It was quite a relief to me (for we men, and especially myself, often find it troublesome to pare fruit). Now I could eat fruit without paring the skin unconcernedly, and should any onlooker laugh at me, or ask the reason, I could lecture him from the point of medical science.'

−'You always view things from a point of vantage,' interposed the younger daughter.

We went into the garden, and took our coffee there in a shaded corner. Meanwhile I noticed a little puppy looking up at us from a corner of the turf. It did not move, and I soon discovered it was porcelain.

−'Ah, I see, I thought it was a live dog when I was here last. It was towards evening, just as I was leaving when I noticed it.'

At this moment a servant brought in a tortoise: it was a very large one and quite tame. The duchess fed it with lettuce, saying:

−'This is my pet, and I am very fond of it. It prefers lettuce to any other vegetable.'

−'I have seen many tortoises,' I said, 'but this is the first time I have seen one as a pet. In Japan, one sees in the ponds or small lakes round the temples, hundreds, nay, thousands, floating in the water, or lying on rocks or boards basking in the sun. Their preservation is chiefly due to the customary kindness and religious sentiment of the Japanese.'

I then told the duchess what I knew of tortoises and their habits, remarking that those amphibians lived more in the water than on land, and it was necessary for them to be put in the water at least occasionally.

And so the soft summer evening glided away as we passed from one topic of conversation to another.

−'Do you find European languages very difficult to learn?' asked one of the young ladies. 'I suppose there is no similarity between our language and yours?'

−'None whatever,' I replied, 'and we certainly find them very difficult to acquire. The difference between the various European languages might perhaps be compared to the difference between a horse and a mule, while the difference between Japanese and the European languages would certainly not be closer in comparison than a horse to an ox. That is to say, the former differs only in species, and the latter in kind. Hence you can easily see how much more difficult it is for an Oriental to learn any European language, than a European to learn a second European language. Even amongst the European languages, there are, as you know, many idioms differing one from the other, and consequently difficult to understand. Only the other day I was not a little amused at a French translation of the English sentence "hold good" in the sense that "one thing had an advantage over another." You can imagine how much more difficult it is for a Japanese to know the value of every word, not to say an idiom, of a European language. Once in Japan, I was watching some European and Japanese children playing Hide-and-Seek together. The European children were making use of the Japanese words meaning "Hot and Cold" in place of "Far and Near." I could only make out what they meant after I had carefully watched the game. I am sure we commit similar errors every day when speaking in a foreign language. More than thirty years ago a party of Japanese ambassadors, including the present Marquis Ito, whom you know, and their suites, made a round trip through America and Europe: perhaps the duke remembers it. The mayor of a large manufacturing town in England, which a portion of the party were visiting, invited the visitors to the play. The party was divided into two and occupied two boxes opposite each other. The mayor and his wife were in a box and their daughter in the other. An Englishman who was in the mayor's box remarked to a Japanese guest, of an eminent fellow-guest seated beside the young lady opposite, "Monsieur K. must be very happy," meaning, no doubt, to pay a compliment indirectly to the mayor and his wife; but the Japanese to whom the remark was addressed understood but little English and replied: "K. must be quite ashamed."

─'It spoilt everything. In our language the word meaning "shame" and "bashfulness" are identical and the sense is only modified by a slight difference in construction. A somewhat similar example is the great difference in the meaning between the phrases fâché contre and fâché de. The results of the misconstruction, as may be imagined, were rather serious. It was only made good by another Japanese who made a timely explanation. I heard this incident direct from that gentleman who made the explanation. That incident clearly demonstrates how difficult and delicate it is to express oneself in a tongue other than one's own.'

−'Exactly,' interposed the young nobleman. 'It is always necessary to make much allowance for a foreigner, and to make a guess at his meaning.'

−'The jiujitsu is being exhibited once more in France,' said the duchess. 'I have seen several advertisements in to-day's papers, one of which states that a physician asked the exhibitor to demonstrate on him, and afterwards declared it quite scientific. People in France know very little of that art.'

−'No wonder,' I answered; 'even in England, where jiujitsu is so much spoken of, it was very little known until quite recently. Not many years ago a lecture on the subject, accompanied by some practical demonstrations, was delivered at a literary society, by a Japanese gentleman, assisted by another Japanese. On that occasion a weekly paper of high reputation commented upon the art, saying that there was nothing in it. The writer added that jiujitsu was exactly the same as the English wrestling, with a few different tricks.'

−'Is there much difference between the two?'

−'Yes, there is a great difference. Of course the combatants in both exercises strive to get the upper hand of each other, but the great difference is that the wrestling relies chiefly on strength, whilst jiujitsu depends on all sorts of tricks, based upon a careful study of physical organism, and therefore physical strength may be said to be of little value, nay, in truth, it uses the strength of the opponent against himself. We, in Japan, have also a method of competition resembling the wrestling of the West, and we apply to that the Western name "wrestling." We do not like our jiujitsu to be confounded with it, though Western people sometimes call it by that name. When our jiujitsu is called "wrestling," it hurts our feelings a little.'

−'Why, how is that?' demanded the duchess.

−'Well, nothing very serious, but the reason is this: jiujitsu has always been regarded in Japan as an art chiefly practised by men of the higher classes. It has never been a profession, still less a public show, and the reason why now and then the art is made an object of exhibition in a public hall of the Western towns, is only an outcome of the altered conditions of the time. On the other hand, the wrestling which we call Sumoo has always been a profession and for public entertainment for many centuries.'

−'I see.'

−'It must, however, be understood that even wrestling is not considered a low profession, and though it is exhibited to the public, is very different from other kinds of shows— those, for instance, given at a fête. Wrestling in Japan has a very remote origin. In its earlier stage it was not a profession, it was one of the military sports, but as time went on it became a regular profession. Tokio is the centre of the Wrestling Association, and therefore it has the best wrestlers. Osaka comes next. The wrestlers are brought up and trained from boyhood: promising youths are picked up from all parts of the country by the principal wrestlers and taken into their private halls. There are two principal exhibitions of ten days, one early in the year and the other early in the summer, held in Tokio, when the rank and order of every member of the association is determined by competition. In the intervals they subdivide themselves into several parties and go about the country exhibiting their art. Men are very fond of seeing the wrestling, though very few women care to see it; in fact, it is only of recent date that one observes any women at all at such exhibitions, and those only of indifferent standing. It is not considered good taste. The last point excepted, wrestling in Japan resembles somewhat a bull-fight in Spain. I do not mean the sport itself, but in the sense of its being a national institution. From this fact you may see that we have more and better wrestlers than you in the West. Sometimes Western wrestlers come to Japan and challenge our wrestlers, but they are no match for ours. It is not worth boasting about, I merely state the fact. Of course, there is also much wrestling in country parts, and young people often perform, but they are, after all, only amateurs. As to jiujitsu, the art has been studied by the Samurai in a similar manner to fencing, with no professional performance or public show. Hence a great difference in the social position of jiujitsu experts and wrestlers. Nevertheless, the wrestlers maintain some trace of their ancient standing, for their position even now is regarded as superior to actors or the geisha, though good actors are rapidly gaining a social position.'

−'Is jiujitsu as old as wrestling?'

−'No, it is not. Jiujitsu is not quite three hundred years old, since it has been systematised into an art. There are many

113

schools, I mean styles, of jiujitsu, and naturally some are older than others. They differ somewhat from one another, the difference having arisen chiefly from the endeavour of the founders to make improvements.'

—'But what is the real purport of jiujitsu?'

—'The masters call it an art of self-defence. You see, our Samurai do not like to be arrogant or offensive to other people, and therefore they profess to use jiujitsu only when attacked, hence the name of self-defence, and this point is one of their ideals; but as a matter of fact, it is an art that can be used for attack equally well, and therefore may be called an art both offensive and defensive. The advantage of knowing this art is that we can throw an opponent without hurting or killing him, because it requires no weapons, not even a stick. It is done by catching hold of various parts of the opponent by the hands. Of course, there are many tricks, and therefore, if both parties be equally efficient in the art, the combat becomes very complicated. The term jiujitsu literally means "soft art," or an art accomplished by "sleight of body," as some people put it, so much so that one school is called "The Willow Mind Style." We have a saying, "A willow knows not a breaking by snow," meaning that a slender branch of a willow is stronger than a branch of a robust tree like the pine, an analogy showing that flexibility is often stronger than stubbornness.

'From all this it may well be imagined that a slender and small man, without any perceptible physical strength, can often become a great master of the art. Once at Shanghai, a Japanese who understood jiujitsu well was attacked by a group of Chinese roughs in the middle of a bridge, but he threw them all, one after the other, since when no Chinaman attempts to attack a Japanese, concluding wisely

114

that we may all be masters of the art. Once in England—I believe it was in Newcastle—a number of roughs attacked a Japanese; he threw them all, one after the other, and went off. The roughs were taken into custody by constables, when they confessed that they would not have attacked the man had they known he was a Japanese, and they believed that all Japanese knew the "devilish trick of wrestling," as they called it. You now see the nature of our jiujitsu, I suppose.'

—'And suppose your best wrestler and a jiujitsu man encountered?' asked one of the young ladies.

—'A wrestler is no match for a jiujitsu man. A wrestler who can lift up a big stone, or catch hold of a bull by its horns, would be easily beaten by a youth of fourteen scarcely able to lift a small cannon ball, provided the boy were well trained in jiujitsu. In wrestling, therefore, all jiujitsu tricks are forbidden. This will explain why no Occidental, even a champion wrestler, has ever succeeded in defeating a Japanese jiujitsu man. Perhaps you remember one of our jiujitsu men, who is in England, won the Gold Championship Cup last year, and yet in Japan he is not considered a first-class man in the art. I do not, however, wish to boast of the matter. Even amongst the most undeveloped tribes one sometimes sees the greatest possible skill shown in such matters, especially in the use of the bow and arrow. I hear American Indians shoot fishes in the rivers with arrows, and that too not by aiming direct, but by sending arrows up in the air and letting them fall in the water. They do not shoot direct, because, as you know, the curve of sight in water is very different from that in plain air.'

115

—'I understand that,' said the duchess, 'but your jiujitsu seems to be very different from mere skill. It is the result of a long and deliberate study of physical organism, systematised upon a scientific basis, as the physician in the paper says.'

—'Maybe,' I answered.

—'But what is that book which you have brought with you?' asked the duchess.

—'It is the book I promised you the other day. It is the Kokkwa, a monthly on art. It contains, as you see, very good photogravures and chromographs of our old objets d'art.'

So saying, I handed the book to the duchess, and continued:

—'You told me the other day, apropos of the conversation of the Marchioness Vivastine and myself, that you were also an admirer of our art, and that you appreciated Utamaro and Hokusai. No doubt they were great artists, and I am delighted, of course, with your appreciation, but we should be sorry if they stood to you for the best that we can do in art. This monthly will give you a good idea why I say so.'

All present were interested in the book, and its pages were gently turned over one by one. Presently the duchess remarked:

—'Do you mean to say that the originals of these illustrations date back thirteen centuries?'

—'Indeed, I do,' I replied.

116

–'And that these prints were really made in Japan?' said another.

–'Yes, surely.'

–'What a softness and feeling here! Look!' the duchess went on; 'and how this part resembles classic Italian.'

–'The art of printing,' I said, 'is well developed in Japan. The other day I showed a copy of the Financial and Economical Annual of Japan to a Frenchman, and he thought the printing was very neat and clear, and could scarcely believe that the book had been printed in my country.'

–'I can quite realise the scepticism of that person; but can you give me a rough idea of your ideal of pictures?'

–'That's a rather difficult question. In your sacred book you have a picture where Christ talks about "lilies." He stands in a field, utters His words, pointing to some pure white lilies blooming, but not in abundance, in the field. There is a perfect picture, the symbolic meaning of the pure white flowers standing out vividly before your eyes. In another place you see Christ entering a boat on a lake. There is another picture. A lake calm and serene, surrounded by undulating hills, perhaps with the shadow of the hills and trees reflected on the surface of the water. There one or two fishermen handle oars in a fantastic boat. A sage calls them from the shore to come to Him. A perfect landscape! An immense expanse and an eternal stillness of the universe almost unconsciously arises before the mind's eye of the onlooker. Such is, then, a type of the ideals of our pictorial worlds.'

−'I can well imagine it,' said the young nobleman. 'Your chromographs of even small objects, such as picture postcards, are very fine and artistic and, at the same time, so simple. Look at ours: they have neither feeling nor taste, and usually are showy and gorgeous, and, indeed, often vulgar.'

−'I must say I agree with you to some extent. I am rather sorry that such monthly publications as Kokkwa do not pay well in Japan. The present publisher of the journal is the proprietor of a large newspaper, and not a regular book publisher. He is himself a great collector of our objets d'art, of which he is very fond, and this is the sole reason why he took up the publication after it had been nearly discontinued by its former publisher. He is now trying to see if an English edition of it will pay, although the end he has in view is to make Japan known to the West, rather than any pecuniary personal gain. Indeed, it is for that reason he has sent me this copy, asking me to show it to those who have a taste for such things. I really think that, for the general good, the publication is worth continuing.'

−'Certainly,' said the duchess. 'Let me see, it is only two yen per number, that is five francs per month; cheap enough. I will subscribe at once.'

The young nobleman now left our party, for he had another engagement. He has a talent for music, and when a private concert was given only a few weeks ago in the garden of an aristocratic family which I know, he was the conductor, although only an amateur. This the young ladies told me, and the circumstance led me to ask if they also were not musical. One of them, she told me, played the piano, and the other the violin, and I said I hoped that one day they would let me have the pleasure of hearing them. I further

118

said that the piano was only known in Japan to a slight degree, and that only recently; but that we had always had an instrument much resembling the violin.

The duke held in his hand an English literary weekly of the highest repute. Turning to me he said:

−'Look! here is a review of two new books, one on the Bushido by a Japanese writer, and the other on Japan in general by an American, I suppose. It is a subject that interests me, as, indeed, it does many people nowadays. I have read it through and noticed that the reviewer speaks of Bushido very sarcastically. He says, among other things, that the discovery of Bushido is of quite recent date, and continues; but listen, I will read it:

'Neither Sir E. Satow nor Dr. Aston even mentions the word Bushido; Prof. Chamberlain in his Things Japanese (1898) does not refer to it; the word is not contained in the admirable dictionary prepared by Captain Brinkley, the able but intensely Japanicised correspondent of the Times; nor is it to be found in the principal native dictionary, the Kotoba no Izumi ("Source of Language").'

−'What nonsense,' I interrupted; 'by the same analogy one might say, because there is no compound noun Christian-morality in an English dictionary, there is no such thing as Christian morality.'

'Bushido, in literal Chinese,' continued the duke, reading, 'is the way of the executioner, and those who were eye-witnesses of the tyranny of the Samurai, in the last three years of the Bakufu [Shogunate], will not regard the name as altogether inappropriate. The Bushi (a Japano-Chinese,

119

but not Chineseform), or Samurai, were neither knights nor knightly; they were "followers" merely; many, if not most of them, petty officials, few of them for two hundred and fifty years possessed any military experience whatever.'

—'How ridiculous,' I interrupted; 'but I cannot make out what the reviewer could have got into his head to make him translate the term Bushi as "executioner." It is an insult to Bushi, of whom we have the oft-quoted saying, "Hana wa sakura ni hitowa bushi": "As the cherry blossoms are the prime of the flowers, so the Bushi is the flower of man." We have a popular drama in which there is a scene where a female prisoner is brought out under the superintendence of a common Bushi; and there the phrase "Keigo-no-Bushi" occurs, meaning, the Bushi who guards. Perhaps the reviewer remembered it, and concluded that Bushi meant an executioner, because he had charge of a prisoner. If this is so, by the same analogy we might say the "Knight of the Garter" is a domestic servant who looks after his mistress's garter. Ah! there is another thing which occurs to me. In China, where military men are little thought of, they are often used for such duties as those of an executioner; some foreigners, who had seen the fact whereby those men were called Bushi, perhaps thought that the term meant "executioners" without knowing its primary meaning. By that analogy one might say that gentlemen belonging to the honourable guild known as "The Worshipful Company of Grocers of the City of London" were common dealers in tea and sugar, because they are called grocers, without knowing the origin of the term. The passages in that review accidentally caught my sight too, and out of curiosity I looked the matter up in a few books which I happened to have by me. It is a little technical, but if you do not mind, I will explain it to you in detail.'

—'Please do,' said the duke.

—'The word Bushi is a noun composed of two Chinese characters, bu and shi, both having a distinct meaning. Bu means military or martial when used as an adjective, but it is also very commonly used as a concrete noun; and in that case it may be translated as martialism. When used as a noun it is used in contradistinction to bun. The last word may be translated as "civil," but I am unable to find out an exact equivalent in the Western terms, because the Western term "civil," still less the term "civism," does not convey the true idea of the word. It may, however, be taken to signify things or affairs on civil lines, as contrasting with those on military lines. Shi means a man of position or a gentleman, which came by evolution to mean a military man rather than a civilian. These two words, bu and shi, were put together and made a compound noun, signifying professional military people. The term has been most commonly used in Japan for over ten centuries. There are two other terms, Bundo and Budo, the former means principle, or doctrine, or teaching, or ways of affairs on civil lines, and the latter means the same on martial lines. They are very antique terms, contradistinguishing each other. The term Bushido is not so ancient as those two, but still it is by no means modern. The term Budo is used when one wishes to refer the matter more to the system or the principle as a unit; and the term Bushido is used when one wishes to designate more the individuals. In China the term Bushi had existed, as is natural from the antiquity of her history, many centuries before it did in Japan; I have seen it used in the history of the Hung dynasty. The term of course signifies military men; nevertheless, it has not acquired so much prominence as it has done in Japan, because in China military men have never attained the same importance and organisation as in Japan, and naturally enough there exists in China no such term as Bushido in its concrete sense, Bushido being peculiarly unique to the Japanese. Bushido consists of three Chinese characters, as the reviewer says.

121

In the colloquial Japanese it is read as Bushi-no-michi, do being the Chinese way of pronunciation, and michi being the colloquial Japanese pronunciation of the one and the same character; and therefore do and michi are both the same thing. In Hogen Monogatari, an historical record of the events which took place in the middle of the twelfth century A.D., and written not longer after that period, a great hero, Tametomo, is represented to have said, in the course of a speech, as follows:

'For a Bushi, an act of killing is inevitable. Nevertheless Bushi-no-michi [i.e. Bushido] forbids to kill an unfit object, and therefore, though I have fought more than twenty battles, and put an end to countless lives, I have always fought legitimate foes, and not illegitimate foes [in modern phraseology combatants and non-combatants]. And more! I have neither killed a deer nor fished a fish.

'In the fourteenth century A.D., a book called Chiku-ba-sho (the reminiscence of the bamboo-horse), which is ethical teaching for Bushi, was written by Shiwa Yoshimasa, a Japanese general, born 1349, died 1410 A.D.

'Within the last three hundred years, when Bushido has made a great systematic progress on its literary and intellectual side, many treatises on the subject have been written by eminent scholars and expounders of that doctrine. Nakaye-toju, born in 1608 A.D., wrote a book called Questions and Answers on Bun and Bu, in which the terms Bundo and Budo are used. In the collection of the epistles of Kumazawa Banzan, born 1619 A.D., the same terms are much used. In Lectures by Yamaga Soko, who was born in 1622, and was the founder of a school of our military science, there is one part called Shido. Shido and Bushido are one and the same thing, for the term bu is added to shi when one particularly wishes to denote the idea of the military profession. Thus, for instance, the old class of Samurai is now known as Shizoku, and not as Bushi-Zoku. Kaibara Yekken, born 1630 A.D., wrote a book called Bukum, namely, "Instructions on Bu," in which the term Bushi-no-michi is freely used. The Elementary Lessons on Budo is a book written by Daidoji Yiuzan, born 1639. In that book the term Bushido is freely used, and we see therein such phrases: "What is most important in Bushido is the three conceptions of loyalty, justice, and bravery"; and "if a Bushi comprehend the two opposing notions of justice and injustice, and endeavour to do justice and refrain from doing injustice, Bushido will be attained." Izawa Hanrioshi, born 1711 A.D., published a book called Bushikun, namely, "Instructions for Bushi." In that book, also, the term Bushi-no-michi is repeatedly used, and at the end of the fourth volume of it there is a short postscript in which he says:

'These four volumes have been written to record the outlines of Bushido, in order to supplement the points left untouched in books published in recent generations, such as ... so that one must not say after reading this book that it is not minute.

'I could mention several more books, but I might weary you. The names I have just cited are, in Japan, no less household words than Voltaire or Rousseau in France, and Johnson or Goldsmith in England. Satow, Aston, Chamberlain, or Brinkley might not have had time enough to touch upon the Bushido, but if one says that because they have not touched upon it there is no such thing as Bushido in Japan, it is tantamount to saying that there is no such thing as a diamond in South Africa because some travellers have not mentioned it in their diaries.'

−'You appear always to be making use of the names Bushi and Samurai indiscriminately. No doubt they signify one and the same category of people. But what is the difference?'

−'You are right in raising that question. The term Samurai is a pure and simple Japanese word, derived from a verb meaning "to wait" or "to serve." In ancient times military men on guard at the Imperial palace were called by that name; but when one wished to make the appellation more concise and appear more scholastic, the term Bushi was used. The Chinese character Shi is uniformly translated in Japanese as Samurai, but one preferred to employ the term Bushi more commonly because it gave more prominence to the military calling. At first the guards were recruited from ordinary people, but in course of time the recruiting became hereditary in certain families. They also began gradually to form a sort of class in different provinces, having their leaders, and at last formed a regular class of military men. Those men were universally called Bushi, and their families, when collectively spoken of, were called Buke namely, "Houses of Bu."'

−'I understand. But what is the difference between Daimio and Samurai?'

−'A Daimio is the lord under whom the Samurai served. There were nearly three hundred feudal lords of different standing in Japan. And the number of them therefore, when spoken of roughly, was called "three hundred." In the broad signification the lords were also included in the category of Samurai. In a popular drama, in which a child lord is represented as being in want of food on account of an intrigue, he pathetically says, "A Samurai does not feel

124

hungry even with an empty stomach." Feudal lords belonged to the category of Buke, in contradistinction to Kuge, namely, noble families attached direct to the Imperial courts. At present, of course, there is no such distinction, all former feudal lords and court nobles form the Japanese nobility as one class.'

−'I see, it is quite plain,' said the duke. 'The reviewer appears to have some knowledge of Japan, but judging from what I have just heard from you, I am more convinced than ever of the saying that "a little knowledge is a dangerous thing." One is apt to commit errors on account of such knowledge, especially if he has any feeling of spite and tries to find fault with others. It amuses me all the more, because he further says:

'If one ignored history, it would be easy to draw a picture of Napoleon as a good-natured man of genius who was kind to his relations, and evolved order out of chaos;

and he himself ignores all the history of Bushido, which you have just given me.'

−'I do not think,' I said, 'the reviewer could have any spite against us, nor do I think he has intentionally committed the error you have just mentioned, but it is unfortunate that it has that appearance.'

−'Again,' said the duke, 'what does this mean? The reviewer says here:

'The meaningless quasi-military formalism of the Bakufu, under which the sword, undrawn from its scabbard, came to be almost worshipped, a system of merciless vendetta, often based upon trivial forms of injury, was established.'

−'Well, I will begin with answering the second point first. In thus giving vent to his vindictiveness, the reviewer seems to have forgotten, for instance, how few decades ago it was that in England a personage no less eminent than the prime minister was engaged, if not killed, in a duel. He forgets how widely duels are practised and connived at even now by the law on the Continent, and that men die, conceivably, in consequence of a sword-thrust or a pistol-shot. In Japan duels have been altogether forbidden by the law, as there were signs of duelling being introduced with European customs, and the prohibition has proved to be very effective. In the feudal period a custom similar to duelling, which the reviewer calls vendetta, existed, as he says; but its purport was very different from what he describes. The act was called Kataki-uchi, that is, "revenge." When a man lost his life on account of an unlawful and malicious injury, the children of the deceased regarded it as incumbent on them to take the matter in their hands, if no legal adjustments could be obtained. In the feudal times redress in such matters was not always easy, because the different clans had autonomy; and the Samurai's fighting generally originated from some quarrel of a political nature, and not from robbery or any other felonious act. On the other hand, Confucian ethics held it unworthy of a pious son to "share the same heaven" with a person who wrongfully murdered his father. From these circumstances arose the notion of the necessary vindication of the father's wrongs by the hands of the son. Thus the Japanese vendetta (Kataki-uchi) came to be officially recognised—a step further than the official connivance of the Western duels. As a matter of fact, our Kataki-uchi was of a far more serious nature, but of much rarer occurrence, than the Western duels. The same sentiments and practices

126

were applicable to a lord and his retainers, though in a lesser degree, as in the case of blood relations. With us the avenger had always to stake much on his own part—life, position, and fortune—for although the principle of revenge was recognised in a measure, the avenger seldom got off scot-free from the responsibility of his act, which by the technical points of law was generally amenable to punishment. Thus you will see in the case of the famous forty-seven "Ronin," they avenged the death of their lord, because the latter had had to put an end to his own life, which was accompanied by an order for the total extinction of his house and clan, the cause of all of which was the injurious acts of the wrongdoer. The action of the forty-seven Ronin was morally approved by public sentiment, but they had to commit suicide because they were offenders in the eyes of the law. How, then, can one say that the Japanese Kataki-uchi was a merciless system, based upon trivial forms of injury, as the reviewer pleases to put it.'

−'But,' said the duke, 'suppose the revenge went on endlessly, to be handed down from generation to generation, as it was with the Scottish clans, that would be awful.'

−'No, in that respect, there was a limit. No second revenge was recognised in any form whatever. Thus, if A. murdered B. and B.'s son killed A. in revenge, A.'s son had no claim legally or morally to avenge his fathers death. I may also add that under the new Imperial régime Kataki-uchi has been totally discountenanced by law. There is no connivance of it at all. The law promises redress to every wrong, and every possible care is taken to protect the sufferers. Therefore, nowadays, if one kills another in revenge, he would be accounted an ordinary murderer in the eyes of the law.'

127

−'What about the sword?' interposed the duke.

−'The sword,' I answered, 'was considered the soul of Samurai. They regarded it as the symbol,—nay, the very embodiment of noble sentiment and spirit. It has been so more or less with almost every nation, but it was especially so with us Japanese. The Japanese swords are known to be unrivalled by those of any other nation. Our sword was the envy of all the continental peoples of the Far East. There is a famous poem composed by a great Chinese statesman and scholar, in which he pays high tribute not only to the sword itself, but to the nation which produces it. Even from a merely artistic point of view, our swords deserve to rank high; but that is not all. A latter-day author writes as follows:

The sword-smith was not a mere artisan, but an inspired artist, and his workshop his sanctuary. Daily he commences his craft with prayer and purification, or, as was said, he committed his soul and spirit into the forging and tempering of the steel. Every swing of the sledge-hammer, every plunge into the water, every friction on the stone, was a religious act of no slight import. Was it the spirit of the master or his tutelary deity that cast such a spell over our sword? Perfect as a work of art, setting at defiance its Toledo and Damascus rivals, there was more than art could impart. Its cold blade collecting on its surface, the moment it is drawn, the vapours of the atmosphere: its immaculate texture, flashing light of bluish hue; its matchless edge, upon which histories and possibilities hang, the curve of its back uniting exquisite grace with utmost strength—all these fill us with mixed feelings of power and beauty, of awe and terror.

128

'Such was, then, the "sword" which our Samurai adored. There were two or three at least of such swords, which were heirlooms of a Samurai family. Just imagine a Samurai going forth to the battlefield and reflecting what a distinction his ancestors had made in similar battlefields, or what devotions he had displayed to his lord by that very sword, now being borne in his hand or in his girdle: why! the very thought would fire his soul and make him emulate the deeds of his ancestors and despise cowardice. No mean thought could enter his mind; the spirit of the sword radiating from the pure cold lustre of the blade handed down by his ancestors could not but thrust such thought from his mind. Such would at least be the sentiments of a real Samurai. The sword was not unsheathed wantonly, but when drawn it was a maxim that it should not be sheathed until its legitimate mission had been fulfilled. No wonder, then, that a Samurai should almost have worshipped his sword, even when undrawn from its scabbard, as the reviewer sarcastically describes. The sword of a Samurai, even when in the scabbard, was not a thing to be trifled with. A Samurai worshipped sword, but not money-bags. If they had worshipped the latter instead of the former, they might have met with the approval of the reviewer. From the utilitarian point of view, if they had done so, it might have benefited their country more materially, and, therefore, their worshipping a sword might have been the weakest point of their ideals, but we do not see cause for regret for all that. The tide of time has brought changes on all such matters. The Government has forbidden not only Samurai, but also all others who were privileged, to wear swords in their girdles. Hundreds and thousands of our best blades have left the houses of Samurai and been either exported, or turned into other implements, for mere trifling sums, often for the gold and silver used for the ornaments of the scabbard. For us, it is sad to think of, though it is of course a necessary outcome of the great changes which have passed over us. It is, however, my earnest desire that the spirit of devotion to the swords with which the Samurai was animated may always be preserved. The same feeling explains why some of our officers carry with them their heirloom swords, even in the present war, as you must have noticed now and then in the press. The traditions of the sword, I am glad to say, have not as yet died in the breasts of the Japanese. There is an association in Tokio, the members of which meet periodically, bringing their own choice swords, and offering their comments on those of others. It may be difficult to appreciate how one can enjoy oneself looking at the blades of swords, but with us it gives great pleasure, if only from an artistic point of view. There have been many different schools of swordsmiths, and even amongst the workers of one school there is some special characteristics of their work. It is the pleasure of the Japanese who are fond of good sword blades to judge of the school and maker by inspecting the blades only. It pleases me to tell you of a gentleman in England who has made the study of Japanese swords a special subject, and his attainment of knowledge in the subject has been recognised by the association in Tokio, which has cheerfully elected him its honorary member. I may add a word or two. When Port Arthur was on the brink of falling, a cartoon was published in the London Punch representing General Stoessel standing at the top of a fortified hill under a half-torn Russian flag. He was holding up a broken sword and uttering a few words of devotion to the Emperor of Russia. That cartoon took the English public very much, and was reproduced on the pages of many papers. It appealed very deeply to the imagination of the Japanese, in particular, though I am not quite sure if Stoessel deserved such sympathy at the last stage of the siege.'

−'That cartoon was very good,' said Lady Modestina. 'I have seen it.'

−'So have I too,' chimed in Lady Dulciana.

−'Let us proceed to the latter part of the review,' said the duke. 'The reviewer says of the author of the other book that "he takes rather a pessimistic view of Japan," and proceeds to say:

'Professor S. takes rather a pessimistic view of Japan. He admits to the full, as every one must, the five noble qualities of Japanese character, viz. bravery, loyalty, alertness, thoroughness, and self-control, to which list courtesy should be added.

But he goes on to quote from the author:

'The two cancers at the core of Japanese character are deep-set dishonesty and abandoned impurity; either would be sufficient to wreck the life of any nation.

And it seems, according to the reviewer, the author tells us that Japan is still a country where the word lie is not a term of reproach, but rather implies a jocular compliment, and then dilates upon the undesirable occupations of some females. The words employed are very strong. Let us have your opinion.'

−'We are at times vexed with some of the occidental writers,' I replied, 'even with Anglo-Saxon writers occasionally, who write in such a strain as though they lived high in the pure air, while we Japanese live in the muddy marshes. They pick out some dark spots in our customs, and magnify them to suit their own purpose, as though for all the world they had nothing similar, or even worse, in their own countries. Some of them do this from an excess of zeal which they display in their particular calling, without any particular bad intention of defaming Japan; but the results are the same. My answer to your question is very simple. The Yellow Peril alarmists may rest assured, for, according to the author, Japan must die a natural death. What an idea, to indict a whole nation as a den of liars! Does he not know that truthfulness and honesty is the highest ideal of our ethical notions? The commonest of our ethical sayings is: "Shozikino atama ni kami yadoru" (Deity rests on the heads that are honest). The commonest of the ethical poems is:

'Kokoro dani makoto no michi ni kanai naba
Inorazu totemo kami ya mamoran.

(If only one's thoughts be in accord
With the way of truthfulness,
Deity will protect him, though he may not pray.)

'Does he not know another forcible and common saying of Bushido: "Bushi no ichigon" (One word of a Bushi), which means that a word uttered by a Bushi shall never be idle; or, expressed otherwise—"A word is sufficient; he will remain faithful to it"? It is the watchword of Bushi, and if ever a Bushi were doubted, that phrase sufficed for an answer. And it still governs our social ideal of truthfulness. "Yes" or "No," when once definitely uttered by a Bushi, was no more alterable than the ebb and flow of the tide. Does he not know another of our sayings? "Ichidaku senkin" (One "Yes" is equal to a thousand pieces of gold). Does he not know "Usotsuki" (a liar) is with us an everyday word of scathing contempt? Does he not know an "untruthful word," namely, a lie, is accounted a great sin in

132

the Ten Commandments of Buddhism? Does he not know "Yamashi" (a speculator), a term akin to "a liar," is with us a common word of contempt? Does he not know that in large European towns waiters and drivers are constantly cheating strangers by giving wrong change or bad money? I particularly mention these incidents because I myself have often been a victim. Fancy the idea of saying that the word lie is not a term of reproach in Japan! I would feign go a step further. This kind of charge is the commonest method which the Occidentals employ when they talk about the character of other races which they generally regard as inferior to themselves. But mere common-sense will tell them that there can be no human community, even amongst undeveloped tribes, where the word lie is not a word of reproach, if only the smallest element of a moral notion exist, and there can hardly be any human community where there is no such moral notion at all. Such, at least, is my sociological view. With regard to the second accusation, the refutation I am going to make may not be quite in unison with social delicacy, but for that I ask your pardon. You say the author speaks of the undesirable life of some females. The matter is ugly enough, we admit. Of course, metaphorically speaking, we could restore by explanation the paint which had been blackened to its original colour, but still it would not be snow-white. Pure such matters cannot be, we admit, but is there any nation on earth which has no dark spot at all? I ask the author: Does he not know the real condition of the Western countries, whence he springs? How is it with Paris, London, Berlin, or Vienna? Pick, for instance, one hundred pedestrians at random, one afternoon or evening, in Regent Street, or on the Boulevards, the best thoroughfares of London and Paris. What percentage of them can be held up as the ideals of "purity" the writer seems to imagine them to be? I might go much further if I wished, but I prefer not. Taken as a whole, I venture to think that the social structure of Japan is in

133

reality far cleaner than that of most countries. Of course, I do not say "two wrongs make a right," but I do say this: It is naïve to accuse us in such harsh terms, as though believing that we Japanese have no idea of the dark spots of other nations. Men after the style of this writer admit such of our noble characteristics as those enumerated by the writer because they have become manifest, not during an epoch of peace, but in the time of war. Could any one say that they were manufactured specially for the war—at a minute's notice? Did not the greatest error of our opponents lie in the fact that they had not perceived these qualities in the time of peace? It saddens us to think that such a writer either cannot see, or intentionally ignores, some of the essential points of our character, unless they are incontestably demonstrated by incessant slaughter.

—'Pardon me,—I have been a little excited, and have spoken, perhaps, more than I should. Once a Frenchman told Lord Palmerston that English thieves were cleverer than Continental ones; whereupon Palmerston answered: "I am glad of that, for it shows that our intellectual faculty is more developed all round." That is one way of looking at things. At any rate, I have no intention of attacking any occidental vices: our writers do not indulge in writing on these matters either. I rather believe that vices are necessary outcomes of modern progress. Every nation has its virtues and vices. I dare say we shall have to add more vices as we make further progress. Cards, for instance, are much played nowadays among our people, since we have learned that they are played generally among our occidental benefactors. Ah! but I must not forget to mention that there are in the West, especially in England and America, many writers for whose fairness we have much gratitude. One does not like to see, still less to acknowledge, any point of superiority in a fellow-creature or a fellow-nation one has been accustomed to look down upon: such is human nature.

134

Our sense of gratitude is, therefore, all the more due to those unbiassed writers.

'Japan is cleaner than most countries,' I continued, 'but she was even better in that respect in the days gone by. Conversely, therefore, the general atmosphere of social morality, I confess, became somewhat tarnished at the time of the great transition, as is bound at such period. There are two reasons for that. In the first place, in the feudal days social discipline was very strict in general, and tranquil enjoyment of the positions of Samurai—above all, those holding official positions—depended a great deal upon their private conduct; but with the introduction of occidental ideas, the private affairs of individuals have come to be viewed very leniently under the name of personal freedom. In the second place, the general condition of society has occasioned laxity in moral discipline almost unavoidably and of necessity. I mean to say that, during the last years of the Shogunate, when the country was in a state of effervescence, and when freedom of speech and meeting had no existence in the modern sense—nay, when any meetings or speeches having a political nature were most rigidly watched and pursued by emissaries, it was almost a matter of necessity that countless young patriots whose lives were as precarious as candle-lights in the wind, as we have it, should resort to a restaurant or tavern, where they could exchange and communicate thought and schemes under the cover of merriment and jocularity. Nay, more: there were not wanting young patriots, who in after years became famous, who owed their lives and success to the heroic assistance rendered by women of uncertain position, to whom they had to repay their indebtedness by personal consideration rather than yield to social scruples.

'The women also were heroic in those days, as is generally the case at the time of revolution in most countries. Add to this the general disruption and transformation, unknown in our previous history, of the whole structure of society, both political and social, and it will be no matter of surprise that a certain relaxation in the usual moral discipline of the people was the result. The Japan which foreigners have seen is that Japan and not the Japan of her normal days. The effect of that great change of 1867—I say "Great Change," because we do not like to apply the term "revolution"—has been subsiding for many years, and now Japan is fast returning to her normal state. I am, therefore, not at all pessimistic in regard to the future of our national life, though the author may be.'

—'And besides,' interposed the duchess, 'foreigners themselves are also spoiling your manners, according to your remarks which I read in one of the English periodicals you gave me. Dulcy, will you bring the English periodical I mean? It is on the small table in my boudoir: I should like to read it once more.'

In a few moments the periodical in question was brought by Lady Dulciana. The duchess took it in her hand, saying, 'Here are the baron's remarks. Listen, I will read aloud.' She read as follows:—

'OCCIDENTAL CIVILISATION IN JAPAN

'"Do you really think," I asked, "that, generally speaking, occidental civilisation is beneficial to Japan?"

'"Well," slowly replied the baron, "that is a question which requires very careful answering. I am certainly of opinion that, from the purely material point of view, this invasion of

Western thought and methods has done us the greatest possible good. I refer especially, of course, to science and mechanics. And as to the mental part of it, the influence also is distinctly good—but still, is not so beneficial as from the material point of view.

'"Remember that for centuries we have had our own way of thinking and reasoning, and so, to a great extent, we are not convinced by Western thought. We keep to our old ways, to our old methods, though the trend of our ideas is slightly altered by European thought. Let me give you an illustration of what I mean, for it is rather a difficult point to explain. For instance, we have always been humane and charitable to our fellow-creatures, but in the old days there was no form of public charity. It was not much needed, as a matter of fact, but now you will find that we are everywhere establishing hospitals on the European system. So you see only the old mode of our charity is changed. It is rather a delicate point to say how far Western thought has impregnated our own. The opinions of Darwin, Huxley, and Spencer, as well as the views of Catholic and Protestant Missions, are spread all over Japan; but our ethical sense is such that it does not allow us easily to adopt the dogmatic points of foreign religions, and though many Japanese have adopted Christianity, yet they are, after all, in a vast minority. But that does not signify that we are averse to religion; on the contrary, I am glad to say we extend the greatest tolerance to all kinds of religionists. I am not a Christian myself, but I know, perhaps, more of the essence of Christianity than some of my fellow-countrymen who profess it, for I had to study the Greek Testament in my Cambridge days. I am always amused when the people here imagine I know nothing about that religion. The Missionary question is always a very delicate one. I am sure missionaries mean well, but sometimes they are very indiscreet. For instance, Miss M'Caul, writing the other day

137

from the front, says that one of her escorts was a Japanese lady of position, who had been specially attached to her by the Japanese Government. One day a missionary went up to this lady and asked her if she was married. 'Oh yes,' she replied, 'and I have three children.' 'But were you married in church?' 'No,' 'Then, of course, you are not really married!' Well such narrow minds do real harm. The missionary did not mean to be offensive, but as your proverb has it—'Evil is often wrought by want of thought.'"

"'Has Occidentalism spoiled your art, baron, do you think?"

"'To a certain extent the Western civilisation has damaged the artistic side of our life. I don't think that your oil-paintings will ever supersede our own light sketches. Our houses are not made for elaborate picture frames, and the price of your pictures is much greater than the price of ours. And why should we pay a large sum when we can get as much happiness and pleasure for a small sum? But undoubtedly the European style is influencing ours, as ours is influencing yours. Although our pictures, as a rule, are excellent on the side of idealism, they are very often defective from a technical point of view. Our perspective can certainly be improved by the European method. Some people are of opinion that European methods will spoil our characteristics. But in my opinion it will be so only while the artists are in a transitory state; if they excel they will be all right. I don't see any reason to reject that kind of improvement. Let me give you a plain and simple example of what I mean. Take that square box, for instance. Now, a Japanese artist, owing to his inefficiency in perspective, would so draw it as to make it appear triangular; well, what harm could be done by showing him how to draw it properly.

"'The people generally move with the upper classes, and all our upper classes in Japan are in favour of Western modes of thought and life. People generally are delighted with the Westernisation of Japan, and especially grateful for the improvement in political and civic conditions. We have now the representative system in Parliament; our Courts of Law are modelled on yours; and alas! the increase of Courts has increased litigation, yet justice can be obtained, and appeal can be made against injustice, easier than under the old feudal system. The general condition of the lower classes is far better than in the days of the feudal daimios. Then every locality differed. In some places, if the daimio was a good man, the poor were happy; in others they were less happy, but on the whole there was not extreme poverty. The same condition is continued and somewhat improved. I fear, however, that the relative position of the poor has a tendency to degenerate as in Europe."

'THE STANDARD OF LIVING

"'Are the people generally better off as regards money?"

"'Well, they make more money, but £10 now is only equal to £1, or less, in the old days. But one thing is certain, they have better food. There is one thing, however, in which Western methods have not benefited us—the demarcation between rich and poor is becoming more marked with the new civilisation. And that is a bad sign, though it can't be helped. Education, I am glad to say, is much more general than it was. In former days the Samurai class were well educated, and there were several very good schools, but education was not so general as it is now, when every community has its elementary schools, although we are still far from well off in the way of universities. However, they will come."

"'In speaking to me of the new civilisation, for which he is mainly responsible, the Marquis Ito told me he was afraid that the reverence of the young for the old, and of children for their parents, which was so much a feature of old Japan, appeared to be dying out."

"'I quite agree with him," replied the baron, "and if the individualistic ideas of Western nations continue to increase in Japan, the old family feeling of reverence is sure to decline. That is our great problem of the future. Young Japan in some ways is departing from the ways of its ancestors, and it is a thing to be very greatly feared and deplored."

"'Do you think that, speaking generally, character is improved in Japan by the Western influence?"

"'Speaking of individuals," replied my host, with great vehemence, "no, it is not. On the contrary, I notice great deterioration from association with foreigners. Take, for instance, our ports, where there are mainly houses of ill-fame, mainly supported by European sailors, who have introduced vices and vulgarities of which old Japan was absolutely ignorant. But, of course, I do not consider that the Western influence is wholly bad merely because certain very low-class foreigners come to our country and behave badly. The general good of the community has been greatly advanced by our contact with the West. Trades-unions, for instance, and the formation of great business companies, which were quite unknown in the old days, have helped greatly to raise the commerical status of our people, both employers and employed. You ask me as to individual morality under modern influences. Well, it is difficult to define. On the whole, I think the morality of the individual was higher in the old days, because those days were more simple and the community was more sober. The more primitive a land is, the better it is morally. But I fear we must move with modern times."

"'And which do you prefer—the quiet feudal days of old Japan, or the modern push and worry and hustle and bustle?'"
"'It all depends on the point of view,' was my host's reply. "Competition with the world is absolutely necessary. But there were many good points about the old days. Although they involved a régime of restriction and there was very little chance of individual development (though not so little as Lafcadio Hearn would make out), men of ability could always push their way to the front even in the days of feudalism."

"'The Marquis Ito, for instance?'"

"'Don't speak of him. He, Marquis Yamagata, and many others, have arisen from an obscure position, but, they belong more to our own time, I am speaking of older days. Take, for instance, Arai Hakuseki, who, born in humble circumstances, became the chief adviser of the Shogun. Many a farmer's son who joined the priesthood rose to greater power and position than that of a middle-class daimio."

"'And do you think that the general level of happiness in Japan is as high as it was in the old days of romance?'"

"'Yes," smiled the baron. "But people were happy in former days because they did not know what freedom meant, still less the enjoyment of the luxuries to which they are now accustomed. To them ignorance was literally bliss. But the idea of happiness nowadays differs in kind and character, and it is difficult to say if modern Japan is as happy as the ancient Japan. One thing, I hope, will always remain with us, and that is our patriotism and loyalty. A country is in a good way which puts loyalty to the sovereign and love of country before all private and meaner considerations."'

Finishing the reading, the duchess continued, 'I suppose you are correctly reported?'
−'Yes, in the main,' I answered.

−'I was reading,' said the duchess, 'the other day, the chapter on Japan in the Far East, by Archibald Little, just issued from the Clarendon Press, which, I think, is the best topographical description of Japan written in a popular style. In it I came across a passage to this effect:

'Whether increased intercourse with the essentially vulgar West will, as many well-wishers fear, at the same time destroy the old simplicity of living, the future will show.

'The Occidentals seem to have begun to perceive vulgarity in things European. There is really vulgarity in many things, I fear. But, baron, had you any particular idea when you spoke about the vulgarity introduced into your open ports?'

−'I am afraid not,' I answered; 'it would be difficult for me to explain it to you, and you would not appreciate it if I did. Look! the last ray of the sun is glittering in the foliage. Time has flown wonderfully quick: I must say au revoir'

V

Some observations fit on peace prospects—Discussion on Anglo-French-Russo-Japanese entente—Russian views of the Japanese—Discussion on religion and Japan—Japan and the International Conventions—The meaning of religion—General Nogi—A high-priest on Japan and Russia—The Japanese conception of death—A quotation from an old book on Bushido—The notion of the name— Further remarks on the Russian views of the Japanese— England and America—The outbreak of the war—A wanton project of the Russian admiral restrained by the French admiral—Discussion on the Yellow Peril and Pan-Asiatic ambition—Japan not a small country —French poor in the caves—Paris by night—Sir Stamford Raffles and his appreciation of Japan ninety years ago—Patriotism and France—La France, c'est le pays de mon cœur—A romantic and tragical story—Discussion on Socialism and Japan—England and America—Discussion on the word 'Revolution'—The Great Change of Japan in 1867—Its political and social effects—A comparison with the French Revolution—Discussion on unity and continuity of authority—An anonymous pamphlet—Discussion on the relative position of the French Nationalists and Socialists with regard to Japan—French thrift

I was once more partaking of tea en famille in the Duchess of Fairfield's garden. She, like myself, prefers to be unceremonious, as there is then so much more possibility of a quiet conversation.

—'What do you think of the prospect of peace?' said the duke. 'The war must surely now cease.'

−'Yes, I should think so too,' I replied. 'Enough blood has already been shed; but, you know, our opponents are such that they do not see things in the same light as other people.'

−'But they must do so now,' was the reply. 'Every one has known for a long time that it is of no use for them to carry on the war. The issue is clear.'

−'Well, we shall see what will happen.'

−'The justice of the cause and the singleness of the aim of Japan are now widely recognised by the thinking people of the whole world,' said the duchess, 'and the part you have played in it is not small.'

−'I thank you very much for your sympathetic words,' I answered. 'On the morrow of the battle of Tsu-shima I received a telegram from a well-known English writer in which he congratulated me on the brilliant victory, as he said, of our fleets, adding thereto "only equalled by your success in Europe." That that victory was brilliant I cannot deny, though the honour belongs to my own country, but as to the part of the telegram concerning myself, it is an exaggeration. The only thing which is true, however, is that I have worked hard all this time—I may say, harder than I have in all my life. I have done so, as every Japanese ought to do, having in view the fact that my fatherland has been engaged in the most gigantic struggle since the famous invasion of the Mongolian Armada, or even more momentous than that. I merely mention this incident to you because you are so sympathetic: I have never told it to any one else.'

−'I can quite understand your feelings,' said the duchess, and continued after a little pause—

'The whole world knows the chivalrous character of the Japanese. Remember, however, I am a friend of Russia, and that is the reason why I am all the more anxious that Russia should recognise the situation as it is.'

−'Yes, I know your views very well. There are many Frenchmen who hold similar views. Some of them sincerely wished to save the Baltic Fleet and advocated peace, as they were sure all the ships would go to the bottom of the sea if they ventured to the Far East, which would leave the Baltic defenceless, and would thus deprive France of the usefulness of the Dual Alliance. But those friendly counsels were not heeded by the Russians; on the contrary, as you know, some insinuations were made regarding the press which had published them. We have a saying: "Good medicine is bitter to the mouth, and faithful counsel is averse to the ear." This is a case in point.'

−'It is often so, I fear,' said the duke. 'But, baron, I must now leave you. I have an engagement to-day, and have to take my daughters with me. The duchess studies diplomacy and politics more than I, so please stay and talk with her.'

The Duke of Fairfield is a typical aristocrat: although not a great talker, he is eminently sensible, unostentatious, and dignified. France of to-day is not for the aristocracy, but the duke is resigned to the circumstance. He has always been as cordial and kind to me as the other members of his family. He now left the duchess and me to our conversation, and went out with his two daughters.

−'I am an advocate of an entente Anglo-French as well as Russo-Japanese: we all four ought to keep on well together, that you know very well,' said the duchess. 'Of course I do not sympathise with the way in which the Russian bureaucracy carries on the administration of that country: that is understood. But what is your opinion of the Russians in general? Do you think you can ever be friendly with them?'

−'Yes, I think so: on our part there is no reason why we should not be friendly with the Russians. I can even say we like them individually. But, you see, they have some deep-rooted prejudices against us which stand in the way. Only some weeks ago, I read a letter written and widely circulated by Countess Sophie, the wife of Count Leo Tolstoy. She is an advocate of peace, and abhors war in general, as does her husband. We have no objection to her, so far as her conviction is concerned regarding war, but in that letter she is pleased to write:

'A spiritually undeveloped, unchristian nation, such as the Japanese, is bound to conquer, for among them is rife the principle of patriotism, which is opposed to the Christian principle of love to one's neighbour, and, therefore, of aversion to war. Russians have not yet grown to this stage, but they are on the way to it.

'You see, the countess says we are not Christians, and therefore cannot love our neighbours: it is a calumny. The great bulk of the Japanese are not Christians in religion, it is true, but we know how to love our neighbours all the same. It is a point of our ethics. For all that, we cannot give up our patriotism. Patriotism is not irreconcilable with the love of one's neighbour. If Christianity is such as the countess represents it to be, then I am fain to think that the less it influences our people the better. Besides, to say that the Russians are defeated by the Japanese because they love their neighbours more than the Japanese do theirs, is a proposition which, however religious it may be, cannot convince us in the least degree.'

−'Neither does it give me a shadow of conviction,' said the duchess. 'On the contrary, I know that intense belief in Christianity has often produced the best soldiers. Think of the Spanish army of Charles V., for instance. They were intensely religious, and at the same time intensely patriotic, and fought well. People often say the Japanese have no religion, but I do not believe it. They have a religion unique to themselves.'

−'Such views as those of the countess,' said I, 'are entertained not only by women like herself, but even by serious men, holding high positions. Only in the autumn of last year, a letter from one who signed himself "A Russian Statesman," and spoken of by the Editor as "A prominent Russian statesman, about whose love of peace there is no doubt," appeared in the Deutsche Revue, stating Russian views which to our eyes were of the most fantastic character. My answer to it was published in the same Revue, when the writer retaliated by another letter expounding notions even more extraordinary. I answered him once more, and there the matter ended. In the course of the controversy he spoke of the difference between the Russian religious views of life and those of the Japanese, and insinuated that our conception of justice and morality was inferior to that of his country. He abused our law-courts and legislation. Fancy! a Russian statesman boasting of the matters relating to laws.

'He even went on to say,' I continued, 'that Japan has not been doing her duty according to the Convention agreed upon at The Hague Conference, whereas Russia (according to his view) had been doing hers for months. But the truth is, Japan has been most scrupulous in those matters from the very beginning of the war; the prisoners' treatment regulations were promulgated within a week's time after the outbreak of the war, and the Prisoners' Intelligence Board was instituted seven days later. The whole world knows the excellent working of the Japanese Red Cross Society, and, I may add, the defectiveness of Russia in similar respects. Yet the so-called Russian statesman can make an assertion of this kind, not in his own country, but in a foreign press, unchecked. His statement regarding the difference in moral thought, and cognate subjects, may be partly due to some political motive, but the fact remains that he circulates false ideas.'

−'I, for one, agree with you that the charge is certainly unfair,' said the duchess, 'and besides, I repeat I do not agree with those who say that the Japanese have no religion. The very ideals which they hold up as models for their soldiers cannot but be a religion, as I said the other day. What does a "religion" mean? It means a conscientious preparedness and practice for the suppression of one's lower nature. Man has all sorts of wishes and desires, temptations and tendencies, which the experience of generations knows must be restrained. Wisdom comes in and teaches him to control such weakness, and the teaching, if systematised at all, becomes a "religion," a cult, if one prefers to call it by that appellation. For instance, man likes to live (what creature likes to die if left to his natural desire), and if he prefers to give up his life for some ideal, is it not an act of self-repression, or indeed of self-sacrifice, and if it forms a characteristic of a nation, does it not become the "religion" of that nation? Some say the Japanese despise life, because they like death for its own sake: I call that a nonsensical observation. On the contrary,

148

I see a religion in the very fact of the Japanese being so patriotic as to so cheerfully sacrifice their lives for their country and for their emperor. A remark which I have read in a paper as having been uttered by General Nogi certainly contains, to my idea, a strong religious strain. It was:

'"Now that my two sons have sacrificed their lives and I am a childless man, I may with an easier conscience face the parents of those thousands of young men who have likewise offered up their lives under my command."

'The expression may be simple,' continued the duchess, 'but nevertheless, it is possible to discern in it a touch of feeling, which to me has a strong religious element. In truth, I must confess that I have noticed more deeds worthy of religion manifested by your country than any nation professing a religion can lay claim to. Some time ago, a priest of very high standing returned from the Far East. He made an application while out there to be allowed to visit the Russian prisoners in order to see how they were treated by the Japanese authorities. He got the permission at once, and saw everything, to his great personal satisfaction. He then made a similar application to the Russian authorities, but was refused. He had some ground to suspect that the Russian treatment of the prisoners was not quite satisfactory. To begin with, he said, Japan, who is not our ally, had given him every facility, and Russia, who is, refused to do so. He almost wept at the thought that a non-Christian nation had more of the essence of a religion than another who professed Christianity. I should not have told you all this, were I not moved by the current of events, which have left a deep impression on my mind. I have no thoughts of being unfriendly to Russia, but I cannot help appreciating Japan all the same.'

—'I thank you very much,' I said.

—'I know the horror of war very well,' continued the duchess, 'and what lamentable incidents occur when the wild, warlike spirit prevails. During our last great war, I was but a girl of thirteen, and I was naturally with my mother. We had to quarter the wounded; I remember how I used to carry about a small table from one to another, writing short notes for them. Little as I was, many awful tales reached my ear during that war, wherein our priests, and our women too, were sufferers. I can never forget them. Compared to it the present war is a lesson; the so-called civilised world has to learn much from the Japanese, not only on points of courage and devotion, but also in regard to morale.'

A little pause, and the duchess went on—

—'Stoical imperturbability appears to be a marked feature in your heroes. There are many people who have seen the character of the Japanese in many lights and appreciate it, and yet are unable to perceive their feelings, or I might rather say, sentimental qualities. They are curious to know if the Japanese nature is much developed in that respect.'

—'Well, I can tell you, as far as I may be permitted to judge my own countrymen, we have much feeling and sentimental elements. At the very bottom of the stoicism of Bushi there flows hidden streams of feeling and sentimentality, often imperceptible to the onlooker. In one way, I am of opinion that our heart is filled with even too much feeling and sentimentality, and I am inclined to believe it is our weak point, for feeling and sentimentality are often accompanied by over-scrupulousness and over-sensitiveness, and with us this disposition exercises much influence, not only in our private affairs, but also in politics and diplomacy. In this world, in which some people say that politics, still more international diplomacy, knows not morality, the fact that we are so scrupulous often hinders our politics and diplomacy, and yet we do not regret it, for the time may come when the just traits of our character will be discovered by the world at large, and receive its approval.'

−'You are,' said the duchess, 'well acquainted with our common saying, "Honesty is the best policy," and my earnest hope is that your country will never imitate some of the European politics. But, baron, let me ask another question: Granted that the moral and ethical training of Japan is a religion, as I do, yet I cannot entirely see how that training could have been instilled in the minds of millions of men so deeply. When one hears of thousands rushing on to certain death at a word of command (as we have often heard of the Japanese troops), one is almost tempted to think there may be something in it which promises a reward in the future life for such a death, as is the case with the Mohammedan creed; but I understand that there is nothing of the sort in your training, and that the fact of your soldiers being so fearless of death has nothing to do with religion in its ordinarily accepted sense. I can very well imagine that this or that group of honourable men, picked out of multitudes, could be of that type, but it almost amazes me when we see hundreds of thousands of men, one and all, being animated by the same spirit, without any exception.'

−'I cannot,' I answered, 'profess that every man of our troops is so high-minded as you say, or at least, I cannot say so myself, being Japanese; but assuming it to be the case, the kind of doubt to which you give expression is entertained by many Occidentals, and questions to that effect have often been put to me. I can, however, give no other answer than to repeat that there is no such religious belief in our case, as there is in Mohammedanism. In Europe one often engages in a deadly duel on account of some dispute, sometimes for public reasons, but often for other reasons which do not appear commendable to outsiders: those who fight surely do not risk their lives from any religious belief in their cause. They do so because, as far as they themselves are concerned, a consideration of honour demands. This sentiment is exactly similar to our sense of honour, only in our case we have, perhaps, made it more rational and more general. To attain this ideal, a long training and preparation is necessary, but when once attained, there is nothing to wonder at. If one imagined that a man killed in a duel on account of a quarrel over a woman sacrificed his life because he believed he would be happy in a future life,—if he died in that fashion, every one else would laugh at him. Why, then, is there anything to wonder at when we say that we Japanese can be fearless of death without connecting it with a religious belief of the future life, for a cause which is far nobler than that of the ordinary Western custom of sacrificing one's life in a duel. The morale of our troops is the result purely of ordinary ethical training and diffusion of national traditions. Loyalty and patriotism are the highest ideals of the Japanese nation. Japanese ethics have taught for centuries how to die an honourable death, and yet one must not think that Japanese ethics teach only how to die: they also teach how to live.'

—'What do you mean by that?'

—'I mean to say, in Bushido, death was not valued for its own sake, even in a battle, for if one died a useless or dishonourable death, it was called a dog's death, which, of course, is a term of contempt. We still have the same notion of death. In a book on Bushido, entitled Chiku-ba-sho,

152

written in the fourteenth century A.D., by Shiwa-Yoshimasa, as I mentioned the other day, we have in the very opening page, as follows:

'Men who handle bows and arrows [military men] should do their part, thinking not only of their own persons, but of the names of their descendants. They should not incur a perpetually irksome name [permanent bad reputation] on account of a greed for life, which is after all of short duration. But, on the other hand, if they cast away their lives when they ought not to die, they will also incur a discreditable name. The chief point is that life should be sacrificed when it is honourable to do so, in behalf of the supreme lord [the emperor], or on account of an affair which is of great importance to the generalissimo of their bows and arrows [the Shogun]. Only by thus behaving can the famous names of the descendants be secured and perpetuated. As a Bushi, one should never be light-minded; on the contrary, he should always be thoughtful and meditative. The majority of men pass their time saying they would behave aptly when time and circumstances requiring it arrive. Such people generally experience great difficulty when any emergency unexpectedly arises, and generally regret afterwards that they had missed the opportunity when they ought to have died. The training of the mind of the best bow-handlers [warriors] and of Buddhists is said to be identical. In all cases, restlessness of mind is deplorable.'

−'The term "name" plays a great part in your ethical notions, as I see from the quotation you have just given,' said the duchess. 'You yourself have also spoken about it in your peroration to the article on Japanese education, which you published in the Independent Review. I was reading that article this very morning, and had intended to ask you for a further explanation about it, but I think I have now caught the idea, though it is somewhat vague to me still. The idea of doing one's part, thinking of the names of one's descendants, as the book you have just quoted speaks about, sounds somewhat odd to our ears. It will be always puzzling to the generality of the Occidentals.'

−'Why so,' I answered; 'you Occidentals seem always to make simple matters difficult to comprehend, when they would be quite clear if only viewed in a light, not deep, philosophical manner. The spirit of the dictum I have just quoted has always been maintained in our ethics, under all circumstances. As you say, no human creature can love death; it is against nature, and, therefore, we Japanese value life no less than other races; but we study how to live and how to die, and when circumstances require, we value our life lighter than the proverbial feather: that's all.'

−'And yet it is a problem for us,' said the duchess.

−'And it is plain to us who have grown up in such an atmosphere, although it may be somewhat difficult for foreigners to understand.'

−'Do you think those noble characteristics will last long under the influence of modern civilisation?' asked the duchess.

−'It is a question,' I answered, 'but I hope and believe it will last; indeed, we must make it do so.'

−'But now, to take up the thread of our original conversation,' said the duchess. 'Politically speaking, I am of the opinion that Russia ought to make friends with you, and that my long, endearing hope for an entente between England, France, Russia, and your country ought to be effected for the security of peace at large and for the benefit of humanity.'

−'I appreciate,' I answered, 'the general trend of your discourse, and I know it has been your line of politics for many years, and not a view invented merely to please me. I sympathise with you all the more when I hear you confessing the weak points of an ally and paying high tribute to my country. The time may come when your cherished idea may be realised, but at present the prospects do not look bright. The greatest obstacle in the path is the pretensions of the Russians. They will not reconcile themselves to the idea that we Japanese are also a nation which deserves the name of a civilised race.'

−'They will and must do so in time,' said the duchess.

−'We Japanese are modest. We do not give ourselves airs. I say this frankly and sincerely. It is neither presumption nor self-conceit, it is my pure conviction; but we like to be treated with proper consideration. A few days ago an interview which I gave to a French weekly was published. The subject was somewhat akin to our present conversation. A telegram from Washington, which was published in some journals, stated that the Russians in America were irritated because President Roosevelt had given an informal reception to Baron Komura. It also stated that the Russians were inspiring the impression that Mr. Roosevelt was annoyed with Great Britain because she had refused to put pressure on Japan to be moderate, and so on. The gist of my observation on the telegram was:—

'It was understood that the plenipotentiaries of both countries should arrive in Washington before the first part of August. The Japanese plenipotentiaries arrived punctually at the prearranged date, but the Russian plenipotentiaries were belated, as we all know, and yet complaints are made that it was Mr. Roosevelt's partiality towards Japan which made him receive the Japanese plenipotentiaries informally. I cannot see why the president should not offer cordiality to his distinguished guests, be they Japanese or Russian, on their arrival. England is not less anxious to see the termination of the present war than any other nation, but I do not see why England should put pressure upon Japan to give advantage to Russia, inasmuch as she knows that Japan is not a nation to make any unreasonable demand upon her worsted foe. President Roosevelt knows all this. I also believe that while the president is determined to be quite impartial in the matter, he is not inclined to oppress Japan in order to give any unreasonable advantage to Russia, nor does he expect to see England do so either.

–'You see, such sentiments as those expressed in the telegram, which I do not consider a misrepresentation, cannot but arise from some idea of prestige, with which the Russians imagine they have been endowed to a much higher degree by nature than Japan has been. There is another point they have made a great deal of fuss about, and which they cannot get out of their heads. It is the first torpedoing of the Russian fleets at the entrance of Port Arthur, which took place, as you know, on the night of the 8-9th of February last year. They always speak of it as a treacherous attack. As a matter of fact, however, it was nothing of the sort, as may be seen from all the circumstances which forced us into the war, and which are known to all the world. Our justification has become more evident since the revelation of the secret history of the Russian politics of the time. There even exists a secret treaty between China and Russia, made at the time when Russia obtained a concession from China for the construction of the Manchurian railways. The purport of the treaty, which is now no longer a secret, is no other than that Russia and China were to regard Japan as their enemy, and to menace her by the use of that railway. China soon discovered the fallacy: she soon saw that Japan had not the disposition represented by the Russians. Russia would perhaps now say that the treaty was only made for the purpose of obtaining the concession: I hope it was so, but who knows that it had been so from the beginning? In spite of all this, Japan had always adopted a conciliatory attitude before the outbreak of the war—a war in which, to use a phrase of President Roosevelt's memorable message to the American Congress, "it was necessary for the aggrieved nation valiantly to stand up for its rights." Remember, I do not quote this in any vainglory. Moreover, when the war became inevitable, we gave a clear notice of war to our opponents (on the 6th of that month). Perhaps you have seen the White Book of Japan relating to the subject.'

−'I saw a French translation of it,' said the duchess, 'and it has modified considerably the early impressions, not only of myself, but of most people.'

−'I am glad of that,' I said. 'It is true that the Emperor of Japan issued on the 10th of that month a formal declaration of war, but it was addressed to his own subjects, and its aim was to make the actual situation known to them and also indirectly to the neutrals. As far as Russia and Japan are concerned, the notice of the 6th, whereby Japan announced to Russia that she would take an "independent action," was nothing else than a declaration of war. It is, therefore, unfair to state that the first attack on Port Arthur was a "treacherous attack" or "an attack by surprise," even if there were no other reasons which justify Japan's action.'

−'And yet the Russian statesman, for instance, wrote in the same remarkable letters that "the whole world knows that

157

Japan and not Russia has provoked the present war," and spoke of Japan, in reference to the first battle of Port Arthur, as "guilty of a criminal breach of peace," and of that battle as a "piratical night attack." He went on so far as to stigmatise Japan as "this bullying and bellicose nation." It is the more remarkable that all this had been done after the plain facts of the truth had come into the possession of the world. In the course of my refutation I stated that torpedoing was not a surprise attack in the sense of International Law, as the Russian statesman affirms; at the most it could only be construed as a tactical surprise, but in reality it was not even of that nature. I gave my reason therefor, to which the Russian statesman replied, that "a Japanese is the only person who can make any difference between a surprise and a tactical surprise, and no educated European can make such a difference." The difference itself is plain enough. Tactical surprises come under no sphere of international question. The Russian troops themselves are daily practising them in the war. In spite of it, he feigns his ignorance. In my reply I had to detail and to develop my argument a step further. If you are not already wearied, I will recall a passage of my letter in question:

'With regard to the Port Arthur question, I should like in the first place to ask the Russian statesman as to what Russia herself did in all warlike engagements before the battle of Narva, and also when the army of his country entered Poland in 1733; when it entered Moldavia and took possession of Chotsin, Bender, and Jassi in 1806; when the Russian ships fired into, and sunk or captured, some Greek ships and made an attack upon Poros in 1831? Further, how was it when the Russian troops made raids on the coasts of the northern islands of Japan unexpectedly and repeatedly in the beginning of the nineteenth century, on which occasions they slaughtered our innocent villagers and burned our villages, or when they attacked and occupied our Island of Tsushima in 1861?—in all these cases there having been no cause or reason whatever for the hostility perpetrated, and that, too, without the slightest warning. Above all, I should like to call his attention to the proposal which his country made through its ambassador, Baron Brunnow, to the Diplomatique Corps of the Great Powers at Constantinople in 1840, concerning Egypt. The Russian ambassador offered various schemes for action, the pith of which was to be found in the following words:

'"To execute all these measures with the greatest promptitude, and with the greatest secrecy,—promptitude, because it is the only means of ensuring their success; secrecy, because the blow must first be struck before it is announced."'

Having read so far, I continued: 'After I had thus written, I proceeded to elucidate that, "with these facts in view, the Russians had no right to calumniate Japan, even if their country were attacked by surprise," and that, "nevertheless, Japan had done nothing of the sort, as is plain from other facts." Such is the case on our side.'

—'That point is now wholly cleared up in the eyes of the world,' said the duchess. 'The Russians certainly ought not to grumble endlessly over the milk which they themselves spilled!'

—'I may remind you of a still more fresh instance of the unscrupulousness of the Russians themselves. At the time of the ratification of the treaty of Simonoseki, did not the Russian admiral commanding the Pacific fleet propose to the French admiral commanding the French fleet in the same water to attack and destroy the Japanese fleet by a deliberate surprise! Was it not only restrained from being

159

carried out by the judicious refusal of the French admiral on the ground that he had received no such instruction from his government! We cannot, of course, be thankful to France for joining the memorable combination of the three powers, but we remember with pleasant recollection the noble determination of her admiral.'

−'Thank God! our action was correct, at least in that respect.'

−'You must be quite sickened,' I said, 'of the hackneyed talk of the "Yellow Peril" cry, and the "Pan-Asiatic" ambition attributed to Japan, because you know they are all groundless. The same Russian statesman dilated on them also: if he really entertains any belief in them his conception is erroneous; if he does not, and still says so, it is most unfair. I assured him that Japan knew no such ambition, and gave vent to my conviction in this manner. I hope you will kindly listen to me.

'There is no possibility of "Panasianism" even if Japan had dreamed of it, nor is there any likelihood of the Western powers being endangered by the ascendency of Japan. The insinuation of your writer that the English and American commerce would be jeopardised by Japan's victory, and, therefore, Japan ought to be thoroughly defeated, is a most absurd proposition. To begin with, Japan's victory would never prejudice the commercial interests of those countries; on the contrary, they would be more safeguarded. But suppose it did, it would be for England and America to look after those matters before the Russians did for them. England and America, however, are amongst those countries which are most sympathetic with Japan. I can put it in another way. Suppose, after Japan's success in this war, Japan's industry should be more developed, it would

160

only serve more to stimulate the commerce between the East and West. Supposing, however, that the development of Japan's industry be more or less detrimental to the Western commerce, is it just and humane—let me repeat, is it just and humane, to formulate a doctrine that she is to be crushed because there is a fear that her industry might be developed? It would be like a rich person formulating the doctrine that a poor neighbour of his ought to be murdered for no other reason than a vague apprehension that he might possibly become a prosperous man.

'That is what I answered the Russian statesman. But even at this moment such speculative opinions are widespread. I can only hope that Japan's real motive and aspiration for emulating occidental civilisation is now becoming better known to the Western nations, at all events to the bulk of the French people.'

—'I believe so, too,' said the duchess. 'But one thing which strikes me is that, while on the one hand many people depict Japan by her huge shadow, even a greater number of people speak of Japan as a small country, as though she were no more than Belgium, Holland, or Denmark. A country which competes with the United Kingdom of Great Britain and Ireland, France, or even Germany, in the size of her territory and number of population, cannot be a small country.'

—'It is perhaps because we Japanese do not parade ourselves. We prefer to speak of ourselves as small in deference to the modern civilisation of the Western nations. Besides, we are not so wealthy as the occidental nations. We always feel it. It often prevents us from doing better things.'

161

−'But your country is not poor.'

−'We are not poor. I am only speaking comparatively with the great powers of the West. The volume of our commerce has risen from a few millions to six or seven hundred million yens in less than forty years. In a way we ought to be satisfied.'

−'I suppose the people are happy.'

−'Well, I may say so. We have no very rich classes, but at the same time we have no extreme poverty as yet. Only the other evening a compatriot of mine who had travelled in the country near Tours told me that the common people there lived in small caves in the cliffs, or on the slopes of the hills, and they were all barefooted when they were at home, or were at work in the vintage. I hear there are many such in Britain also. It sounds rather odd for France. And more! Paris is a wonderful town. It is a place of the agglomeration of everything extreme. A little time ago, accompanied by a few Frenchmen, I made a round of visits to all sorts of places through the whole night in order to see Paris by night. I saw many night shows to begin with: I saw many gay places: I saw several dens of the poor. Among the shows, that of Niente struck me most. It seemed so strange to entertain visitors with beer at tables which are coffins, and in a room lighted by a chandelier constructed of human bones. A small cave tavern made right in the ground, where the poor were enjoying bocks of beer, and listening to some indifferent musical performance, was also interesting. I asked from where they got the air into the place. The answer was "nowhere." But what impressed me most was a den of the destitute, where the poor get permission to sleep for one night, and to receive a basin of soup, at a total cost of twopence. When I visited the dens, it was far on in the night. I saw some four or five hundred men, clad in rags most of them, leaning on tables, asleep, in different cellars connected by narrow passages, right deep in the ground. Naturally also many were lying on the ground, and several on the stone staircases. These cellars could not have been made for such a purpose, and I was unable to divine for what they had been originally used. Perhaps they had been the cellars of some great wine merchant. I don't think you yourself can have seen such a place, but you can imagine the awfulness of the sight. Indeed, the French gentleman who was with me said he began to feel upset. I am happy to say that we have not such extreme cases of poverty in our country up to the present generation.'

−'I am afraid it is such cases as these that give good pretext to the socialistic movement,' said the duchess. 'It is a great problem. But to return to our subject, you have no embassy in Europe, as all other great powers have. You have only legations, with ordinary ministers, like secondary powers. It might have been one cause why ordinary people think Japan is such a small country.'

−'It may be so,' I answered, 'in one way; but you see we have not had any particular reason to make ourselves ostentatious, and besides, the matter does not rest with one side only.'

−'It is rather singular,' said the duchess, 'that the world has not discovered the real character of the Japanese for so long a time. But yet there was at least one man who realised it ninety years ago. I have read an account about him in a recent issue of the English press. It was in the year 1813, and, therefore, at the time when Java was under English occupation. Lord Minto (ancestor of the new viceroy) was

163

then Viceroy of India, and it seems Sir Stamford Raffles was the chief representative of the British East India Company out in the East. The latter sent in that year an Englishman, Dr. Daniel Ainslie, to whom was attached a Dutchman, Wardenaar by name, to Nagasaki on a mission to look after English interests, and to make a confidential report on the situation in Japan. The mission was a failure; the time was not ripe enough. But the impression Sir Stamford obtained through Dr. Ainslie is interesting. It reads as fresh as though it had been brought back from Japan only yesterday, and speaks for itself:

'The refusal of the Japanese, instigated by the prejudiced and stiff-necked Dutchman, Hendrik Doeff, to trade with the English, did not bias Sir Stamford's mind against them. Dr. Ainslie, in whom he had implicit confidence, sent him voluminous reports, and on them he formed a judgment most favourable to the Japanese in every respect. Expression was given to these opinions in Sir Stamford's presidential address to the Batavian Society of Arts and Sciences on September 11, 1815. The following extracts are those of the most direct importance; "I need only offer a few notices on the character which they appeared to Dr. Ainslie to display during a residence of four months, and as far as he had the opportunity of judging. They are represented to be a nervous, vigorous people, whose bodily and mental powers assimilate much nearer to those of Europe than what is attributed to Asiatics in general. Their features are masculine and perfectly European, with the exception of the small, lengthened Tartar eye, which almost universally prevails, and is the only feature of resemblance between them and the Chinese. The complexion is perfectly fair, and indeed blooming, the women of the higher classes being equally fair with Europeans, and having the bloom of health more generally prevalent among them than is usually found in Europe. For a people who have had very few, if any, external aids, the Japanese cannot but rank high in the scale of civilisation....

'"The Chinese have been stationary, at least as long as we have known them, but the slightest impulse seems sufficient to give a determination to the Japanese character which would progressively improve until it attained the same height of civilisation with the European....

'"The Japanese, with an apparent coldness like the stillness of the Spanish character, and derived nearly from the same causes—that system of espionage and that principle of disunion dictated by the principles of both Governments— are represented to be eager of novelty and warm in their attachments, open to strangers, and, hating the restrictions of their political institutions, a people who seem inclined to throw themselves into the hands of any nation of superior intelligence. They have, at the same time, a great contempt and disregard of everything below their own standard of morals and habits, as instanced in the case of the Chinese."

'These remarks, uttered ninety years ago, show that at least one discerning mind had appreciated all the difference between the Japanese and other Asiatics, judged according to the accepted views among Europeans. It was the apathy of the home authorities that alone prevented the establishment nearly a century ago of an entente cordiale between England and Japan as the consequence of the strenuous effort of Sir Stamford Raffles to promote commercial relations at Nagasaki.'

At this juncture the duke returned with his two daughters; joining us very soon, he said to me:

—'Have you noticed the controversy about French patriotism waging in the papers just now? I wish all Frenchmen were as patriotic as your countrymen.'

—'I have noticed,' I said, 'but I believe that whatever opinion one may entertain, or whatever views one may express, in the innermost shrine of the heart of every Frenchman there is treasured a phrase, "La France: c'est le pays de mon cœur." It cannot be otherwise.'

—'I hope so,' rejoined the duke. 'To love one's own country, which is patriotism, is almost a natural instinct. The only difference is the degree of intensity.'

—'Let me tell you,' I proceeded, 'how I came to remember that phrase, and excuse me if my talk is somewhat delicate. It is now more than twenty years ago, perhaps you remember, when a young cantatrice, together with her companion-maid, put an end to their lives, under romantic but tragic circumstances, beneath the windows of the chateau of a young foreign nobleman in his country. It created a great sensation at the time. I was then staying in England. She left a letter in which she expressed her desire that her enfant d'amour should be brought up and educated in France, adding thereto the phrase I have just quoted. We have a saying, "Do not cast away good dictum on account of the person who uttered it." Those words—I mean "La France," etc.—though uttered by a female of her type, left a deep impression in my mind. They are so fine and touching. I dare say many a Frenchman has used, and still uses, that phrase, at least in his mind. Apropos to that story, I will tell you an incident. Several years after that event I was in Japan, and dined one evening with some friends, the party including a few foreigners. There were no ladies present. As is usual, a good deal of merry chatting went on among us after dinner. On that occasion I narrated to them the story of the event just mentioned, and, of course, recalled that phrase to their remembrance. One of the foreigners suddenly said, "I was the man concerned in it—I was the man." You can imagine how awkward I felt. It is always necessary to be on one's guard in society. One never knows who a person may be. The incident, however, will serve to show how vividly the phrase remained in my memory.'

—'Now, baron,' interposed the duchess, 'permit me to ask you to explain a problem which I am unable to solve myself.'

—'What is it?' I replied. 'I am always ready to answer your questions as far as possible.'

—'The ideals as well as the whole structure, both political and social, of your country,' continued the duchess, 'seem to differ, as far as I can judge, from the ideals and doctrines of some of the Socialists of the West. According to these latter, there can be no patriotism, as the essence of their teaching is cosmopolite and not national, and there can be no such social and political structure as, for instance, those which your country adores. And yet, on the Continent, the Socialists are disposed to be more friendly to your country than the other sections of the communities. On your part, also, you appear to be more intimate, or at least more acquainted, with people belonging to that class. Excuse me if my remarks are too personal.'

—'I am not intimate,' I interposed, 'nor am I even acquainted with many. But please continue.'

−'Well, in England, for instance, it is the Conservatives who are more enthusiastic about your country, and the Liberals only rank second. I cannot make out how all that comes about on the Continent.'

−'I do not think English sympathy for Japan has anything to do with their home politics. Look at America! The form of the government and their political ideas are totally different from ours, and yet they have shown great sympathy to us, as you must have observed.'

−'American democracy, nevertheless, is more apparent than real,' said the duchess. 'Their methods are more monarchical than republican. When once a man is elected President, he is like a monarch. He has a wide scope for political movement in his hands. He chooses his ministers independently of the Congress, and the ministry is not dependent on the Congress; in other words, there is a concentration of power and also the continuity of it, though the person of the President may change after a certain lapse of time. Look at Mr. Roosevelt, what a position he occupies in his country.'

−'For all that,' I said, 'America is a republic. American sympathy for Japan cannot be explained by the theory you put upon the American polity. The sympathy of the Anglo-Saxons arises, in my opinion, chiefly from their perception of the justice of our cause, and from their appreciation of the humane and enlightened behaviour of the Japanese. This is my plain opinion. No one can fail to perceive a great contrast in these respects between the two countries engaged in the war. The sympathy of the European Socialists is somewhat similar, I believe. The conditions of Japan are much nearer to their own ideals than are those of our opponents.'

−'That is very likely,' said the duchess, 'but Japan as she is cannot be an ideal object of admiration to them; their sympathy appears only to be based on comparison. Why, there was even an assertion by some Socialists that Japan was liked only because the autocracy of the other side was disliked. By the bye, you said the other day, that you did not like to apply the term "revolution" to your great change of 1867.'

−'Yes, I said so.'

−'And I agree with you,' continued the duchess. '"Revolution" means upsetting and destroying everything, but you never had anything of that kind. Your emperor assumed a new authority, but it was only a restoration, or, in other words, unification of power; then, too, the sovereignty of his majesty's family is so antique that there is again a great continuity of power: those are the points which make Japan so fine a nation.

−'Well,' I continued, 'we do not like to apply the term "revolution" to our great change, because that term is usually applied to a big, popular movement against established governments, which, while destroying one, sets up another. That is to say, the term is generally used in a political sense. The history of our great change differs from that, because, although the Shogunate Government was upset, the other Government, namely, the Imperial, which was reinvigorated and had come to exercise again its full authority, had always existed, and the sovereignty had continued to rest with the heads of that Government, namely, the emperors; that you know very well. Nevertheless, with regard to the social aspects of the change, one cannot say there has been no upsetting of

169

things. As a matter of fact, almost everything has been upset; restoration and innovation were the two currents of thought then prevailing. The main work was restoration, but almost everything else was innovation, or at least renovation. Hence, almost every institution and material object which was old was destroyed, or nearly destroyed, beyond all necessary limit, almost in the same way as was experienced by England under the Long Parliament, and France in 1789. I don't mean there was in Japan any such sanguinary deeds perpetrated as those by the Jacobins, but the general social currents of events were something like those of French and English experience. There was even a suggestion made by serious people of cutting down the big trees of a fine park in the middle of Tokio and turning it into mulberry fields, on the argument that the latter would be beneficial to the nation, whilst the former was a useless luxury. At one time, indeed, even the word civilisation was much abused: of course, not in such a way as Madame Roland lamented the abuse of the term "liberty," because our abuse of the word "civilisation" was neither political nor serious. It was chiefly so with small social matters. For instance, when one wished to dispense with some of the old customs and manners, which he deemed too rigid and inconvenient, he would cast them away light-heartedly, with the remark that "it was not a civilised method." Of course, a great change like the one we have made can only be carried out under such circumstances as those, accompanied necessarily by great sacrifices. Without doubt, it would not do if the same thing went on endlessly. Fortunately we have managed to tide over that transitory state, and have produced the Japan of the present day.'

−'Whatever may have been the social aspects of your great change,' said the duchess, 'one thing is undeniable, and that is, that its best results have been brought about by the unification and continuity of the pouvoir—I mean, authority. But by saying this, I must not be misunderstood, especially in this country, as saying that a continuity of authority is necessarily to be connected with heredity, for I maintain, for instance, that the Catholic religion is a specimen of continuity in the person of the Pope. But, baron, was there any outcry for "Liberté, Egalité, and Fraternité" at the time of your great change?'

—'No, not exactly,' I replied. 'Our struggle was not one of the lower classes en masse against the upper classes. Besides, our lower classes were not in such a desperate condition as those of France in her troubled days.'

—'You know already,' proceeded the duchess, 'that those three terms contradict each other if carried out literally.'

—'That is true. But by similar reasoning, all terms of virtue are contradictory if carried out to the letter. Thus, the extremity of patience makes one a fool; that of bravery, foolhardy; that of charity, lavish; and that of extensive love of all things, makes one a sentimental weeper. Forgive me if I am a little polemic. However, there is one thing that I think I have not told you, and that is this: Although there was no definite cry for the three "té's" during our great change, some vague notion of them was observable during that event and some time after. It was during that transition period that the French notion of personal right based upon the civil law got into the Japanese mind a little too strongly in opposition to the idea of public laws based upon the principles of State and common good. Thus, for instance, a man did not scruple to cut down whatever forests belonged to him, no matter whether or not by doing so irreparable public injury should be occasioned; his notion being that his proprietary right of the forests stood over any other right. In other words, the notion of private laws was not reconciled with that of public laws. We have had to bring about an amelioration, and to enact fresh laws to regulate the forest question, much on the same lines as the old regulations which had previously existed in many parts of the country. There have been many other matters much similar to this. I may also add that proper respect between inferior and superior, and younger and elder, was also slackened at one time, which is a sort of misuse of equality and fraternity.

'But to return to our discourse: all the arguments I have heard from you to-day remind me of an anonymous political pamphlet which I happened to glance at. It speaks of the necessity of unification and continuation of authority. It speaks of the advisability of non-dependency of the Ministry on the Chamber, and it speaks of the self-contradiction of the three terms. I almost suspect that the writer of the pamphlet is influenced by you, or you by him, or is it a coincidence?'

−'No matter,' said the duchess lightly, and continued; 'I think there are no Socialists in Japan—at all events, not worth speaking of, as a party?'

−'Very true,' I interposed.

−'I thought so,' continued the duchess; 'Japan is not a country compatible with the ideas and doctrines of Socialism: she does not want it.'

−'And yet, some points of her aspirations,' I said, 'deserve attention. It is the duty of an enlightened Government to anticipate the legitimate requirements of the lower classes, and to make the spread of dangerous doctrines useless.'

−'And Japan does so, I suppose,' said the duchess.

–'Well, we are doing our best,' I answered, 'more especially because the introduction of Western methods of progress tend to produce all sorts of evils, though, of course, the benefit derived therefrom is comparatively far greater in its way.'

–'The freer a country is, the less it is likely to be disturbed by socialistic or nihilistic movements, you mean, I suppose,' said the duchess.

–'It is not all, but something like it,' I said. 'England and America are free from those movements.'

–'France is a free country,' said the duchess, 'and yet she labours under an overpowering influence of Socialism.'

–'It seems true,' I said.

–'You might say because she is too free, perhaps,' said the duchess.

–'Or, rather,' I replied, 'she might be paying the penalty incurred during the ancient monarchy of the misuse of its power.'

–'Maybe,' she answered. 'But I am far from believing in real power of that party. It is, of course, foolish to ignore an existence of such an element. They have, however, never been in office. Suppose they have formed a Government, what do you think will come out of it? At all events, I can never agree with some of their extreme views which, if carried out literally, would mean an abolition of the army and navy, the Government, even the State.'

173

−'The subject is too intricate for me,' I said; 'I give it up.'

−'At all events,' she replied, 'there being no socialistic party in Japan, as you say, is it not all the more strange that no cordiality seems to exist between Japan and the French Nationalists, whose notions and ideas resemble those of the Japanese.'

−'We can have no sympathy, still less concern, with any political aspiration of a section of other people as far as their domestic politics are concerned. But I do not see why the Japanese should not be willing to be friendly with the Nationalist section of the French people. Of late, the Japanese have not seemed to be persona gratæ with your Nationalists, if there be any such section. But it is not our fault. They have shown through their partiality to our opponents much antipathy to Japan. It is another reason why the contrast between the Socialists and other sections of the French people has become, or rather, once became, so manifest as regards their attitude to my country.'

−'But the Nationalists are not enemies of Japan. In fact, it was the Nationalists who disapproved ten years ago the action of the Government, which joined in the combination of the three powers against Japan.'

−'Maybe,' I said, 'but the general tendency of that section, since the outbreak of the present war, has not been so favourable to us as you would have liked.'

−'But you must make some allowance for the fact that France is the ally of the other side.'

−'I do so, but the contrast in tone between different journals is so marked, and the papers which are most bitter against

174

us, at one time were those reputed as the organs of the Nationalists.'

−'That may have been so,' said the duchess, 'and there have even been some which were rather misleading. I confess I was rather surprised when once asked by a member of a respectable family, "how it was that the Japanese were near Moukden, whilst we had been informed by the press all these months that the Russians had been constantly gaining victories." Probably that family happened to take in some exceptional journal, and perhaps only one. But you cannot read journalistic opinions only and regard them as the real views of the Nationalists. They have, in reality, very little influence over the papers; I wish they had more. Journals generally go their own way: I cannot and must not explain why. Besides, the socialist journals also have not been friendly to Japan from the very beginning. They became so only when the contrasts between the belligerents had become somewhat manifest. They were shrewd in the matter: the Nationalists were slow; one had to awake them.'

−'I was not here at that time,' said I, 'so I cannot offer any observation thereon. But, madam, is it too impertinent for me to ask if French interest in Russian bonds are much in the hands of Nationalists?'

−'Oh no,' answered the duchess. 'I wish they were; but you see our old families are not like those of some other countries. The interest of the Russian bonds mostly concerns petty people who have invested in them their hard-earned savings. It is, therefore, all the more unfortunate that the present war should be protracted.'

−'I envy France,' I said, 'that she has such a saving people: it is in consequence of this that she has, as I am told, some billions of surplus francs every year.'

−'That, I believe, is the case,' said the duchess.

−'As to the friendly relations between your country and mine, let us hope that a time happier than the present may arrive soon, and the sooner the better.'

−'I hope so, too,' said the duchess, 'and we must try to make it so.'

VI

I found myself once more in a group of people, including some ladies. The group was very incongruous, as is usual in dreamland. The conversation went on merrily and very light-heartedly.

—'Now, baron, it is your turn. You must now tell us something interesting,' said one of those present.

—'I have nothing worth telling,' I answered.

—'But you must: you were in Europe for many years, when quite young, I have heard. You must have had some experiences to interest us.'

—'Well, I can remember only one or two amusing incidents. I once knew a charming young lady, called by her friends "the modest Violet." She lived with her mother and sisters in a country home near London. I was often invited there to

177

take tea and play tennis, or accompany them for a drive. On one occasion, I was walking with her round the garden, when we came to a nook where there was a garden seat. We sat down. But the seat, being old, the part on which I sat gave way all of a sudden, and I found myself flat on the ground, the other part of the seat remaining intact.'

—'Does she still remember you, or rather, have you seen her since your arrival in Europe this time?' asked another.

—'Yes! I have seen her, and I noticed when I visited her she was still using on her table a silver trinket, of which I made her a present years ago, on the occasion of her wedding.'

—'That is one—and another.'

—'Well, I was at Brighton one summer, and met there a young lady with whom I was acquainted. We went for a walk together on the Parade one bright afternoon and then went down to the beach. She sat on a small rock and leaned against the stone wall. She had a book of select poems in her hand and read a good many of them while I reclined on the sand by her side. When she rose from her seat, I noticed that the back of her white summer dress was stained green by the moss on the stone against which she had leaned, and she was obliged to go home with her sunshade open over her back.'

—'Let me again ask if you have met her since?'

—'No, I have lost trace of her altogether. She was the daughter of an astronomer. If she is still living, she will remember me when she sees my Summer Dream.'

—'What?'

—'I don't know.'

—'But I have heard you utter those words once or twice. Surely they must have a meaning.'

—'No! I think not. You must know that I was formerly a Deputy of the Japanese Diet.'

—'What has that to do with the subject?'

—'Well! Deputies often talk about things which they know nothing about. Just observe the deputies who talk most in the chamber. They are sure to be those who have never read through the documents they hold in their hands.'

—'What a pleasantry! However, we have had the second tale. What next?'

—'No more amusing ones. But I remember another which was somewhat chivalrous. In a large town in the north of France, there was a group of rich manufacturers belonging to the same family, originally English, though some of the younger members had been born in France. A bosom friend of mine, and another compatriot, were staying there, and they were both on intimate terms with all the members of the family. I spent several summer days in that town, and also in Dunkirk and Ostend, with my friends and most of the people I am referring to. They were all very cordial, and it goes without saying that I spent a very jolly time. There was a young lady belonging to one branch of the family, who in age, to say the least of it, was past the first bloom of youth. I noticed that she and the members of another branch of the family never spoke together, which aroused my curiosity, and as a result of discreet inquiry, I found that some discord existed between them, the cause of which was

179

she had not married the man of her choice on account of the interference of an uncle, who was the head of the other branch of the family. I felt rather sorry about the matter, for it was the only rift in the family lute, otherwise most happy and harmonious. A strong desire came over me to bring about a reconciliation. One day at Dunkirk, I accompanied the young lady to the sea-coast, where, after a long persuasion, I obtained her consent to be reconciled. The chief individual having been won over, I had no great difficulty in persuading the others; and peace was proclaimed then and there at Dunkirk.'

−'But you were only a young man, then.'

−'Certainly I was younger than I am now, but I am not quite so young as you may imagine. The Japanese, as a rule, appear to European eyes many years younger than they are in reality. Thus, for instance, when Marquis Ito and Count Inouyé came over to England as students for the first time, they were both "over twenty," and Count Inouyé was older than the Marquis Ito by some years.'

−'Their relative ages, however, must have remained the same always,' said one jestingly.

−'That is so: but that is not my point. They were then considered as young students of seventeen or eighteen. When, therefore, they told their teacher that they would return to Japan and counsel their Prince to change his anti-foreign policy into a pro-foreign policy, he laughed at them, saying, "You boys, what can you do?" And Ito and Inouyé only succeeded, after great perseverance, to obtain the necessary consent. However that may be, I am glad to have heard since that the lady in question was happily married.'

−'Allow me to ask a very delicate question. Have you never fallen in love, or something like it, with any European lady during your long stay in Europe?'

−'Well, I have always preferred to keep my heart well in hand, so as not to be hampered in the more serious duties of life; and, moreover, I do not believe in the desirability of intermarriage between foreigners. There have, of course, been many intermarriages between the Japanese and the occidental races, and the results of some of them have been apparently very good, but there have also been many failures, and I do not think, in general, happiness can be secured in intermarriages of this kind, so much as those between people who have greater resemblance in customs and manners and everything else to each other. Even if the couple are happy, it often happens that it is not so between them and their relations. You know, perhaps, that the late Commander Hirosé was a bachelor. He was a man of stoical character. There is, however, a rumour about him that while he was staying over here he met a young European lady whom he liked very much. He did not propose to her but for one reason, and that was because he was afraid she might feel unhappy when taken to Japan for the reason I have just mentioned, in addition to the fact that he was a naval officer, in consequence of which he would have to leave her to herself more than ordinary married women—and that in a country to which she was a stranger in many things!'

−'But your success in the war will make your countrymen very popular among young ladies,' interposed another laughingly.

181

−'I have no fear. Western young ladies are cautious enough. But, nevertheless, there is a slight danger of the name of Japan being taken advantage of. I heard a story only the other day that in California some Chinese cut off their plaits and dressed in European costumes while they were staying at an hotel, and were passing themselves off as Japanese. They were discovered when a real Japanese addressed them in his language, to which they were unable to reply. I have heard of another incident which took place in a town in the north of England. A foreigner, professing himself to be a Japanese, tried to take an apartment. The landlady, who had had some Japanese lodgers before, somewhat suspected the nationality of the man from his way of bargaining for the rent. She asked a Japanese to call in on her, and the foreigner was soon discovered to be a European whose nationality belonged to a country where the climate is very hot, and whose complexion alone bore resemblance to the Japanese.'

−'What is the Japanese climate like?' asked another.

−'Well, that is a question I am asked so often. You see Japan is a long, narrow country running from north to south-west; therefore, if you take the northern and southern extremities, there is much difference of climate, but as to Japan proper, that is to say, the middle part, the climate does not much differ from yours. The latitude there is much lower than England or France. The latitude of London is fifty-one degrees, one minute north; that of Paris, forty-eight degrees, fifty minutes north; whilst that of Yokohama, which is the port of Tokio, and about twenty miles south of the latter, is thirty-five degrees, twenty-six minutes; and, therefore, people taking an analogy from Egypt or Algeria often wrongly imagine that Japan is a tropical land, but it is not so. We have our seasons: spring, summer, autumn, and winter, at the same time as you. We have snow, frost, even hailstones, much similar to you. We have occasional rain and showers also, as you have, or perhaps a little more frequent. We have a rainy season in June, although we do not have so much fog as in England. The weather is generally fine; our summer lasts longer than yours, and is somewhat hotter, but not so hot as people generally imagine. Our autumn lasts longer and is finer than yours, because you seem to jump almost from summer to winter, and winter to summer. In fact, in Japan, we almost doubt which is the better season of the year, spring or autumn. In autumn, in many parts of the country, almost all the foliage, as well as the maples, turn to all shades of red and scarlet intermingled with yellow. It is the result of the brilliant sun shining on the frosted leaves—a grand sight, which you seem not to have in this quarter of the world.'

−'The chrysanthemums are also very fine too, I think,' said another.

−'Yes, but in that respect we cannot now boast so much, as it is cultivated so extensively in the West, and the blossoms are, as a rule, much bigger than ours. Everywhere in society nowadays chrysanthemums are plentifully used for table decorations. Indeed, people say the introduction of that flower was a great boon to the florists of Europe, as the chrysanthemum season happens to fall just at a time when the scarcity of flowers is most felt. There is, however, one difference in its cultivation between the Occidental and Japanese horticulturists. The latter strive to keep all the leaves fresh and green from the bottom of the stalk to the top, which is no easy matter, and do not trouble to produce very large blossoms, but in the West the size of the flower appears to be almost the only care, in consequence of which I have seen almost all the flowers exhibited at shows without any stalk at all. I may add a word concerning the rain in Japan, especially in Tokio. The shower is often very heavy, and falls in a slanting direction on account of a strong wind, which often prevails in Japan; therefore, the roofs of the buildings have long eaves; even the buildings in European style must have eaves and windows specially designed, differing from the ordinary Western architecture, otherwise the rain would soak through. The reason why the climate of Japan is temperate in comparison with its latitude is chiefly due to the effects of two great currents, one coming from the Behring Strait and the other coming from the south, one cold and the other warm; and between those currents is produced the climate of Japan. Strangely enough, in Manchuria and the northern parts of China proper, that is to say, the regions surrounding Pekin, the summer is excessively hot and the winter extremely cold.'

─'Do you say the climate in every part of Japan proper is pretty much the same?' asked one.

─'Pretty much, but not exactly. You see Japan proper has a range of mountains, which divides the country into two parts, one side facing the Pacific Ocean and the other the Sea of Japan. The former is more bright and cheerful, and conversely the latter is less bright and less cheerful. Perhaps, owing to that disadvantage in climate, the Japan Sea side is less advanced in all respects. Then, again, the development of Japan seems to have proceeded from west to east, beginning at the north-western part of Kiusiu, thence along both sides of the Inland Sea, thence along the Pacific Ocean on toward the Plain of Kwanto, where Tokio is situated. All travellers can discern this very easily by the general development of these regions in comparison with other parts of the country.'

─'Is the summer so hot as to be unbearable?' asked another.

184

—'I would not say "unbearable," but, of course, it would be far more comfortable if one went to good summer resorts. There are many places in Japan suitable for spending the summer, and are visited by a large number of Occidentals, not only from all parts of Japan, but also from most of the open ports of the neighbouring countries. For instance, Karuizawa, where I have a small villa, is over three thousand feet above sea level, and there nearly one thousand foreigners spend the summer every year. Apropos to Karuizawa, I may tell you en passant an incident which occurred there a few years ago. Early one morning I discovered two foreigners had got into a corner of my garden and were cutting down branches of my favourite trees; they were not very refined, and evidently belonged to some irregular mission. On my asking for an explanation, they told me the branches were for the decoration of the house of God. They did not know to apologise, but appeared to assume that they could do anything in the name of their mission. I had to explain to them that they were doing what they ought not to, and that if they did the same thing in the grounds of less tolerant people, trouble might ensue. I then formally gave them the branches already cut down, in order to exonerate them from any possible infraction of the Ten Commandments. I mention this incident in order that other people engaged in similar missions might take it as a warning. But to return to my subject: well-to-do Japanese also resort to the mountains or to the seaside places for their summer holidays. For the people in general, however, spring and autumn are the best seasons of the year. It is then that countless groups of men and women indulge in innocent picnic parties to see all sorts of flowers and tinted leaves, and to visit places of interest, with which the country abounds; indeed, some of the people who are more æsthetic and poetic often travel

185

great distances simply for those objects. The fire-flies also are a sight in many parts of Japan.'

−'I have read some accounts of those excursions,' said one, 'and their fondness for hanging down from the branches of trees their quaint but simple and innocent effusions of poetic thought, written on slips of paper.'

−'But what are the general pastimes of the Japanese gentry at home?' asked another. 'Are they fond of open-air sports as the English are?'

−'No, I am sorry to say they are not. In England, more than elsewhere, all sorts of open-air sports have been invented and played, perhaps owing to the condition of the climate. Mr. Balfour, the Prime Minister, as everybody knows, is a great golfer. Professor Balfour, his brother, was a great cricketer. His premature death years ago, by an accident on the Alps, was lamented very deeply by the scientific world; and I, for one, grieved much, for he was very kind to me when I went up to Cambridge, and smoothed my way considerably for the University study. With us, however, outdoor sports have always been considered childish, and the rude sports of children have never been improved to suit grown-up men. In recent years, of course, Western open-air sports, such as base-ball or lawn tennis, are played by students very widely (at this moment some Japanese teams of base-ball players have gone to America to play against the Americans). But older people seldom indulge in that kind of sport. Billiards also is only of modern introduction.'

−'But surely you must have some kind of pastimes?'

186

−'Well, we have some, but before entering on that subject I will say a word about a letter written by an American on kindred subjects. It caught my eye accidentally in the Japan Times. It is rather interesting and, therefore, I will recite it to you verbatim. The heading of it is "Japan is a queer country."

'Such was the heading of an article in one of our American papers of recent date. As an example of the country being "queer" the writer stated among other things that "old men in Japan fly kites and spin tops, while children look on." Now, I for one have been in Japan a good while and have seen many flying kites and spinning tops. Yet I have never had the fortune of seeing the picture described above. It is easy to conceive how the kind-hearted Ojiisan might show his little grandson how to fly a kite or to spin a top while the little fellow looked on, but that is in no way peculiar to Japan. The same thing might be seen in almost any country.

'Again the writer says, "Japanese writers use paint brushes, not pens, and write from bottom to top," in which he has gotten his ideas more topsy-turvy than the Land of Topsyturvydom itself. And further, "in Japan there are no lawyers, and Japanese doctors never make any charges." Comment is unnecessary.

'These are only specimens of much that has for years flooded our Western newspapers about Japan. Not a great while ago I saw an article in which it was said that Japanese babies never cried, and if a dog barked at night he was taken off next day and killed. It is high time that Western people were beginning to have a few sane thoughts about Japan, and stop speaking of it as "an Oriental puzzle, a nation of recluses, a land of fabulous wealth, of universal licentiousness, or of Edenic purity, the fastness of a treacherous and fickle crew, a Paradise of guileless

187

children, a Utopia of artists and poets." Japan has some superficial oddities, but what country is there that has not? To be a bit humorous, if people wish to say ludicrous things about Japan, it may not be so bad, but to put such things out as sober truth makes a false impression and does the people an injustice.

'Imagine a Japanese going to America, for example, and writing back something like this: "America is a queer country. The people clothe themselves with the hair and skins of animals. They fasten their clothing on by means of little knobs hung in holes; the women go about with the arms and upper part of the body nude. Owing to the peculiar make of their shoes, they all walk on tiptoe. The people eat dead pigs, and drink a white, thick fluid called chichi, which they squeeze out of the body of a large animal. When eating they stick long iron instruments in their mouths. When moving about they are obliged constantly to set one foot out in front in order to keep from falling on their noses. Sometimes when there is a company of them together they open their mouths very wide at each other, utter loud, inarticulate cries, and jump about in a very curious manner, shaking from head to foot."

'Now what would the Japanese people think of such a story, and what kind of impression would they get of the American people? But this is a fair specimen of the style in which many have written about this country. We cannot quite speak of it as lying, yet it amounts to the same in that it deceives and makes a false impression. The people of Japan are much the same as the world at large.

'And finally, what is true of the customs of Japan is also true of the Japanese language. A Westerner, for instance, will poke fun at the expression, "For the first time, I hang upon your honourable eyes," and perhaps with the next

188

breath say, "I knew him as soon as I laid eyes on him." Literally speaking it is hard to tell which is the more "okashii" (ridiculous), to hang upon the honourable eyes of another, or to lay your eyes on somebody else. Or which is worse, to "stick" to the end of the street in going to your business, or to "stick to it" when you get there? All languages must be explained and understood in the light of their idiomatic use and meaning, otherwise they become idiotic, and in this the Japanese language is no exception.

'There is one point in that letter to which I must take exception, as is remarked in the editorial notes, too, but otherwise I quite concur with the writer. The matter I refer to is that of the kites. On that point neither the writer of the original article nor the writer of the letter hit the mark. As a general rule, of course, kites or tops are played with by children as in the West, but there is one particular method of flying special kites which is indulged in by grown-up men. It is done in Nagasaki. The kites are made in a particular shape so that a slight pull or loosening of the line makes a rapid movement, and if one pulls when the kite is not in the right position it falls to the ground with lightning-like rapidity. It requires great skill to manage, and therefore cannot be done by mere boys. Those kites are well known by the name of Nagasaki kites. In that town people fly them in a certain season of the year, making the kites fight one against the other high up in the air. The method is as follows: A certain portion of the line is gummed over with a mixture containing fine particles of glass, so that it would cut another line which might come in contact with it. A skilful flier manages his kite in such a way that his line will cut the line of others without hurting his own, and, therefore, during the competition all the kites are making rapid movements to and fro high up in the air. In recent years Nagasaki men, a large number of whom are residents in Tokio, have instituted a display of kite-flying of their method. The performance takes place on a certain day in spring in a suburban park of the capital.

'But to return to the subject of the pastimes of the Japanese gentry in general. Some are fond of handling Kakemono. Some are fond of collecting old curios. There are, therefore, a far greater number of curiosity shops in Japan than in any other country. Some are fond of performing orthodox tea ceremonies, but by far the greater number are fond of playing at the game of "go," and "Japanese chess."'

−'What are they like?'

'"Go" is a game which you have not in the West. Our chess is different from yours, but the principle is similar. With us "go" is considered more refined than chess, and in consequence "go" is more generally played by the upper classes, and chess by the lower classes. In such games, ours seem to be more scientific and complicated than those in the West. I do not like to appear to boast of our own "things," but my conviction, founded on fact, enforces me to tell the truth.

'I will begin with "chess." In all parts of the world the game of chess exists in some form or other. They must have descended from a common origin: we profess to have derived our game from China. It seems there have been several kinds of chess in China. In Japan also there were three kinds in earlier days—the great, the middle, and the ordinary. The last is the one which has survived and has become a national game. Many improvements have been made since its introduction into Japan, so that it now differs considerably from that of China. We all know of improvements which have been made on the Western guns and rifles, because they belong to our own day: but we do not know when and by whom the improvements in chess were made. It is said, until some hundred years ago, there was an extra piece on either side called the "drunken elephant," having almost omnipotent power—I suppose something like your "queen." The experts of that time agreed that the problems of the game would become much more interesting without that particular piece, because its omnipotency overshadowed the action of other figures, and it was accordingly abolished by Imperial sanction. We consider our game more scientific and complicated than any other of the kind. A single fact will go far to demonstrate my assertion. Bring together at random a number of ordinary Japanese chess players and the same number of ordinary European players. Let the movements of the "men" of the European chess be shown to the Japanese, and let the Europeans and the Japanese play the European chess, you may be sure that after the second game, the Japanese will be on the winning side. When I was staying at Munich over twenty years ago, I learned the European moves from a lad living in the next flat; after the second game I won continually, and the lad gave up in despair. Mind, I am not at all a good player as I play rarely, and, when I do play, I prefer to play "go." On the way to Europe last year, I played European chess on board the mail steamer, learning again the movements of the figures, which I had not practised since my Munich days. After one or two games, I became one of the best players among the passengers. This was not the case with me only, for there were several other Japanese on board, and they also became excellent players. The same is the experience of all the Japanese travellers.'

−'What is the reason of that?' asked one of those present.

−'Because ours is much more complicated than yours. The only danger we have to watch against when we play your game is to be caught in an unguarded moment by a movement which is foreign to us. I mean, for instance, your knights move sidewards or backwards, and we are often caught by it, because our knights move only forwards.'

−'But what do you mean by saying, your chess being more complicated?' asked another.

−'I will only outline the reason, for it is impossible to demonstrate it in the short space of a Summer Dream.'

−'What!'

−'Well, I mean to say that it would take a long time were I to describe it in detail, but listen: In the first place, the squares of our boards are nine by nine, therefore there are seventeen more squares than yours: the number of our men are twenty in all on each side, two rows of nine each, and two extra, and, therefore, four more men than yours on each side. Then, again, in your game, when you take one of your opponent's pieces, you put it aside and never make any use of it except under one particular circumstance, which I need not describe. With ours, however, either side of the players can make use of any of the captured pieces of his opponent and add them to his own men, at any time and place, and under any circumstance, provided that he brings them on to the board, one at a time, in his turn of move.'

−'But how can you make any distinction between your own men and those of your opponent, if you put down the opponent's men as your own?' said another.

'Well, we have no difference of colour between friends and foes and our men are made flat ab initio, and are laid on the squares with their heads turned towards the enemy, so that one can easily distinguish friends from foes by the position in which they are placed.'

—'How can you turn the head towards the enemy?' asked one.

—'By the head, I do not mean the head and tail you use when tossing. Our men are made in such a way that one of the four sides has a projected part; and that side is the head. In other words, the head does not mean the flat surface, but rather one of the sides of a flat object. Call it the top, if you prefer.'

—'I see,' said one.

—'The methods of making use of the captured men makes the whole play much more intricate. As a rule, of course, if you take a man of your opponent, possessing greater power, it is better than taking one possessing less power, but this does not always follow, because according to the vicissitudes of the game a man which has less power may be utilised for some particular purpose to greater advantage than one of greater power. This is the point in which our chess has far more interest than yours. Then, again, in your chess one does not seek so much to take a man of one's opponent as one does in our chess, because with yours mere exchange of men is to be avoided as it does not affect the relative force of either side, but with ours one often plays in such a way as to capture a piece or two, even more, even though he loses similar or identical men of his own, in the same process, because by the cleverer use of the captured men a better issue can often be obtained. Another peculiarity of our game is that, when a piece gets into the third row, or beyond, of the squares on the opponent's side, the player has the option of changing its power in certain ways. This is another source of interest. But remember, this method differs from one which is employed in your chess when a pawn gets into the last row of the squares on the opponent's side. As a consequence of all this, you can easily see that there cannot be such a result as a drawn game in our chess.'

−'Can you describe the kind of men and the moves of your chess?' asked one.

−'Oh, that would take too much time; but I will tell you an incident connected with it. After a dinner party in England, I had some talk on the subject with a bishop, who happened to be present. He asked me what our "castles" (tours) were like. I answered we had no castle, because we did not believe a castle could move about on land. We call our corresponding figures "light chariots," or, more commonly, "lances." He next asked me what our queen was like. I answered, we have no queen, because we do not believe in the advisability of making a queen work hard, not only harder than the king, but than all other subjects. You may call it "keeping a woman in seclusion," but we think it respect and consideration for the fair sex not to expose them to such a task as fighting. We have two generals, between whom the power of your queen is divided. One is called "diagonal dasher," and the other "flying chariot." He then asked me what our bishops were like. I answered, we have no bishop, because we do not consider it good taste to make a venerable bishop fight a sanguinary battle, besides, the same moves with which your "bishops" are empowered are bestowed on our "diagonal dasher."'

−'You fabricate the story,' said one.

−'Not at all,' I answered. 'It was a true and genuine incident. In fact, I do not think the names of most of your "men" very commendable.'

−'Well, then, what are your names, and how do you arrange the position of the men at the commencement?' said another.

−'We place the king in the centre of the last row. We can do so because our squares are nine and not eight, as yours. On each side of the king we have the gold general, silver general, knight, and lancer respectively. On the second square of the second row from the left we have the diagonal dasher; and in the second square from the right in the same row we have the flying chariot. The third row is allotted to the pawns, which we call foot-soldiers,—the same signification as yours. Thus you can see the starting position is entirely identical on both sides, which is not the case with yours, because your squares being eight, you cannot place the king in the very centre of the row.'

−'But how do you manage when a weaker hand plays with a stronger hand?' interposed another.

−'Well, in that case, the stronger hand takes off one or more men from the board at the beginning, just as you do, and thus equalises the relative strength.'

−'What is "go"?'

−'It is a game which you have not, and, therefore, it is rather difficult to describe, and it would not interest you much, if I described it, because I could make no comparison. When I was in England before, now many years ago, some people played a childish game called "go-bang." The board and the pieces used are the same as our "go," though those I have seen in Europe are very simple and cheaply made. In Japan they are rather expensive. The materials both of the board and pieces are generally choice kinds of wood, and rare black stone and shells, which make them expensive,—in fact, some people regard them as an ornament for the room. The game, which is the same as your "go-bang," is also played by the name of "gomoku narabe," that is, placing five pieces in a row. We call the board for "go" "go-ban," which literally means the board for "go," and from that I conclude that your game of "go-bang" came from Japan, only you have misapplied the appellation of the board to the game. In Japan, it goes without saying, that game is only fit for boys and girls, though occasionally some people show, even in that game, great scientific skill. Unlike chess, the pieces of "go" are placed on the top of the cross, and the end of the lines which mark the board into squares. There are nineteen by nineteen of such spots, and, therefore, there are three hundred and sixty-one black and white pieces altogether, though in practice, the more skilful the players the less the actual number of pieces used. From the simple fact of the pieces being white and black, and having no difference of value, casual observers might think the game of "go" does not possess so much interest and variation as chess, but according to the opinion generally accepted, there is much more in "go" than in "chess," though some who are more partial to chess profess that there is a little more in chess than in "go." At all events, there are more people who understand chess than "go," because the latter is more difficult to learn. "Go" has also been introduced to us from China in the earlier days of intercourse, more than ten centuries ago, but no one knows the exact history of its introduction. In Japan the game has undergone many changes. It is known that the board used in China in ancient times contained a less number of squares, but I am not sure if it had already the present number when first introduced into Japan. It seems the present number of the squares is most productive of all sorts of problems. In ancient times in China, the black pieces were offered to the person who held a better social position than the other, or to the stronger hand in case of a match between those of equal position. This was so in the earlier stage of the game in Japan, but later the white pieces came to be used uniformly by the better player. The methods of starting, and the rules for equalising the relative strength of the players at the beginning, and for counting, have all undergone improvements. For three centuries there existed an academy for "go," and also for "chess," under the superintendence of the best players of the empire, who received certain annuities and personal distinction from the central government in order to maintain the interest in the games. Indeed, diplomas of different degrees were given to champions, according to their deserts. The ceremony of the competition by the best players was annually performed in the castle of the Shogun. From this you can well imagine that we have had better players in those games than in the country whence they were originally derived. Great geniuses were occasionally produced. Since the inauguration of the present Government, these institutions have disappeared (though they still exist as private institutions), and the positions of the best players, whatever their genius, are no longer lucrative nor distinguished. I am not, therefore, sure if we can keep up our former standard of skill. In all the games I have seen and heard of, there is none which has so many degrees of skill as the game of "go."'

−'Are there no more games of a similar nature?'

−'There are several more, but mostly childish, and played by young girls or children at certain seasons of the year, such as "poem cards."'

−'What is that?'

'The Japanese name for "poem cards" is Uta-Karuta. Strangely enough, the term "Karuta" is not Japanese. It is of European derivation, being the same as the word "Carta" (card in modern English). There had existed poem shells before poem cards came into use. One half of a short poem was written inside one half of a shell, and the other half of the poem inside the other half, there being usually one hundred shells with different poems written in them. The game was to find the one half of the shell which belonged to the other. The shells were often richly decorated, as one may see from the remnants of old ones. A little more than three hundred years ago, when the Island of Hirado was the trading port for Dutch and English vessels, the European traders brought with them their cards with which they were in the habit of playing. The Japanese who happened to see them seem to have thought that the shape of those cards had some novelty and were more simple than their shells. They, therefore, substituted cards for shells, and hence the original name "Carta" came to be used by us. I will now explain the game of "poem cards"; it is played at the time of the New Year, generally by young girls. There are two sets of cards. One half of short poems is written each separately on one set, and the other half is written in the same manner on the other set as at poem shells. One set is either thrown in the middle of the players or dealt out in equal numbers. While one person is reading the first part of a poem, each of the players picks up a card on which the other half of the same poem is written, or turns it upside down, when the numbers are equally divided, as the case may be. In the one method, whoever has picked up the

198

most is the winner. In the other, if one were slow in turning over her card and it were picked up by another of the party, she would have as penalty a card from the one who had picked hers up. Thus the one who has turned all her cards upside down first would be the first winner, and one who has any cards left unturned at the end, is the last loser.'

—'Surely you must have some kinds of cards played more seriously,' said one.

—'We have another game called "flower cards."'

—'What's that like?'

—'Well, the flower cards is a more difficult and serious game. In times gone by no game of cards having any resemblance to gambling was played among the gentry; moral discipline forbade such. Since the introduction of European ideas, the rigidity of discipline has somewhat slackened and cards are now played to some extent. Nevertheless, people do not consider card-playing good taste. If they play they do so with some diffidence, somewhat in a similar way as smoking is done by ladies in European society nowadays. The "flower-cards" is a game thus played; our name of it is Hana-karuta. The term "Karuta" is, as I said before, of European derivation. The principle is taken from your cards, but so altered and improved, that scarcely any similarity can be detected in its present form. To begin with: the pictures represented on your whist cards appear to us rather incongruous and vulgar; ours are more poetical and consistent. With ours some significant objects of each month, mostly flowers, such as the blossom of the cherry and plum, the iris, wisteria, and peonies, are represented, variegated by birds, the moon, or falling rain. There are four cards for each

199

month, and, therefore, the number of the cards is forty-eight in all. There is a different value assigned to each card. Naturally there are several methods of playing the cards, as is the case with your whist cards, but the method which is used most is very intricate and interesting. I do not care for playing at cards, but I know the methods. I am also acquainted with various European games from whist to bridge as far as the methods are concerned, but none of them equal in intricacy and variation our game of "flower cards," though there is a certain resemblance between flower cards and bridge. But please, I repeat, do not think I am saying all this from any sense of vanity, because such a thing is scarcely worth boasting of; I am merely stating a fact as I see it.'

−'What is, then, the method of playing?'

−'Well, to describe it in full would require at least a pamphlet, but I will give you an outline of the game. The proper number of players engaged at one time is three; the game can be played by two, but it is as slow as playing dummy whist. The advantage of our game lies in that a party could consist of up to six players. The limits of the players engaged at a time, as I have just said, is three, and therefore the number exceeding three is obliged to stand out for one game, namely, for the play of one deal. But no particular person is obliged to stand out, so that one must either be bought off or allowed to play by the resignation of any other player, unless he himself prefers to stand out. This takes place after the cards have been dealt. Here, therefore, comes in much consideration and often "bluff." Naturally, each one plays for himself and for his own advantage, therefore there is no partnership as in whist; and yet in the course of playing one has often to form a sort of alliance for a moment with a second player in order to prevent the common calamity against the probable stratagem of the third player. I may also add, that as each one plays on his own account, he has the option of standing out for one game, as I have already indicated, in which case, however, he has to pay a certain penalty. Should all players but two thus stand out, those remaining two would play the game. One deal sometimes finishes without any play at all, when all the players but one throw up their hands and pay penalty rather than play with bad cards, in which case, of course, the penalties go to the one who remains. The penalty paid varies according to the relative positions of the payers to the dealer, as well as the kinds of the six cards which are thrown out on the table at the beginning of the game, and therefore paying penalty and standing out from the play for one game requires much consideration. The prices for buying up the surplus number of the players also differ according to the six cards on the table and to the cards the seller holds. Similar to bridge, certain rewards are given to the player who holds certain sets of cards and also to the player who gets in certain sets of cards. It is the latter point which requires, as is natural, the greatest skill, inasmuch as one who aims at getting in one such set loses much when he fails, and it often happens that while he is striving to get in a certain set, another player gets in a far better set; therefore one has often to sacrifice his own chance in order to hinder an opponent. Twelve games make a rubber. The method of counting the issue is as follows: Each player must have in his hand in the case of quit one hundred and twenty points at the end of the rubber, and therefore it would seem that each receives one hundred and twenty points in counters at the beginning, but, as a matter of fact, he only receives seventy-two points or sixty, as the players agree upon. The counting in this game generally goes by dozens, though odd numbers also come in. Thus counters are made of two kinds, one is a dozen points and the other single points. The balance between the points which one actually receives when

201

starting and ten dozens which he has to make good in his hand at the end of the rubber goes to the person who is the greatest winner of the rubber, and therefore the more players, the greater the rewards for the winner of the rubber. Of course it is most difficult to play in such a way as just to quit oneself, because there are so many tricks, and one often has to float a loan in the course of the game, or in other words, to borrow a requisite number of counters from the banker, which must be repaid at the end of the rubber.

'The "rain" cards are another source of fluctuation in the game, because every one of them, whatever value it possess, may be counted as a single point card somewhat similar to what you sometimes do with your aces. I almost think the invention of your bridge is in some way based upon our flower cards.'

—'It is dreadful: one could never get a clear idea only by hearing the explanation. You have, after all, wasted your time in trying to make us understand, though I asked you for the explanation,' said one cunningly.

'Thank you very much,' I said.

—'You say your social atmosphere in respect of such matters was far better in times gone by,' said another.

—'I do,' I answered.

'But I hope it will not get worse.'

—'I hope so too,' I said, 'but the influence of Western civilisation is so overwhelming.'

−'Pierre Loti's description of some of the features of Japanese society is very fine from a literary point of view, but I understand it is not a true representation. Is that your opinion too?' interposed another.

−'I have not read it, but from what I have heard, I can decidedly answer in the affirmative. The main facts therein contained are nothing else than exaggerated stories of exceptional incidents often practised by foreigners themselves. Do you think we Japanese could not have the same experience in the West if we liked? Nay, more: can you say that similar incidents do not happen in some parts of the West? I don't expect an answer. I shall be doing greater service to the West by letting such a delicate subject drop.'

−'Perhaps you may think me a little abrupt,' remarked a gentleman; 'but may I ask you rather a delicate question? People say that in Japan men and women bathe together, and talk about it as a sign of immorality. Is it a fact?'

−'Not exactly,' I answered; 'in public baths, in times gone by, both sexes bathed together, but you must remember, even in those times, those who went to public baths were people of the lower classes, for the better classes always managed to have their own bathroom, and in Japan houses having such bathrooms are very common. Moreover, even in those days, there was nothing more indelicate in the matter of public baths than a sea-bath by both sexes in occidental countries. I should like to remind those who write about such matters of many customs in their own countries to which they may be too much accustomed to perceive any impropriety, but which appear very indelicate to the eyes of strangers. I may go a step further: we are sometimes even astonished to notice that the most indelicate performances—such that, if it were in Japan, would not be permitted by the police to go on two minutes—are given, under the name of dances or suchlike, and men and women of respectability go and see them without showing the slightest embarrassment. I confess I have personally seen some of these performances while visiting out of curiosity different places of interest. But, in reality, there is no necessity for me to set up such matters against our former customs of public baths, because, for several decades, such bathing has been forbidden, and every public bath has long since had one division for men and another for women. Those who think that the former custom still exists are mistaken, and are labouring under a false impression given by travellers of former days.

'Apropos of a bath, I prefer in a way our system, be it public or private, to the ordinary Western method. With our system, a large space of the floor of the bathroom is made either of wood or concrete, in such a way that water may be poured on to it. There is, besides the main bath, also a small tank containing fresh cold and warm water in separate sections, so that one who bathes can make free use of the water, warm or cold, both before getting into the bath and before dressing.'

−'I think, on the whole, I like your country,' said another. 'It seems very different from what many people have represented it hitherto, but you have not yet given us a comprehensive survey of your people, in respect to social and moral organisation.'

−'I think I have done so often,' said I; 'but if you do not object, I will do so once more by repeating to you the exact words of an interview which I gave to a representative of the London press:

'"You remember the story of George Washington and the cherry tree?" said Baron Suyematsu, with a smile, to our representative. "Well, that is very often told to the children in the Japanese schools."

'The distinguished Japanese statesman, who is at present in London, was explaining how the moral virtues, and especially patriotism and bravery in battle, are not merely considered desirable things in Japan, but are actively propagated in the schools and in the army. For, as Mr. Lyttelton, the Colonial Secretary, remarked to an audience last week, they teach patriotism in Japan.

'"You see, there is no religious teaching in the public schools in Japan," said Baron Suyematsu; "but the teaching of morality occupies an important place in the curriculum. From the Western point of view it may seem difficult to teach morality without connecting it with religion, but we do it!"

'This patriotic bravery, as one of the virtues, comes into the code. The teaching is based upon the Confucian ethics, and the "cleanness of conscience" which is the essence of Shintoism, the national religion of Japan.

'THE CODE OF HONOUR.

'"Then there is Bushido," said the baron, "which may be called the code of honour of Japanese knighthood. This Bushido had a tight grasp of the military class, which consisted of the retainers of feudal lords, who had not to work for their daily bread. These retainers were not rich, but they had something to live upon, and frugality was one of their virtues. Their only business was to do their duty to their lords, which meant in time of war to fight for them. But as for more than two centuries and a half the country

205

had been at peace, and as the military class had no fields of ordinary occupation, they naturally gave their energies to intellectual pursuits side by side with military training. In a word, their business was to make themselves as much gentlemen as possible. Thus grew up a code of honour which was primarily founded upon military duty alone, but which later on was extended to the acquirement of gentlemanly conduct, and then to be a true gentleman, and loyal to their lords.

"'After the opening of our country to other nations, there was a time when we seemed to lose the guiding influence of our old morals, for Confucianism lost its influence to some extent, and intercourse with strangers gave some shock to our old morality, and led our people to imagine that freedom from restraint and obligation was the characteristic of European ideals.

"'It was at this juncture that the emperor issued an edict defining our ideal of morality. In accordance with his edict, the curriculum of the schools includes the teaching of morality, and the moral virtues are explained and expatiated upon in lectures and discourses. The teachers introduce sayings and maxims of great men of all nations.

'WASHINGTON AND SELF-HELP.

"'As I have told you, the story of George Washington is often quoted. Smiles's Self-Help is often used, and I have no doubt Nelson's signal at Trafalgar. The principal examples are naturally the great heroes of our own country who served the emperor and Japan. In that way both boys and girls are imbued with the moral virtues, among which loyalty and patriotism are prominent.

206

'"But this teaching is not limited to the schools. It is carried on in the barracks in the form of what we call 'spiritual education.' The aim is to make men capable of appreciating their duties as soldiers. This barrack teaching is in accordance with an edict issued by the emperor when universal military service was introduced, and it is based upon the moral virtues. We have no chaplains. The teaching is undertaken by the officers themselves as part of their regular duty, and they deliver exhortations in the barrack-rooms.

'"But you must know that, man for man, Europeans recognise that Japanese are superior to Russians, and I am not surprised that that is said. In Japan education is universal, and there is scarcely a soldier who cannot read and write, or who has not had some kind of education. For that reason they ought to be intellectually superior to the Russians. And as we have universal service, all sorts of people are found in the ranks, without distinction of social position or vocation. In the barracks you find the son of a nobleman and the son of a coolie, and there is no aloofness between them. That makes the company so efficient.

'MILITARY TRAINING FOR BOYS.

'"In the schools we not only have the national flag, but the boys are drilled in military manner. If the municipality can afford it, real arms are used in the higher grade schools. In the peers' school and many others they have regular firing manœuvres.

'"It is not generally known, I suppose, that I was once an English volunteer?" said Baron Suyematsu, with a laugh at the recollection. "That was when I was at Cambridge. I joined the University Rifles."

'As to Chinese soldiers, the baron said that the moral teaching of the Japanese army constituted one of the great differences between them. Then he pointed out that in China soldiers are rightly looked down upon, for they are recruited only from the worst classes, and respectable men will not enter the ranks.

'Baron Suyematsu does not approve of the efforts of the Christian missionaries to discourage the national custom of committing suicide rather than be captured in battle, for he thinks the effect would be to lower the soldiers' high ideal of patriotism and courage.

'"There is all the difference," he said, "between wanton suicide and voluntarily sacrificing one's life for the honour of the nation. Our ideal is to die for one's country rather than bring upon her the disgrace of being taken by the enemy. What can be nobler than that? It is the same as being killed by the enemy. And the missionaries are trying to teach our soldiers that it is wrong. It is a great pity."'

—'But that only covers one phase, the method of your education,' said one.

—'True, but it covers a good deal!' I said. 'Do you think I can write a big book on Japan at a moment's notice?'

—'Well, I will leave you alone then,' said he.

—'Every one of the Russian soldiers who returned wounded from the battlefield, when asked the cause of their defeat, said that the Russians were defeated because the Japanese soldiers were great scholars compared to themselves. I have it on good authority,' interposed another.

—'Perhaps it looked like that to them,' I answered.

VII

*Some talk on superstition—A remark on earrings—
Japanese troops after the war; no fear of Chauvinism—
Generals and officers—How the system of the hereditary
military service was abolished and the new system was
introduced—Its history—Japan after the war—Views given
to the American press—Mr. Seppings-Wright and his views
on the Japanese character—The Japanese navy and its
history—Origin of the shipbuilding yards—The difficulty of
a thorough reform in China and Russia—How Japan
managed to bring about the consummation of the great
reform—The feudal system was a great help—Explanation
of the Japanese feudal system and the clans—The re-
shuffling of the feudatories under the Tokugawa régime—
Difference of grandeur of the feudatories—Exceptional
formation of the Satsuma clan—Financial system of the
Shogunate—-Finance of the Imperial Government at the
beginning of the Great Change—How the affairs of the
governments of the feudatories were wound up—The old
system of taxation—Thorough reform—The old notion of
land   tenure*

I found myself once more in a very incongruous group of
people whom I had met on various occasions. I noticed a
number of them engaged in a lively conversation.

−'Ah! Monsieur A.,' said a lady, 'you are acquainted with
many Japanese, and have been in contact with them for
many years, so that you will be able to explain to me. Some
say the Japanese are superstitious, others again say they are
not. Which do you think true?'

−'I have known,' said Monsieur A., 'some hundreds of the Japanese, mostly young men, of course. They are extremely free from any sort of bias or superstition. I have never known people so unbiassed and so little superstitious.'

−'But,' said the lady, 'I have heard from a gentleman who was resident in Japan for some years that there existed in that country some sort of superstition. He told me, for example, that "some people disliked the number "four," because shi, which is four in Japanese, means also death, as far as the pronunciation is concerned. Consequently when, for instance, one gives a tip, he would give either threepence or fivepence, and not fourpence, even in the case where fourpence may be more appropriate; in other words, either less or more, to avoid the number four. And the same is generally the case when one makes a present of a number of articles which are identical, unless they are two pairs; is not that funny? In the whole world there can be nothing more natural than numbers. No one can make the four cardinal points of the compass less or more because he dislikes the number "four." The same reasoning holds good with everything.'

−'I do not think,' answered Monsieur A., 'the superstition of four is very widely believed in. But what do you say to our dislike for the number thirteen.'

−'But,' said she, 'that is a different matter. That originated with religion.'

−'Is it so?' said Monsieur A. 'I wouldn't dispute it. But let me tell you an incident I met with some time ago. I was present at a meeting of a literary association. There was a good deal of conversation on the subject of the superstition of less civilised peoples. At the refreshment-table I had to sit next an elderly lady. I placed, accidentally or not I don't remember, my knife and fork crosswise. The lady immediately noticed this, and told me quickly to alter them. I remarked that the dislike of that position of knife and fork was perhaps also a sort of superstition, whereupon the lady told me that it was not a superstition, but a tradition, and therefore it differed very much from the superstitions practised by less civilised peoples.'

—'She was right, of course,' said the lady.

—'Well, I can scarcely see any difference,' observed Monsieur A.

—'I can tell you another incident,' remarked a different gentleman. 'When an occidental missionary was once telling some women of savage tribes that their wearing rings in their noses was barbarous and unhealthy, he was asked by them how it was that his wife and daughters were wearing rings in their ears, and he had great difficulty in explaining to them that the method adopted by the civilised races for wearing rings in their ears was very different from their wearing rings in the nose.'

—'Oh!' exclaimed some ladies.

—'But stay,' said another, 'let us have some more serious talk. I wish to ask Baron Suyematsu his opinion on a few important points of which I am anxious to be informed.'

Turning to me, he said:

—'I do not entertain any wild notion of the "Yellow Peril" cry. One thing is certain, however, that your country has been winning all this time brilliant victories unprecedented

212

in history, and there is no doubt that your success will continue to the end of the war. Don't you think after the fighting is over your army will become chauvinistic, or, in plain language, unruly, and constantly ready to pick quarrels with foreign countries.'

—'I do not think so,' I answered. 'In the first place, the discipline of our men is very good, and they are most orderly and obedient to the emperor and his government. Then, too, the very nature of the organisation of our troops makes such matters differ greatly from hereditary troops or volunteers of long service. You see by the universal system, which we have adopted, men serve in the ranks only for a limited time, and therefore in the course of a few years the old soldiers retire, and go back to their original avocations in the country or the town, as the case may be, and the new ones fill their places. While the newcomers would be inspired by the traditions of their regiments, they could not, at the same time, be personally bombastic on account of the deeds of their predecessors.'

—'But what of the generals and officers?'

—'Of them I entertain no fear of their becoming jingoes. After having undergone all the hard work, and having achieved many brilliant victories, it is only natural that generals and other officers, indeed the army itself, should win greater popularity and higher estimation in the people's minds, and it is possible that their weight may be felt indirectly in internal politics. But it would never go so far as to make any difference in our external relations with foreign countries. As a matter of fact, our generals and officers are as little inclined to meddle with general politics as they are intent on fulfilling their professional duties. Above all, as I have so often said, it is a great misconception on the part of some Occidentals to suppose the Japanese at large to be an aggressive and bellicose nation.'

—'Your army is now organised under the universal service system,' said another. 'Before the present Imperial régime came into existence you had, as I understand, a very deep-rooted hereditary system of military service. It must have been very difficult to abolish the old and substitute the new. Your Bushi were regarded as the flower of the land, and surely it was a most bold conception to substitute sons of peasants and tradesmen in their place, and to believe they would do service equally well, or better. Your statesmen must have had strong convictions to induce them to make such a radical change as the new régime. Please let us have some explanation on that point.'

—'Well, roughly speaking,' I replied, 'I can only say that it was an outcome of the changed conditions of the time, but there were, of course, some circumstances which facilitated its formation. The Samurai, our hereditary military class, was the pick of the Japanese population, more refined and more intellectual than any other. Nevertheless, the long-continued peace and the effects of inheriting their occupation made them somewhat inclined towards effeminacy—in other words, less martial than their ancestors. Besides, as I have explained elsewhere, the hereditary military system has one very weak point. Such shortcomings as these were already felt before the inauguration of the new régime, and it was noticed that the best soldiers who engaged in battles before the Restoration were those organised under methods differing from the old system. Let me explain it more in detail. Chosiu was the clan which fought more battles than any other. The Chosiu troops which fought best were different kinds of voluntary regiments, consisting of bands of adventurous young men enlisted from the lowest classes of Samurai, as well as peasants and tradesmen. There was even a band which consisted of Yeta, who were afterwards emancipated and became new commoners, as I have explained elsewhere. At the time when an internal dissension broke out in Chosiu and its government was overthrown by the more radical elements under the leadership of such men as Takasugi, Kawasé, Ito, Yamagata, Inouyé and others, it was those voluntary bands just mentioned that sided with them against the troops of the government, who mostly belonged to the higher classes of the hereditary military families. Shortly after that event Kido, who was a participator of the same idea and the Senior of those men, had returned to Chosiu after an absence of about ten months as a fugitive, and had become the moving spirit of Chosiu. It was just at the time when Chosiu was on the eve of being surrounded a second time by the Shogunate troops, and it was a very critical period for the Chosiu, who had to make every preparation for fighting against great odds. At Kido's recommendation, Murata was intrusted by the prince to organise in the European style all the troops of Chosiu, including those bands. Murata (who afterwards changed his name into Omura) was originally a medical student, and had studied the Dutch language and subsequently the Dutch military system. In the early days of the new Imperial régime he occupied a high post in the Imperial Army Department, and his bronze statue is standing high in Tokio, before the shrine of warriors. But to return to my subject. Chosiu defeated the Shogunate troops on all sides. Thus in Chosiu the weakness of the hereditary military system had been practically seen very early. Most of the Shogunate troops were organised according to the old system of the Middle Ages. Many of them, being clad in heavy armour, were no match for the Chosiu troops with their light equipments. On the Shogunate side there were also some regiments which fought well, but they were those

215

which had been organised and drilled after the European style. In that war, and the subsequent ones, it was well known that the best troops on the anti-imperialist side were also those which had been organised something like volunteer regiments and drilled after the European system. These facts will show that even before the Restoration the credit of the hereditary military system had already considerably declined. Marshal Yamagata was originally a person belonging to an insignificant class of the Chosiu Samurai, and was the leader of the most powerful band of Chosiu I have just mentioned. You may well imagine that he would not be a man to advocate the continuation of the hereditary military system. The introduction of the system of universal service founded upon the European Continental system is due to him.'

−'That goes a long way to explain the matter,' said one.

−'But do you conscientiously believe,' said another, 'that Japan will not suffer from "swollen head," and will continue to have sufficient control of herself?'

−'I do. Why not? I know it. No sooner had I landed on the American soil last year, having left Japan immediately after the outbreak of the war, than I gave my views to the American press on the then existing situation, as well as on our probable future, showing the true motives and aspirations of my country. They were widely circulated. My meaning was identical in every case, though the words and matters touched upon were not necessarily identical. I will recite you one specimen which was then published in an American weekly.

'As to our fight with Russia, we are as able to meet her army on land as we are her fleets on the sea. We have just the same confidence in our army as in the navy. But we would be very sorry to be regarded by the world as only fighting men. We have been for many years striving for the assimilation of everything materially and mentally good that belongs to the best type of the American and European civilisation. We aspire to be a nation, but our endeavour for the realisation of that idea is based on a larger peaceful acquisition of intellectual culture. We have no ambition for territorial aggrandisement. We have not the least idea of making any difference on account of race. We desire to govern ourselves and advance in the world in peace—not to conquer and tyrannise over another people. We come into the comity of nations, but that entirely on the occidental basis of civilisation. Some people speak of us as pagan, but the conscience of the people is perfectly free in our country, and it is guaranteed by our constitution. We believe in toleration and absolute liberty of religious conviction, and I may safely say that religion is many times freer in our country than it is in the country which is now our foe. We are disposed to be, and earnestly wish and strive to be, liberal and tolerant in all things. This fact, I am glad to see, is already so widely recognised by those Americans and Europeans who are connected with and know about such matters. We hope to advance to that place in the world where our beautiful little country will be a leader among the nations of the world in science, industry, arts, and intellectual achievements, and an example of peace and harmony towards all races, all nations, and all men.

—'I still hold the same views. I have no reason to fear that I shall have to change them after the war. It might perhaps be more interesting and convincing if you were to see what some people, other than ourselves, who are capable of giving an idea on the point, say. Mr. Seppings Wright, an English ex-naval officer and an artist, is one. He was on board one or other of the ships of Admiral Togo's fleet for many months under exceptional circumstances. He returned to England quite recently. An interesting interview with him was published in a recent number of the English press. Here is the part bearing on the subject:

'THE MOST WONDERFUL PEOPLE IN THE WORLD.

'"I gather that you formed a very high opinion of the Japanese character?"

'"They are," said Mr. Seppings-Wright, with animation, "the most wonderful people in the world. I make no exception. Neither the statesmen nor the peoples of Europe have yet learned to estimate the Japanese at their true value. They are destined to play a magnificent rôle in the future development of the world. At present people are talking of their courage, their great military qualities. These are, indeed, now sufficiently self-evident. I rate the Japanese army above any other army in the world. As for the navy, I cannot use language too strong to express my admiration for it. Yet what most impressed me was not the personal bravery of the Japanese soldier and sailor, or the splendid organisation of their naval and military forces, it was the character of the people—their unique simplicity, their chivalrous courtesy, their kindness of heart, their sweetness of disposition, their unaggressiveness. They have none of the lust of conquest for conquest's sake. They have never fought save to protect their territory or their vital interests—but they have never been beaten. Chinese, Koreans, and now Russians—they have resisted all, and beaten all in turn; and now that they have proved their right to be regarded as one of the Great Powers of the world, their influence will, I am convinced, be all on the side of peace and peaceful development."

"'You make the Japanese out to be a new variety of the human race?"

"'No, not a new variety—an old variety—a variety untainted by the commercialism of European civilisation. They have not yet learned the creed of individualism—of every man for himself. They will lay down their lives cheerfully and willingly for their country—for their emperor, who is almost a god in their eyes, since he embodies their fatherland. What new traits they may develop I cannot pretend to say."

'WHAT JAPAN CAN STILL DO.

"'It would be strange," I interrupted, "if, after the unbroken series of victories they have won on land and sea, they did not develop some symptom of 'swelled head'?"

−'I saw not the slightest sign of that. Very rarely you see even incipient symptoms in an individual. Their great successes have not apparently turned their heads in the least. They began this war in the most absolute confidence of victory. They can, if need be, do much more than they have done. No one knows the number of men Oyama has in Manchuria—no one, that is, outside the Government and the Headquarters' Staff.'"

−'Of the navy,' said another, 'it is truly amazing that you should have such an efficient one, which you have built up in the course of no more than two or three decades. Assiduous and energetic as you must have been, there must have been some other circumstances which have helped

219

you in arriving at that result, or at least I cannot think otherwise when I reflect calmly on the matter.'

−'Your views are not far from fact,' I answered. 'It would be certainly amazing if a people who had only known perhaps canoes in a small stream, having no seafaring experience or tradition, built up a new navy as we have done. Many people have carelessly looked upon Japan as such, hence the misconception. Japan abounds in history and traditions of the sea from the dawn of her history. Our fleets often made distant expeditions, and fought battles far out of our own waters. The ships were, no doubt, rude and primitive compared with the modern ones. From the model of a warship made about three hundred years ago, which I have seen in a temple not far from Tokio, I think that our ships of those days were not much inferior to those of the West of a corresponding time. From the period when foreign intercourse was suspended, the construction of large ships was prohibited, be it a warship or a merchantman. The country was in perfect peace, and the navy was in use even less than the army, and this, therefore, is why such an enormous difference between the European system and ours had come into existence. Nevertheless, some feudal lords whose seats were situated on the sea-coast had a certain number of retainers specially destined for seafaring purposes. And, moreover, Japan being a country surrounded by the sea on all sides, merchantmen and fishing boats, rude as they were, were abundant; hence the stock of sailors has never been wanting. With the new advent of the Western nations to the Far East some fifty years ago, with their "black ships," the country awoke to the necessity of having strong ships, and the Shogunate, jealous as it was in the ascendency of the feudal lords, abolished the prohibition against building large ships. Towards the later years of the Shogunate it possessed a small but creditable navy in the European style. Many

220

feudal lords also possessed some kind of Western ships, several of them possessing eight or nine ships. Of course, many of these ships were only corvettes, or schooners, or ordinary commercial steamers, but they were all used by those lords and manned chiefly by their retainers, and were called their navy. They differed from ordinary merchantmen. These ships were mostly bought from Western merchants; a few were the presents of the Western monarchs to the Shogun; some were constructed in Japan. The earliest steamship constructed in Japan was a steam-launch built about 1862 in the province of Ise for the Prince of Chosiu. It was navigated from there to Hagi, the old capital of Chosiu, on the coast of the Japan Sea. I do not know what became of it after that, but the fact that it navigated that distance would show that the Japanese were already gaining some capacity for building steamships after the European style. When the Shogun submitted to the Imperial order and vacated the castle of Tokio, the navy of the Shogunate, declining to share the fate of the Shogun, raised anchor and fled to Hakodate under the leadership of Yenomoto. Several of the best ships were lost by storm and some in fighting, and practically no ship was left of the revolting fleets. With the submission of Yenomoto and his participators, the country regained a complete peace. Then began the construction of the new navy. The feudal lords presented to the Imperial government their ships, most of which had already done their service during the preceding war. Most of the officers and sailors took service under the Imperial government just as they were. Many men who were engaged in naval affairs under the Shogunate were given suitable positions under the new government; even Yenomoto, the chief of the rebel fleet, was made an admiral after he had been pardoned. The navy being more expensive in every way than the army, we had more difficulty in its development; but in one way or another the Imperial government has exerted its energy until we have obtained the navy of the present moment. It has required much patience and ingenuity from both technical and political points of view, but somehow or other we have managed so far. I may add a few words more. In the early days of the Imperial government a large number of English naval officers were engaged by our government, who did much service in the organisation of our navy, for which we feel much indebtedness. I may also add that later on Monsieur Bertin of France, whom we have engaged for some years, has also done much service in the matter.'

−'You now have several shipbuilding yards, both governmental and private,' said one, 'and you can construct big ships yourselves. How was it brought about at first?'

−'Yokosuka is our oldest dockyard. It was begun when the Shogunate was already tottering. Oguri, an able man, was the finance minister of the Shogunate at the time. It was due to his efforts that the Yokosuka dockyard was constructed. It is said Oguri told his friend one day, "When one becomes a bankrupt it is desirable he should leave behind a Dozo, so Yokosuka will be the Dozo of the Shogunate when it comes to an end." "Dozo" is the name for a storehouse, constructed very solidly; with us almost every house, excepting those of the lower classes, has one or more such buildings, and it was considered an additional disgrace to a man of better class if he became a bankrupt without any such storehouse for the creditors. Oguri evidently foresaw the downfall of the Shogunate, and yet ordered the construction of the dockyard, so that it would be useful for the future rulers of Japan. Such is the early history of our dockyards on the European style, which has expanded itself in the course of time, so that we now have several shipbuilding yards, as you know.'

−'What do you say about the future of China?' said another. 'Don't you think she will also renovate herself like your country and become a formidable power.'

−'She may do so,' I answered, 'in one way or other in the course of time, but I do not think a sudden and thorough transformation of the kind that has taken place in Japan is possible in China. I do not think it is possible even in Russia, where so much movement for internal reform is going on. To begin with, they have no feudal system in existence.'

−'That sounds very odd,' said he: 'I must be enlightened on the point.'

−'Well, Japan has been swayed by a feudal system before the great change of the present régime. That fact helped our success to an extent that one cannot easily imagine. Of course, there was a possibility of procrastination of the old system, if the reform movements had miscarried; but when the winds blew in the right direction, that very fact became the most important factor in conveying our ship of state to the harbour where it wished to go. To explain in less metaphorical language: the introduction of a great political reform in a country against an existing government is most difficult. A revolution with a tremendous force like that of France must be regarded as an exceptional case, but ordinary revolutionists seldom succeed in overthrowing existing governments and introducing better and more progressive ones on a firmer basis. When, on the other hand, the existing government is only obliged to introduce some reform by external influence, the reform it introduces cannot be very radical and thorough. With our great movements previous to 1867 the matter was taken up by several powerful feudal lords. Naturally, there had been several precursory movements against the Shogunate by the bands of zealous patriots gathered here and there, but the Shogunate had no difficulty in suppressing them. The revolt against the Shogunate became grave only when some powerful feudal lords with their clans assumed an antagonistic attitude. As you know, our clans were, in fact, autonomic principalities, as far as our own country was concerned, and therefore, when a prince and his government decided to take a certain step in one way or other, it was an act of state, however small it may have been, and not the act of a gathering of private individuals. It follows, therefore, that when a great feudal lord became an open enemy of the Shogunate, his opposition was an organised power. When, therefore, Chosiu took up the cudgels against the Shogunate, the latter found a formidable foe; and when, further, Satsuma and others began to sympathise with Chosiu, the Shogunate began to totter, and in the course of a few years came to an end. If it had not been on account of the existence of a feudal system, such phenomenal change would have been most difficult. Of course, there were several other causes which gave facility to that great change. The system of the Shogunate had existed in Japan over seven hundred years, but the family which held in its hands the authority of the Shogun changed from time to time. The family which ruled Japan as Shogun for the longest time before the Tokugawa, viz. the last Shogunate, was the Ashikaga family, which lasted two hundred and forty years, with sixteen Shoguns in succession. Next to the Ashikaga family was the Hojio family, which, though not actual Shoguns, exercised the actual power of the Shogunate for one hundred and thirty-four years, with nine representatives in succession. Now Tokugawa lasted as Shogun two hundred and sixty-four years, with fifteen Shoguns; therefore Tokugawa ruled as the Shogunate longer than any other family. In the natural course of events popular imagination had already begun to think, that the time was approaching for Tokugawa to cease to be the Shogunate.

'Then, again, public opinion and sentiment were fast growing in favour of the restoration of the Imperial authority. It was a perfectly legitimate movement; it differed very widely from those cries which are generally raised in other countries at the time of revolution by the lower classes, based on the mere dissatisfaction of the conditions of existence. Add to this the great shock given by the advent to the country of the Western black ships one after the other. It was sufficient to stir up the heart and soul of the whole nation, and to prepare the way for any change or reform, provided they were good for the preservation of self-existence. Such was the tide which occasioned the convulsion of the Japanese, previous to the great change of 1867. No country, neither China nor Russia, would ever get such a splendid opportunity as this for a radical and thorough reform.

'Then again, the fact that the Imperial court had existed, and yet had had no intricate organisation, was also a great help in assisting the completion of the task. Because the Imperial court had existed, and that too from time immemorial, and it had always commanded the greatest possible reverence of the people, all the new movements knew where to rally; and because the court had not an intricate and crystallised organisation before the restoration, as the administrative government of the country, the tablet was almost blank, so that nearly all institutions could be introduced with greater facility than they would have been otherwise, the only requirements being the capacity and forethought with which the matter was to be executed.'

─'Viewed in the light you have just represented to us,' said another, 'the prospects appear to have been very bright; but there must have been a great danger of the matter miscarrying, and the anxiety felt by responsible statesmen must have been very great.'

─'Certainly it was so. But we were very fortunate. Patriotism and loyalty went far to do the greater part of the work. Suppose the different princes and their clans had been more selfish, and had begun to quarrel among themselves, perhaps with some latent intention of placing themselves in the position of the Shogunate, the country would have indeed fared very badly, and great hindrance would have been placed in the path of reform. In that respect, however, the two most powerful clans, Satsuma and Chosiu, who had the best rights to covet the Shogunate, if such a right were permissible at all, were determined above all others not to embark on such an enterprise. Their princes and statesmen all directed their whole energies to the revivification and consolidation of the Imperial authority. Satsuma and Chosiu being so disposed, all others had to follow their examples. Indeed, they had no thought of doing otherwise.'

─'It was the general spirit of the time,' said one, 'but in what way was the new Imperial government organised, and how did it begin to work? Surely the spirit of the time cannot work itself out alone; political wisdom must have played a great part in leading that spirit to the right goal.'

─'When the last Shogun resigned his authority,' I continued, 'the Imperial government on a new and firmer basis was immediately organised. In it were gathered the ablest men of the empire from all sources. Able court nobles, able feudal lords, and able Samurai of different clans, were all

226

given suitable places side by side. There were many court nobles, with Sanjio and Iwakura at their head, who had done much in bringing about the great change. The Imperial court before the change had no military power, as you know, but the court, including the nobles, always stood in high social estimation. For that reason, as well as for their personal distinction, they were given high places in different branches of the government. Side by side with them, several feudal lords, who were endowed with personal ability, were also given high positions. After them came distinguished Samurai of different clans, to whom various positions, high and low, were assigned, according to their fame and ability. At that time there existed two appellations designating those Samurai who became officials of the Imperial government: Choshi (summoned Samurai) and Koshi (tributed Samurai)—the former meaning those Samurai who were specially summoned by the emperor to serve in his government; the latter meaning those who were taken into the Imperial service at the recommendation of the feudal lord, whose retainers they had been. Thus you can see the intelligence and ability of the different clans were gathered together around the Imperial throne, beneath which all of them, court nobles, feudal lords, and ordinary Samurai, worked together for the common good of the empire, a sight never seen before. Such disinterestedness and such avidity for ability were subsequently extended even to the men of those clans and of the fleet who had fought against the Imperialists.'

−'Very fine,' said one; 'but I should think it must have been very difficult for them to get on well together.'

−'True,' I answered; 'but when men with a vital common aim work together, putting aside self-interests, they can achieve great things. Besides, there was a centre of gravity in the political force, resulting from a combination of the

227

preponderant influences of Satcho, viz. Satsuma and Chosiu. That centre of gravity acted the part of a pendulum or regulator in the new government, and kept all the forces working in unison. You know already that the Satcho were two powerful clans which were the chief factors in bringing about the Great Change. In addition to their natural claim to influence, they produced men of ability, far greater in number than any other clans. Naturally, therefore, Satcho men occupied more important positions than men of other clans. Next to Satcho, the clan having similar influence was Tosa. Next to Tosa, Saga came to share influence under the new government. Satcho kept their mutual harmony well together, and Tosa and Saga joined in the concert. There could be no other clans able to beat their own drums separately. Of course there was a possibility of the Satcho themselves coming into conflict, but for that the statesmen of the clans in question understood each other, and each felt a great responsibility, and accordingly did their best not to produce any discord between them. The chief representative of the Chosiu statesmen was Kido, whilst there were two such on the side of Satsuma, Saigo the elder, and Okubo. These three were popularly called the three great men of the restoration. The types of Okubo and Saigo somewhat differed one from the other, for Saigo, unlike Okubo, was more of a soldier, and represented more the military elements of Satsuma, and therefore we may say that the reins of statesmanship in the new government, as represented by the Satcho, were in the hands of Kido and Okubo. It was chiefly through their efforts that the abolition of the feudal system was ultimately brought about.'

'That part of your history,' said one, 'is a most important and interesting point for us to know. Let us be further enlightened by some of your own observations.'

'Well, the inauguration of the Imperial régime took place in 1867. In the course of a few years a disinterested opinion was mooted and soon spread amongst the lords themselves to the effect that, now that the Shogun had resigned his function and had restored his administrative authority to the Imperial government, it also behoved the lords of all the clans similarly to resign and to give up to the Imperial court the administrative authority of their' clan governments, together with the lands and people they governed. With such reasoning all the feudal lords, headed by the lords of Satcho, vied one with another in voluntarily taking that step. The offer was accepted, and the lords were duly nominated the governors of the different clans. Thus the nature of the position of the lords was changed. They now became mere officials appointed by the new Imperial government, and delegated to carry out its administrative measures. This was an event which took place in 1869. In the course of another few years, viz. in 1871, the clan system was finally abolished, and the prefecture system was introduced in its place. The former lords were ordered by the emperor to reside near him in the capital, and new governors were nominated in their places, chiefly from amongst the Samurai, who were already in the government service. Of course those perfectural governments were newly organised, with suitable subordinates nominated either from amongst those who were already in government service, or from amongst local celebrities. Thus was abolished our feudal system without any murmur.'

—'That is the official history,' said one, 'but there must be also some inner history which you know of in connection with it.'

—'Well,' I answered, 'the new Imperial government was inaugurated as you have already seen. It had no regular revenue as yet; it had neither army nor navy properly belonging to it. Okubo was planning a scheme for Satsuma, by which a portion of its revenue or territory was to be given up to the Imperial government, and that other clans might also be induced to follow the example. Simultaneously with Okubo, Kido was also meditating a project for making the new Imperial administration effective. He schemed the total abolition of the feudal system, the initiation of the idea having been impressed on him by Ito. He returned from Kioto to Chosiu, and presented his views to the Prince of Chosiu, who being a person of extreme loyalty, willingly gave his assent to Kido's proposal. On the return of Kido to Kioto, Okubo gave up his own plan and immediately accepted that of Kido. The matter having been thus agreed upon between the two most influential statesmen, it soon became a question of practical politics, and was successfully carried into effect in no time, as I have already told you.'

−'Can you give me,' said one, 'some idea of the clans of the Japanese feudal system? You make use of that word, as do other writers on Japan, but to me, somehow or other, it does not appear to give a clear idea.'

'The word "clan,"' I replied, 'which is used in place of the Japanese word "Han," does not convey the exact meaning, as you imagine. The word "clan" in English signifies "men," whereas our word "Han" signifies more "a territorial community with its government," including lands and population, somewhat in the same sense as the word "principality" or "duchy." Then, too, the word "clan," strictly speaking, implies the meaning of a collection of families bearing the same surname, and supposed to have descended from a common ancestor, but with our word "Han" no such meaning is implied in the word itself. Every feudal lord of Japan had a large number of retainers, and it was natural that a certain number among them were descended from the same ancestors as the lord himself; but those were, after all, in a very small minority, and the overwhelming number were in nowise connected with their lord, as far as blood relationship was concerned. Thus, you can see, the word "clan" does not represent the exact meaning of the word "Han." The technical term for the acts of giving up and restoring the clan governments to the Imperial government was "Han-seki Hokwan," which meant "restoring the Han records," whereby the giving up of the territory and its population was implied.'

−'I see the difference between the term "clan" and the term "Han,"' said one, 'but I wish to know something more about the process by which the "Han" came to be formed.'

−'That question requires a long answer, because to explain in detail would amount to writing a history of the feudal system of Japan, but I will give you a succinct answer. Feudal lords originally were local celebrities, with some landed property and retainers. In the sixteenth century the country had reached the height of disorder: it was then that countless warriors appeared in the arena, all fighting their way to distinction, some on their own account, and some under the leadership of greater men. The leaders as they became greater had to enlist more followers, and the greater of those followers had in turn to enlist their own followers. These followers were generally enlisted from all sources, some being fortunate sons of mere peasants, some being masterless fighters of a former lord, whose house had become extinct, either through war, or from some other reason. Those who offered service and those who accepted it necessarily entered upon a new relationship of master and servant. The best example of this was the famous Hideyoshi and his followers. Of course, there were many who had better antecedents and pedigrees, but the process by which the cadre of their military organisation had become enlarged was similar. After the country had returned to its normal condition of peace, and those leaders became feudal lords, those followers, viz. retainers, formed their cadre of Samurai. Each lord established his government in his province, to govern the land and people under his authority, and the executive officials were appointed by him from amongst those retainers. All those feudal governments enjoyed autonomy, subject to the general control of the central government of the Shogun. There were also several feudal lords who were made such by virtue of their close relationship with the Shogun, or for their distinguished services, other than military, but the method by which their government and military cadre were formed was much the same. I may add that the word "Han" was originally Chinese, and its literal meaning is a "fence." It was used figuratively to signify an idea of protection or defence, as a fence serves to protect a house, for the central government against external aggressors.'

–'That explains very clearly,' said one, 'the difference between your "Han" and the Western "clans," but I should like to know more about the evolution of your feudal system from its earliest stage.'

–'Very well,' I answered, 'under the ancient Imperial régime, local governors were despatched from the central government. Imperial guards were taken from amongst the provincial youth, there were also several military stations, at different strategic points of the country; the soldiers having been similarly taken from the neighbouring provinces. In the course of time, first with the growth of luxury in the capital, then with the decay of the Imperial authority, the governors themselves ceased to go to their respective provinces, and deputies came to be appointed to discharge their provincial affairs for them. These deputies began to settle in the provinces and to make their functions hereditary, or local celebrities came to be appointed as deputies, often by heredity also. In the meantime, as I told you once before, a sort of hereditary warrior families gradually sprang up in the provinces. The more enfeebled the Imperial court became, the less effective the administrative authority of the Imperial government became in the distant provinces, where fighting between those warrior families was often waged without any knowledge or any recognition of the Imperial government. When, towards the end of the twelfth century, Yoritomo defeated his foes, the Taira, and made himself master of the situation, he established his seat of government at Kamakura, and began to control the whole empire. At first he did so on the pretext of keeping peace and order with Imperial sanction. He called himself, in that respect, Sotsuibushi, which means nothing else than police-master-general. He appointed new local governors, chiefly from amongst the leaders of the warrior families. The official names for these new governors differed from those instituted formerly by the Imperial government. He did not try to do away with the Imperial official organisation, which had become almost nominal, but, in fact, he introduced a new organisation in the provinces. Needless to say, these new governors soon became the real governors in all respects, though their ostensible duties at first were for police affairs in its broad sense. This was the beginning of our system of the military governments. Although there were several vicissitudes, that system in the main lasted down to the great reform of our own days. This period of the system of military power is the period called by the writers in the Western languages the "feudal period," and the system is called the "feudal system." There was, of course, much resemblance in customs and manners, and even institutions, between the European feudal system and our military system, but I do not think the words themselves convey exactly the meaning of our appellation for the system. We call the system "Hoken," which was originally Chinese. That term, which is a combination of two words, means to "create and install" and signifies an act by which some particular person is created a hereditary prince of certain districts. Thus the idea that the persons so created were only made so by the favour of the central government is implied in the term itself. I have already told you that in the sixteenth century, Japan laboured under a condition of the greatest disorder. Many feudal lords rose and fell. When the Tokugawa family assumed the Shogunate, the country was brought to a perfect peace, and that system of "Hoken" was brought to a state of perfection. It was then that a total re-shuffling, so to say, not of the cards but of the feudal lords, was effected. Many old lords retained their positions by acknowledging the supremacy of Tokugawa, but many who were the followers of Tokugawa itself, were newly created lords. The former were called "Tozama" (exterior) Daimio, and the latter were called "Fudai" (adherents) Daimio. Those who had been created, on account of blood relationship to Tokugawa, formed a somewhat different category. The tenure of the lords was not looked upon in the light of private property in its strict sense. The Shogunate freely exercised its authority, to confiscate or to transfer to another place, when political expediency demanded it, though of course such steps were taken only when some blamable action had been committed, or on the offer of some higher and better position. The feudal lords had no right to sell or alienate any portion of the land. In the early part of the Tokugawa régime, the tenure was confiscated in case of default of male heir to a deceased lord, though later on the system of adoption came to the rescue and an adopted heir was allowed to succeed.'

―'I understand now the nature of your feudal system,' said one; 'but it must have been a great sacrifice for the feudal lords to give up all their possessions.'

'It was so in one sense, no doubt,' I answered, 'but, as I have already told you, the lands of our feudal lords were never regarded as private properties. The Shogun had the power to dispose of those tenures, but the Shogun was supposed to have possessed that authority by the delegation of the Imperial prerogative. "Even the remotest sea coast is the emperor's land, and even the humblest creature is the emperor's subject." This was the politico-ethical maxim of China, so also in Japan. This notion had been brought into special prominence, in recent centuries, and patriotic lords and statesmen kept the maxim very vividly in their minds, especially at the time of the great change. The lords had their feudal governments in their locality. They regarded themselves as being the heads of those governments, acting for the emperor. They did not, therefore, feel so much pain as when one gives up a property which is one's own private possession in the strictest sense. Besides, the deep sentiments of loyalty and patriotism swayed them and animated them to adopt the step without any hesitation. I may also add that all the lords used to be invested with some titles of distinction, which were names of some official function of the Imperial court, and also personal ranks, resembling Western orders. These they received through the Shogunate, but the giver was the emperor. Thus you can see that the fountain of honour had always remained with the Imperial court, nay more, the Shogun himself received his function and title from the emperor.'

―'What do you mean by the re-shuffling of the feudal lords?' asked one.

—'I mean that in the early stage of the Tokugawa régime a complete rearrangement of that system, which is generally called feudal, was effected, by transferring all the old lords from one place to another and by creating new lords, to whom new localities were given to govern, whilst many of the older lords lost their possessions. By removal also, some lords were made greater and some smaller. In making that rearrangement, the Shogunate took great care to distribute the lands among the lords in such a way that a combination of several lords against the Shogunate might be impossible. Smaller lords were placed round large ones, and the more trustworthy against less trustworthy, and so on. This rearrangement or shifting I called "re-shuffling." The same thing was done even down to the last days of the Shogunate, though on a limited scale and less frequently. I can therefore say that there was no feudal lord who continued to possess the same seat from the pre-Tokugawa period. There were, however, a few exceptions, and Satsuma was the most significant example. In the earlier state of the feudal system, the lords and retainers did not necessarily reside side by side. The lords had their chief seats where they resided, but the custom of building strong castles had not yet come into existence, and their retainers lived here and there on their domains. From the middle of the sixteenth century, the custom of constructing large castles came into existence. The lords resided in the castles and the retainers lived in houses around them. This became more markedly the case when the re-shuffling of the lords was made and the lords removed, together with their retainers, from one place to another like swarms of bees. It was also at that time that the separation of the Samurai, that is, the retainers, from the ordinary avocations of the people became more thoroughly distinct. The Samurai received their annual allowance from their lords, and did not carry on any commercial business nor trouble themselves about agricultural pursuits. There was great difference of

236

grandeur between the different feudal lords. Our usual way of estimating their relative grandeur was by measuring the reputed quantity of rice produced on their land. According to that method, the degree varied from ten thousand to one million koku. There were some two hundred and seventy lords, and their grandeur varied between those quantities. There were also many petty lords, whose produce of rice from their lands did not amount to ten thousand koku. They were called quasi-lords. Such being the variety of grandeur of the lords, large retainers of great lords often exceeded in grandeur the smaller lords.'

−'You said Satsuma was an exception. Will you explain how it was?'

−'Well, Prince Shimazu was the lord of Satsuma. The greater parts of the provinces Hiuga and Osumi were also included in his dominion. His family had been great lords in that part of the country for some seven hundred years. When the famous Hideyoshi invaded Kiusiu, and reached Satsuma, the prince, namely, the lord of Satsuma, surrendered to that great hero after several battles. Hideyoshi did not consider it politic to push the matter to extremes, so the prince retained his former position. When Tokugawa assumed the Shogunate, the prince was left undisturbed in spite of his having once taken up cudgels against Tokugawa at the famous battle of Sekigahara. His seat of government was Kagoshima, but there was scarcely any establishment worth calling a castle. A certain number of his retainers lived around his residence, but a large number of them lived in different parts of his territory, their lives being partly devoted to agriculture. Satsuma was one of the few strong clans, and its combination with Chosiu resulted, as I said before, in the restoration of the Imperial régime.'

−'Will you please explain in outline the financial system of the Shogunate, and how it was transferred to the Imperial government?' asked one.

'The Shogunate had under its immediate control territorial possessions which were roughly reckoned, in the terms of rice, eight million koku. The Shogunate was clever enough to have the lions share of the landed possessions, which included the best parts of the country, generally comprising prosperous towns, as, for instance, the city of Osaka. The expenditure of the Shogunate was maintained by the income from those territories. No feudal lord had to contribute anything to the exchequer of the Shogunate, except that they were at times ordered to undertake some public works allotted to them; for example, the reparation of some river banks or damage done to the Shogun's castle. The revenue of the Shogunate was scarcely sufficient for maintaining the Shogunate in its normal state, and towards its latter days, when the external relations and internal disturbances began to press heavily, the financial difficulty was much felt. As to the Imperial court, it had no regular revenue at all, except a comparatively trifling sum contributed by the Shogunate, which was supposed to be the equivalent to the taxes collected by the Shogun's officials in the provinces in the immediate vicinity of the Imperial seat. There was no land under the direct control of the court; even the city of Kioto itself was under the administration of the officials of the Shogunate. Consequently the Imperial court was always in a needy condition. It follows, also, that the court nobles were also in an extremely needy condition, though high in personal rank. They only received paltry annual allowances out of the Shogun's contribution, though a very few high court nobles had small landed possessions. Such being the case, it was natural that the Imperial government, when it first

238

came into a renewed existence, should have met with much financial difficulty.'

—'But how did you manage to tide over the transitory period?' asked one.

—'The troops,' I answered, 'which fought for the Imperial cause were generally supported at the expense of their own feudal clan-governments. For the current expenses, some rich merchants either contributed or advanced the necessary sum of money, and also new paper money was issued. By such means as these the government managed to carry on its affairs, and in the course of time some revenue began to accrue to the Imperial treasury from the regions which had been under the control of the Shogunate, but the sum was insignificant. It follows, therefore, that for financial reasons only some great change was necessary, and thus a double impetus was given to the idea of such men as Kido and Okubo for the abolition of the feudal system.'

—'Let us assume that the feudal system had already been abolished,' said another, 'the winding-up of the affairs of the different feudal governments, and the consolidation under a uniform system of central government must have been a very difficult and delicate matter.'

—'Yes, it was so,' I answered. 'To begin with, most of those governments had debts of all kinds which had to be liquidated, above all, their obligations for paper money floated by them. The coinage of gold and silver was the monopoly of the central government, but all the feudal lords had the privilege of circulating paper money under different forms in different clans. The actual value of this paper money in gold and silver varied according to the financial condition of the feudal government by whom it was issued, and that money was legal only in the districts which were under the jurisdiction of the lords by whose governments they were issued. You can therefore easily imagine how troublesome and inconvenient the matter must have been to travellers and traders in localities where those feudal governments stood in close proximity to each other. Then again, the lords and their retainers could not be made penniless immediately on the abolition of the feudal system. To them, therefore, certain means of support were given, in proportion to their former rank and income; that support was ultimately converted into the form of government bonds. The income thus given was not enough for many of the Samurai to support themselves and their families, and they, therefore, had to seek some new occupation to which they were not accustomed. A large number of them even lost the bonds thus given, through their incautious or incompetent management. The government had to prevent things getting into a worse condition, and to make the transition state a smooth one, if possible. For that purpose the government often had to organise for them some kind of common work, for which sometimes some special funds were given. Somehow or other, we have got through those trying times. The credit of winding-up the affairs of the feudal governments is chiefly due to Count Inouyé, who was the acting Minister of Finance at the time.

−'How did matters stand at the time with regard to the system of taxation?' asked one.

−'It was also one of the most difficult problems which the Imperial government had to solve,' I answered. 'Perhaps you know that the economical theory of the Far East had always been essentially physiocratic. Agriculture was the foundation of national existence. Commerce and industry were very little considered. Curiously enough, on that

240

account the land had to bear public expenses almost entirely, and commerce and industry contributed almost nothing; in other words, taxes on land were the main source of public revenue. People engaged in industry and commerce paid no tax, except perhaps some trifling amount in the form of licences occasionally, and except that they were often ordered by their lords to contribute irregular sums of money to relieve their financial difficulty. The land taxes were paid, as a rule, in kind, namely, rice, but the burden of the tax-payers was by no means uniform throughout the country. There was a vague measurement expressed by the words "four public, six private," that is to say, four tenth parts of the produce was to go to the government, and the remaining six, together with any supplementary produce, was to remain in the hands of the producers. But this was by no means uniformly practised. Roughly speaking, the burden of the lands under the direct control of the Shogunate was lighter than that on the lands under the different lords. But there was much difference in the burden on the lands held by the different lords. As a matter of fact, all sorts of additional burdens, besides the pure land taxes, were instituted and levied on most lands. It was necessary for the Imperial government to unify these burdens and equalise them, as much as possible, throughout the whole country. It was also desirable to change the whole system of paying taxes in kind into a uniform system of money payment, because, in the case of the former, revenue is subject to variation on account of the condition of the harvest and the market price, besides, that system is more liable to abuse. The Imperial government undertook this tremendous work of reform. The valuation of all lands was carried out, and the system of payment in money was effected. I may here mention that, under the ancient Imperial régime, no proprietary rights were recognised in lands. The tillers of land obtained the allotments of them for life, and new allotments were made from time to time.

That system, however, was not strictly enforced in the case of newly reclaimed lands, especially so in the far-off provinces. As time went on, the system entirely fell through, and hereditary proprietorship of the tillers came tacitly into existence. Nevertheless, the idea of the supreme domain of the sovereign from the points of public law and proprietary rights of the possessors from points of private law had not been brought into a very distinct light, and the vague notion had still remained that the possessors held the lands only by favour of the sovereign. As a matter of fact, in most parts of the country no rights of sale of lands were legally recognised, though the matter was widely affected by some fictitious means, such as long mortgages or long leases. This state of things was entirely changed by the reform made when the nature of the land tax was changed, as I have just described, because by that reform the full proprietary rights from the point of private law were completely recognised. I said that industrial and commercial people contributed almost nothing to the public expenses, and yet the denominations under which they had to pay something were various. Add to this numerous other miscellaneous contributions; there were several hundred different kinds of contributions, but each of these separately amounted to a very small sum, and was not worth the trouble it involved. These, therefore, were altogether abolished. Of course the government had, as time went on, to introduce some new taxes, such as the business tax, the income tax, etc., but these are the results of the progress made in our economical and financial conditions, and based on broader and more universal lines, so as to fit the altered state of the country. The annual budget, which amounted to seventy or eighty million yen before the Sino-Japanese war, amounted to some five or six hundred million yen before the Russo-Japanese war: that will perhaps show the expansion of the financial system of the country.'

−'It is very interesting,' said one; 'but let us have a cup of tea, and then continue the discussion.'

VIII

Commerce and industry—Old methods of communication—Roads and ships—How they have been improved—Railways, post, telegraphs, and telephones—Progress of the financial system—The Satsuma war—The Bank of Japan—The National banks—The monetary system one of the causes of Japan's success—Further remarks on the military reforms—Evolution of the mode of fighting—All reforms at much cost of blood and money—The cause of the Satsuma war—Saigo the Elder—Social condition of Japan to-day—Evolution of legislation—Chinese jurisprudence—The Japanese are not good correspondents—My future—An operatic singer—Japanese stages—Danjiuro and Irving—The old school and the new one—Kawakami and Sada Yakko—The opera Maritana—The end of the dream

I was still in the same incongruous group of people, and carrying on a conversation on the same lines. Though the subjects were rather technical, they seemed to have interested the people who took part in the discussion, because they relate to the important part of our history, wherein the foundation-stone, so to say, of Modern Japan was laid.

−'I suppose, 'said one of the group, 'your country had to take much pains in encouraging commerce and industry to attain the stage you have reached.'

'Well,' I replied, 'we could not do anything which resembled a protective system if we wished, because we were bound by the treaties forced upon us, whereby our custom-house duties, all prefixed, could not exceed five per cent. ad valorem; but as far as it lay in the competence of

244

our Government and people, we did all in our power. You cannot imagine what money, what time, and what labour we have had to waste in many ways, because there were many things which we tried and in which we failed. What we have achieved is insignificant, but it is the result of all those exertions. By the bye, the question of the revision of the old treaties was a long protracted subject of our diplomacy and politics through which we had to struggle. It wrecked several ministries. One minister for foreign affairs, Count Okuma, lost one of his legs and only miraculously escaped death, in consequence of having been inclined to accept terms of revision which the people considered insufficient and irreconcilable with national dignity. The aim of the revision was to regain the tariff as well as judicial autonomy. America had shown very early its inclination to accede to our demand. Italy also showed a similar inclination. But on the whole the matter proved very difficult. About ten years ago Great Britain took the lead in recognising the justice of our demand, other powers followed England's example, and thus the revision was at last effected. That revision restored to us our judicial autonomy completely. You must, however, remember that the tariff autonomy has not yet been entirely restored to us, for we are still bound by one-sided conventional tariffs. But I must now return to the original thread of my discourse. You have already seen that we were hampered by the treaties, but in spite of that we have taken every pains to promote our commerce and industry, without falling into the error of over-interfering or being officious.'

−'And you have made wonderful progress in your commerce in a comparatively short time,' said another.

−'Well, not wonderful,' I answered; 'but it is a fact that our commerce has increased from a few million yen to some six hundred million yen. That is something. I will add a word more. It is a mistake to suppose that the stage we have attained is the mere result of natural growth. We must venture to ask for sympathetic appreciation of our endeavour. Some Western people appear to entertain a sort of apprehension in regard to the growth of our commerce and industry, and even show a desire to check our progress. It would be very hard lines for us, for our conviction is that the growth of our commerce and industry can only be beneficial reciprocally to others as well as to ourselves; and, moreover, what is after all our commerce and industry when compared with that of the Western peoples?'

—'I quite sympathise with you on that point,' said one.

—'Thank you!' I said, and continued. 'Some foreigners speak of our commercial probity very disparagingly. I admit there were some shortcomings, but I deny that the faults were wholly ours. You know that the greater bulk of our Japanese commerce is done in Japan itself by the Western merchants who come out there. If we were always cheating them, and they were always blameless, why should they continue to trade with us and make such great increase of commerce in a comparatively short space of time? It is my opinion that the blame attached to the commercial probity of the Japanese merchant has far less foundation than the reality warrants. A good deal of the blame, I think, is a hearsay, originally circulated by interested persons and innocently magnified by others. Time was when our merchants wellnigh revolted against oppressive dealings of foreign merchants out there, and tried to export direct to foreign countries, but then want of capital and experience stood in their way as a barrier. On the whole, I am satisfied with the progress our commerce has made, as well as with the fact that its volume has increased in spite of the war, though we must endeavour to still further it.'

−'That your country will have to do,' said another; 'but will you tell me the condition of the communications of the country at the time of the abolition of the feudal system, and the improvements you have made since then?'

−'The means of communication,' I replied, 'were not good in those days. We are surrounded by seas on all sides, but we were unable to make the fullest use of the water, because the building of large ships was prohibited for centuries, and therefore our ships had much difficulty in navigating the eastern coasts, as well as the Japan Sea, especially in winter. They often had to remain several months in some port on their route. On the land, roads were not good, they were often badly made on purpose by the different lords for the defence of their territories. Thus, even where a straight road could be made on flat land, it was purposely made high up on the hills in a winding way. Rivers were often left bridgeless where bridges could easily have been constructed. Foreign visitors may think our roads even now bad when compared with those of the Western civilised countries; but in our eyes our present roads are beyond any comparison with those of some thirty or forty years ago. This also means that our central Government, as well as our local governments, had to take much pains and spend much money in the matter. We had also to encourage the building of large ships, both steam and sailing vessels. We have built many lighthouses round the country for the benefit of the navigation of foreign ships as well as for our own.'

−'What of the railways, telegraph, and telephone lines?' asked one.

'Not many years after the restoration we began the construction of the railways. The line between Yokohama

247

and Tokio was the first and most expensive of any of the railways constructed in Japan, for, owing to the lack of experience, we had to pay whatever price we were asked by foreigners for the materials. The next line was one between Kobe and Osaka, and the system has been gradually extended as the finances of the Government have allowed. But finding that the rapid extension to every part of the country was beyond the financial expediency of the Government, private enterprises were encouraged, and many private railway companies were established one after another. Thus we have two kinds of railways, one belonging to the Government, the other belonging to private companies. When I was Minister of Communications eight years ago, the whole length of the railways, state and private, reached three thousand miles. There was some talk of celebrating the occasion, but both Matsumoto, Director of the Board of Railways, and I discountenanced the idea, because three thousand miles of railway were nothing compared with other advanced countries. The extension at present is between four and five thousand miles, I think. The length is not much, but because the country is narrow, every part of it is within easy reach of the train. The telegraph lines belong to the Government entirely, and are managed in conjunction with the general postal system. Soon after the inauguration of the Imperial Government, we began to remodel the postal system which had existed previously, and it has been gradually expanded and improved on the European method. I can say without much diffidence that our postal and telegraph systems may be compared in efficiency with any country, even the most advanced in those matters. The telephone system is comparatively new, but most of the populous towns have it, and large towns are connected by distant telephones. Needless to say that we have managed from the beginning to maintain the system in the hands of the Government.'

−'The Imperial Government seems to have required much money,' said one, 'for winding up the feudal Governments, and for introducing, side by side, many reforms. You also mentioned that the Government had to issue paper money. I should like to know more about how you got through it all.'

−'We had to undergo much financial difficulty. Before the Imperial régime gold and silver constituted practically double standards. At the early stage of the new Government gold was adopted as the standard in theory, but it took a long time before it came into actual operation. The Government had to issue much paper money, and that, too, inconvertible, hence much depreciation of the paper. The strenuous efforts of the Government had been successful in improving the situation when the Satsuma war broke out in 1877. The expense of that war occasioned more issue of paper money, which caused a further depreciation. At one time the difference between silver, which was practically the legal tender at the time, and the paper rose to 100 : 180.

'There was another cause for the depreciation of paper money. It was the issue of notes by the national banks, which were established in all parts of the country after the abolition of the feudal system, and which numbered at one time more than 150. The Government had to meet with these difficulties, and to place the financial and economical condition of the country on a firmer and more satisfactory basis. This the Government began to undertake a few years after the Satsuma war, without hindering the necessary works for the development of the national resources. The Government decided to apply strict economy in all branches of its administration. The money thus saved was partly used for the redemption of the over-issued paper money, and partly to accumulate reserve funds for making the paper currency convertible. The Bank of Japan was established with the view of making it the sole central economical organ of the empire. A scheme was provided for redeeming the notes issued by the so-called national banks, and for converting those banks into strictly private banks in due time.

'The process began in earnest in 1881; it made far quicker progress than was contemplated; thus in 1885 the difference between the silver and the paper money disappeared. From January 1886 the total redemption of the paper money was begun. In 1899 the circulation of the Government paper money and the notes of the national banks altogether ceased to exist, the convertible notes of the Bank of Japan having taken their place. In the same year all national banks ceased to exist, most of them having become private banks, and a few having wound up their business. Two years previously gold had been at last effectively adopted as the Japanese national standard of currency, which was the realisation of the idea cherished by the Imperial Government from the beginning.'

−'What was the nature of the national banks?' asked one; 'and have they proved quite meaningless?'

−'The law for the establishment of those banks was promulgated soon after the abolition of the feudal system. It was modelled after the national banks of America. In the course of time a large number of them came into existence in different parts of the Empire. They were private undertakings, except that they enjoyed the privilege of issuing their own notes, and were subject to Government superintendence. At first the notes were to be convertible into specie, but a modification was introduced in the law by which they could issue notes with Government bonds as security and convertible in Government paper money. Therefore the notes were in reality incontrovertible ones

250

from the point of view of hard money. Previous to that, the Government loan bonds, amounting to one hundred and seventy million yen, were issued for the capitalisation of the feudal lords and their retainers in consideration of their feudal incomes, after the feudal system had been abolished. These bonds were used widely for establishing the banks. The banks enjoyed special privileges of issuing paper money, but in lieu of it they did good service in encouraging and stimulating local industry and commerce, so that we do not regret that those banks were once instituted. Besides, they led to the foundation of the modern monetary system of Japan. You must have observed the efficiency of the monetary system of Japan during the Sino-Japanese war. The success of Japan in great wars is due a great deal to that system. I mean to say that because we have that system, the money possessed by the public could easily be made to serve public purposes in time of emergency. Look at China: as far as individuals are concerned, there is a far greater number of people who are richer than the Japanese, and yet they have no sound banking system in close connection with the state. When the Chinese deposit their money, they prefer to do so with foreign banks. The consequence is that the Government cannot fall back upon the wealth of private individuals. Neither is there much likelihood of home loans being popular in China. Of course there may be some other reasons for this. In Japan nothing but regular taxes and dues regulated by law are levied. No illegal exaction is or could be made. In that respect there exists a perfect understanding between the Government and the people, who know that if they respond to the Government call for loans their dues would be made good in future. No such confidence and usage exist in China, still less in any other part of the East.'

−'You told us that in the beginning of the Imperial Government, the Imperial troops were supported at the expense of the clan governments,' said one. 'Will you tell us a little more about it?'

—'Under the Shogunate,' I answered, 'the feudal lords had to support their own troops, even when they were ordered to send them out somewhere. This was the duty they had to render in return for the tenure of land. Just before the battle of Fushimi, Satsuma and some other clans had their troops stationed in Kioto. Chosiu, which on all sides had come triumphantly out of the war against the attacking forces of the Shogunate, also sent some troops to Kioto; not indeed by order of the Shogun, but rather against it. These troops were all supported by their clan governments. After the battle of Fushimi, the troops of the Satcho and other clans which had become Imperialists, were ordered to the front in the North-Eastern provinces. They now fought as Imperial troops under the "brocade banners," which was the emblematic banner used solely by the Imperial forces, and much reverenced by the Japanese in general, because with us those who fought against those banners had been, and were at all times, universally stigmatised as disloyal subjects. The leaders of those troops were generally commissioned by the Imperial Government. The cohesion of the troops of different clans in one direction was maintained by a generalissimo, who was a high court noble, assisted by a certain number of staff officers, specially appointed by the Imperial Government. In that manner, troops of different clans fought for the cause of the Imperial Government. After the war, the troops of some of the clans were still used for the Imperial purposes, whilst others of them were all sent home. The future of the military system was, however, a great problem. Immediately after the war, the present Marshal, Marquis Yamagata, who was the leader of the Chosiu troops in the province of Echigo, visited Europe, together with Saigo the younger. On his return to Japan, he advocated the adoption of the European

252

system of universal service. He succeeded in his advocacy, and in 1870 regulations were promulgated relating to the subject, by which the system was experimentally put in force in five provinces in the vicinity of Kioto; and the system was made universal and more complete soon after the total abolition of the feudal system. It has undergone further improvement from time to time, until we have come into possession of the army which the world has come to see during the present war. I may add, that in the earlier parts of the new organisation, many French officers were engaged to instruct our men and officers in different ways, and afterwards some German officers were similarly engaged, as you know.'

'Can you roughly explain,' said one, 'the evolution of your modes of fighting before it reached the efficiency of the present day?'

−'It has been pretty much the same as yours,' I answered. 'Putting aside the remote antiquity, I will briefly tell you how it has been since the commencement of the chivalric period. The sword was always our chief weapon of honour, that you know very well. Then bows and arrows were also regarded as honourable weapons, so much so, that the families which made military affairs their constant occupation were called "the houses of bows and arrows," The phrase "bow-handlers" came to signify "leaders." Thus when the famous Takeda Shingen, towards the end of the sixteenth century, spoke of Iyeyasu, his junior contemporary, as "the first bow-handler of the Tokai provinces," he meant by the phrase "first bow-handler" a general of great ability. The spear which was used by the leaders was also held in high esteem. Thus "distinction at the point of the spear" was a phrase commonly used to denote distinguished deeds of warriors. "The seven spears of Shizugatake" is a phrase constantly used by people at large. It refers to the gallant fighting of the seven famous captains of Hideyoshi at the battle of Shizugatake. They all used spears. The Naginata was a weapon with a long curved blade, with a handle a little shorter than that of a spear: it was considered a proper weapon for women and monks, and was not, therefore, looked upon as being so honourable as a spear for ordinary warriors to use. The decisive battles were necessarily hand-to-hand combats. There was even time-honoured heraldic etiquette, that when two combatants were about to fight they announced their names and positions, etc., to each other. I believe a somewhat similar custom existed in Europe also. Warriors of position considered it a disgrace to be killed or captured by "nameless common soldiers," as they were called. The hand-to-hand combat, being the chief feature of battle, it was natural that a person who had overcome an enemy of greater distinction or of higher rank was regarded as having done a correspondingly greater action; hence the custom of bringing back the enemies' heads by the combatants, and submitting them to the inspection of their leaders, came into existence, and in the sixteenth and seventeenth centuries, the modes of such inspections had become an elaborate part of the heraldic ceremonies. The measure of the boxes in which the heads were put, the manner in which to place them and how to take them out, what attitude to be assumed by the one who submitted the heads for inspection, and what composure the one who inspected should assume, and what glance he should give to the head—all these matters had fine and minute rules, though when taking place on the actual spot at a hasty hour, much of the formality was necessarily simplified.'

−'How was it with the firearms?' asked one.

−'The use of firearms in Japan,' I answered, 'dates back only about three and a half centuries. A Portuguese trading-vessel which arrived in 1543 at the islands of Tanegashima, off the southern coasts of Kiusiu, is reputed to have brought a few firearms, and it is said they were the first firearms introduced into Japan, and that they served as a model to us for making others. Hence the name "Tanegashima" had come to signify sometimes "firearms" even down to our own time. A few years afterwards more Portuguese ships arrived at the province of Bungo, in Kiusiu, and brought with them more firearms. At the time a great deal of foreign trade was carried on in that province by Chinese and Portuguese trading-ships. Otomo, the prince of the province, even became a Christian convert, and it is said that he was one of the converted feudal lords who sent missions to Rome. Repute gives it that those firearms were brought by the missionaries, and the prince took his first fancy to them on account of their bringing such useful weapons. In no time the manufacture and use of firearms made their way into many parts of the country. It is said that at the war of Nagasino, which was fought in 1575 between Takeda on one side and Oda and Tokugawa on the other, there were three thousand firearms on the latter side, which seems to have been the war in which the largest number of firearms was used. Of course, the firearms of those days were all matchlocks, and, moreover, they were not considered arms of honour. Firearm companies were formed of the commonest soldiers, and generally used for skirmishes before the commencement of regular fighting. Cannon were also known soon after the introduction of ordinary firearms, but they do not seem to have been much in use. As a matter of fact, before much improvement had been made in the use of firearms, peace returned, and lasted over two hundred years, so that we had little more than matchlocks, which were chiefly used for shooting game. Since the latter part of the eighteenth century, when the Western ships began to appear on the Far Eastern seas, the "coast defence question" had aroused public attention, and the necessity for having strong firearms presented itself. Cannon began to be cast and ordinary guns also, by the different feudal lords. It was then that the bells in most of the temples in most provinces were confiscated, to be thrown into the furnace and recast as, cannon. Perhaps you know that the Japanese temple bells are many times bigger than those ordinarily used in the Western churches and temples. They have no tongues, but are sounded by a large wooden pendulum suspended close to them. The sound, therefore, is deep and sonorous, quite different from the tinkling noise of the Western bells. Those bells used to report certain hours of the day, and it was a charm, especially in country parts, in the midst of nature, to listen to their soft clang. Those chimes were favourite themes in poetry, but most localities are now deprived of that charm for the reason I have just given. As time went on, the Western guns of modern type began to make their way into the country. They were commonly known as the "bayoneted guns." They were a rude kind of gun compared with the modern ones, and, of course, not breach-loaders. In those days the making of guns was not much advanced, even in Europe itself. When the English squadron bombarded Kagoshima, the English ships fared rather badly. They had anchored too near the fortress, in defiance of our cannon, and one ship left behind her anchor in trying to escape the firing from the land. Our skill in casting guns and cannon was not much advanced then, and yet, as one may perceive, we were on the road to success. Looking back in general at the changes in the mode of fighting, the latter days of the Tokugawa régime was the great epoch. It was then that war recommenced, after more than two centuries of peace, and its mode had entirely changed from that of times gone by, and the notion of single combat was totally discarded. At present no one remembers bows and arrows, except perhaps for sporty and still less spears. Swords, indeed, we still value, but rather as a reminiscence of old times, and not as an effective weapon. We have made many new guns and cannon, improved on the Western models, and they are our weapons of to-day.'

−'And all those reforms,' said one, 'in polity, in finance, in the army and navy, were effected with the perfect concord of the whole nation, without a hitch?'

'Not exactly. On broad lines the bulk of the people was with the Government and followed its lead. But we reaped all these fruits at much expense of blood and money. You could not but expect to see among the people at large some who did not exactly approve the methods pursued by the Government. To them the policy of the Government sometimes appeared too radical and hazardous, and thus one group or another showed from time to time their dissent. In those days when people were determined to assume a dissenting attitude, it generally took the shape of physical force, in other word, "revolt." Chosiu itself had had two such revolts, but they had been easily crushed. Chosiu had had a civil strife before the restoration, and in consequence the elements of political differences within the clan had been almost thoroughly unified. Most of its able men devoted their services to the Imperial Government. The old territory of the clan was one of the prefectures which thoroughly submitted to the Imperial administration with perfect confidence, from the very moment when the feudal system was abolished, so much so, that the first governor despatched there by the Imperial Government was originally a retainer of the Shogunate and had fought against the Imperialists. The revolters had therefore not much sympathy from the people, nor had they any means, guns, or ammunition, to turn to their advantage against the Imperialists, and yet it shows that even the Chosiu men themselves were unable to get on altogether harmoniously. The saddest and the gravest case, however, was that of the

Satsuma war, which took place in 1877. It was only after that war that the progressive administration of the new Government was placed on a firm and solid basis, and the surviving influence of the old feudal time disappeared altogether.'

—'Since your explanation has reached as far as that stage,' said one, 'I am anxious to know something about the real cause and circumstances which occasioned that war.'

—'It requires some explanation,' I replied. 'You already know that Satsuma was one of the few most powerful clans. Its history and organisation were different from other clans. And also, unlike Chosiu, it had not had an outbreak of civil strife within the clan before the Restoration period. Its clansmen fought many battles, but it never had any occasion to form voluntary bands as did Chosiu, and therefore it had had no opportunity of observing that the troops recruited from all classes were equal, if not superior, to the Samurai troops. The two greatest statesmen of the clan were Saigo the elder, and Okubo, but as I have indicated already, they differed in the course of their career, as well as in their natural propensity. Saigo had been a devout Imperialist from the beginning, and there were several romantic episodes about his life. Once, in despair, he, together with an Imperialist monk, jumped into the sea. He was rescued, and had to spend years on an island in banishment. Okubo always played the part of a politician. His imperialism had not become quite marked and decisive until almost within the last few years preceding the Restoration. Naturally, therefore, there were in Satsuma some men who were more partial to Saigo and others more inclined to Okubo. There was another group of men, differing from both, namely, the partisans of the real father of the Prince of Satsuma. The late Prince of Satsuma, the predecessor and uncle of the prince in question, had been an able and enlightened man, almost unparalleled by any of the contemporary feudal lords. He had had much leaning towards Western enlightenment. An incident is told of his strength of character in regard to the visit of a Dutchman whom he had invited to Kagoshima, the capital of Satsuma. He went to the port and rode with him side by side back to his residence. At the time an anti-foreign spirit was still strong among the Samurai, and by his riding side by side with the Dutchman he intimated that if the Satsuma Samurai were determined to attack the foreigner, they must also at the same time attack him.'

—'But stop,' said one, 'was not the time you are speaking of before the bombardment of Kagoshima and Simonoseki? I have always understood that Satsuma and Chosiu were fierce anti-foreign clans.'

—'Yes, it was before those bombardments. The Prince of Satsuma, whom I have just spoken of, died somewhere about 1860. I do not remember the exact date. It is true those two clans were anti-foreign towards the latter days of the Tokugawa régime, but it does not follow that they had always been the same. The acceleration of the idea was much due to the circumstances of the time, which require explanation. At the time of that prince, he and his government had shown much inclination towards Western intercourse. As a matter of fact, it is even said some trade was secretly carried on between Satsuma and the Dutchmen at an island in the Southern Sea. The old bottles marked Soy, which one sometimes finds in Holland, are said to have been the bottles which contained our Shoyu and to have been imported into Holland at that time. Even Chosiu was not at first so fierce an anti-foreign clan as it became later on. The Prince of Chosiu had a few medical retainers who were well versed in the Dutch language. He used to collect information about Europe from them. They even translated for him some European extracts, and compiled them into the form of a periodical pamphlet, which may be said to have been the very beginning of the Japanese newspapers. He was one of the few feudal lords who first introduced the system of vaccination in their territory. He established a glass factory in his province. He also made experiments in the art of photography. All this took place before the bombardment of Simonoseki. It is, therefore, wrong to suppose that either Satsuma or Chosiu knew nothing of the West before they were bombarded. Besides, the fault which had originated the bombardment of Kagoshima lay in reality in the miscalculation which had been shown by an Anglo-Saxon. Nevertheless, we had to pay the indemnity all the same, in addition to having been bombarded. But to return to my subject. The Prince of Satsuma, who died somewhere about 1860, as I have just told you, had no heir of his own, and was succeeded by the young son of his brother, whom he had adopted. That brother was the famous Shimazu-Saburo, who acted as regent for the young prince. For that reason, he also exercised much influence in the clan, and at one time played the part of the real ruler of Satsuma. His character, however, differed very much from that of his deceased brother. He was also a man of ability, but rather conservative, and his sympathy was not much with the sweeping reforms of Japan on European lines. He sometimes held office in the new Imperial Government, but spent more of his time in retirement in Satsuma. Saigo the elder, also was not a man who cared to toil in ordinary administrative affairs, and after the cabinet crisis in 1873 on the Corean question, he retired to Kagoshima. From all this you can see that there remained in Satsuma strong conservative element, which could not be looked upon as a negligible quantity. As a matter of fact, Satsuma was the only locality where the Imperial Government found it not expedient to enforce rigorously all the new progressive measures, which it did in all other localities. Unlike Chosiu, the governor and his subordinates, though officially nominated by the central Government, were men belonging to the province and sharing those conservative sentiments, and therefore at heart not the faithful executors of the will of the central Government. At last the province rose in revolt against the central Government in 1877.

−'To detail the matter a little further,' I continued, 'when Saigo retired to Kagoshima in 1873, many of his admirers and followers, especially those in the army, also resigned their offices, and retired to Satsuma, whilst many others, including Saigo the younger, namely the brother of the elder Saigo, remained in the service of the Government with Okubo. Thus Satsuma men were practically divided into two parties, many near relatives and friends having taken different sides. As time went on the distance between them became greater and greater. In Satsuma the so-called private schools were organised in different parts of the province by the chief followers of Saigo the elder, though he himself mostly indulged in hunting. Those schools in reality were utilised for gathering together young men to serve latent designs of the organisers. It is a doubtful point of history how far Saigo himself was cognisant of those matters, but one thing is certain, that he did not exactly discourage them. When some time back Yamagata mooted the proposal for the universal service system, Saigo, who was then fulfilling an important position in the army, was persuaded to agree. Again, when the final abolition of the feudal system was decided upon, he joined the cabinet almost for that special purpose, and his weight went a long way in achieving that aim. It has always remained doubtful whether Shimazu Saburo was in accord with the scheme, but the matter was carried out by Okubo and Saigo in conjunction with influential statesmen of other clans. Hence we can see that Saigo was also in the main on the lines of progressive policy. It may, however, be presumed that, intelligent and well educated as he was in the Oriental sense, he had not any deep insight into the European civilisation. Besides, his personal character and proclivity were not exactly fit to appreciate radical changes, which to him must have appeared somewhat frivolous. Then, too, after his retirement to Kagoshima, many governmental measures were often misrepresented to him as the result of thoughtless actions of Okubo and others, and it was also possible that many personal scandalous misrepresentations were made about those in power. Hence it is to be presumed that Saigo also felt some desirability of modifying the trend of the national policy. When, therefore, his followers committed an act which was irreconcilable with the peaceful observation of the laws of the land and which soon assumed attitudes of revolt, Saigo became their head without any overt action and almost as a result of the natural course of events. The revolters numbered forty-five thousand. Individually, Saigo was the most popular man in the whole empire. The Imperial army at the time did not number much more than the revolters. It was a most critical time for the Government, which only succeeded in suppressing the rebels after many sanguinary battles. It is well worth remembering that in the case of the Satsuma men, many near relatives and close friends had to fight one against the other, because a large number of them was on the side of the Government as well. Casual observers of the outside world may say it was barbarous that such people should fight one against the other, but such is often the case when a nation undergoes a great change. I may reiterate that it was a very critical time for Japan, for if the rebels had been victorious, there was a grave fear that the progressive policy would have been seriously hindered and a military despotism would have reigned in the country. It was absolutely necessary to crush the rebels at the point of the bayonet, however great and popular Saigo might have been and however meritorious his antecedents. I for one have some consolation in saying that I have done some little service to my country by being the first to formulate and publish the views of the situation I have just spoken of, and to lead the public opinion in that direction, before any other dared to do so. I received several threatening letters at the time, but suffered no actual attack. Towards the latter part of that war I was on the battlefield, and was one of the few who assisted at the last hour in washing Saigo's head, which had been found and dug up. The head had been buried hastily in a small ditch by one of his captains, who, when Saigo had been fatally wounded in the last battle, cut it off at his own request, while the fray was still raging, to prevent it falling into the hands of the enemy. I remember there were present Marshal Yamagata, Marshal Oyama, and General Nozu.'

−'What had become of Shimazu Saburo at the time of the war?' asked another.

−'He was in Kagoshima,' I answered, 'but he kept aloof together with some devoted followers: the rebels also seem to have preferred to leave him alone. In the course of years he died a natural and honourable death, to the great regret of the emperor and the nation. Okubo was assassinated a few years after the war by a small group of young men who had been zealous supporters of Saigo. Taking into consideration all that I have related, you will clearly see that the present-day Japan has by no means been built upon a bed of roses.'

−'How does the social condition of Japan stand at present?' asked another; 'from the political point of view, for instance, who is the ruling class?'

—'The social condition of Japan,' I answered, 'is satisfactory. We have aristocracy and commons, as you know, but no class animosity. The distance between them is not great. The commercial class also is making its influence felt: many people who formerly belonged to a class which despised business occupation are now engaged in business. The official positions are occupied almost all by men of ability belonging mostly to the middle class. Almost none of the old nobles occupy any official positions. You must have heard many statesmen and generals called by some titles of nobility, but they are only new nobility, given by the emperor for meritorious services rendered to the new Imperial Government, and therefore their modes of thought and their inclinations are not far different from that of the ordinary people at large. All the Government officials and officers of the army and navy are taken by examination without any distinction of class or locality, and therefore young men belonging to any class of society or to any province have equal chance. It is true that immediately after the restoration some powerful clans, especially that of Satcho, exercised more influence in political circles, but it was only natural as the results of the great change. Even at this moment there are several statesmen, who originally belonged to those clans, who exercise great influence: it is because their services to the country have been great, and consequently they enjoy greater prestige. In the army and navy, also, the majority of the generals of the higher class are in a similar manner men who have risen from those clans. With the rest, the clannish landmarks are already almost indistinguishable; even amongst those of the highest positions the disappearance of the clannish traces must be only a question of time, for most of the personages occupying those positions are already far advanced in age. It is not, therefore, fair for some foreigners to say that the Satcho men placed themselves in the place of the Shogunate. As a matter of fact, the Satcho statesmen themselves have introduced many important regulations for giving equal chances to every class and province. Then, again, what is most worth noticing is perhaps the fact that all public affairs are governed by laws and regulations, and not by any arbitrary will; so much so, that in some instances people think that there are too many laws and regulations. On the whole, I approve the present system, as every one must, because it leaves no room for class or bureaucratic oppression.'

—'Can you explain,' said one, 'how all those psychological changes have been brought about? People in the West have always thought that the Orientals little cared for laws and regulations, their modes of government being based upon customs and traditions.'

—'You may think so,' I answered; 'if you take the generality of the Orientals, but it is not the case with Modern Japan. Even in China the matter was never exactly as you have just said. China has always been wanting in the matter of civil law. But there is one particular feature worth noticing. In the same way as the Romans were rich in the notions of civil law, the Chinese were rich in the ideas of criminal law. I do not, of course, say their system was good from the Western point of view, but in its way it had very good jurisprudence and codes, which were handed down with some necessary modifications from dynasty to dynasty. They knew the importance of separating ethics from jurisprudence for more than a dozen centuries, namely, from the Tang dynasty, when a very good criminal code, which was an improvement and enlargement upon that of the preceding dynasty, was enacted. Thus, for instance, torture is looked upon by the Occidentals simply as barbarous, but it has its raison d'être in the Chinese jurisprudence. According to that jurisprudence, no person is to be punished on mere circumstantial evidence, or on the

265

words of witnesses, unless the prisoner himself makes confession of his guilt. The act of confession is technically called the "completion of self-acknowledgment." The object of this is to make sure that no innocent person shall ever be punished. In some cases, if punishments be inflicted, despite the prisoner's strong protest of innocence, on mere circumstantial evidence, or on the evidence of witnesses, great injustice may be done, as was well illustrated in the Beck incident, which recently created so great a sensation in England. Torture is resorted to only in the case where, although the evidence is conclusive, yet the prisoner obstinately refuses to acknowledge his guilt. In other words, the application of torture is only to be resorted to in order that a prisoner whose guilt is quite evident might not be allowed to escape unpunished merely because he obstinately refuses to confess. The raison d'être of the torture, therefore, is not so bad as casual observers imagine. The blame of the method lies in its abuse. We Japanese once followed that jurisprudence, but have given it up because it is liable to misapplication, and we have adopted the European system of judgment by evidence, not because we believed in the infallibility of that system, but because we believed that less injustice would be committed by that system than the other. China has also been very rich in codes of governmental organisation, not indeed in the Western style of constitutional laws; but still, from a literary point of view, they are all very good. Now to return to our subject. If Japan were a country which had not known the usefulness of laws and regulations, and yet had begun to imitate the methods of European legislation with success as she has done, such a result might indeed be a matter of some amazement. She had, however, had much experience in making laws and regulations during the ancient Imperial régime when we had frequent intercourse with the Tang dynasty of China, and therefore, when we began to formulate new legislation on Western lines, it was

266

only necessary to grasp the spirit as to the method, and to make some modification in form of what we had done previously. And besides, scholars well acquainted with the Chinese codes were not wanting, and their ability was ready to be utilised for new legislation.'

—'It would be very interesting,' said one, 'if we could obtain a new book which would scientifically treat of the history of the evolution of all those great changes which have taken place. Really, we know little concerning Japan.'

—'That may be,' I answered, 'but there are several books, especially in English, from which one can gather a good deal of information on Japan, though they are not always correct to our eyes. The French are the people who interest themselves the least in such matters, and yet complain that they are without any information.'

—'I do not care,' he replied, 'for those unscientific books. I am anxious that a good, scientific, and authentic book on those points should be written at first hand by some competent Japanese.'

Here a compatriot of mine turned to me, and said privately that the gentleman who had just made the above remark was one who could not be persuaded to believe that Western civilisation had taken root in Japan, and who did not until recently believe that Japan could cope with the Russians. His reason was not on account of any bias against Japan, but because he could not believe Western civilisation could be transplanted to an exotic soil in so short a time, as in the case of Japan. He had only recently begun to think otherwise, after close observation of the progress of the war, and therefore wished to know the true history of the evolution of all the important changes which had taken place in our country.

–'Now you gentlemen have had enough time,' said a lady. 'It is our turn now. I suppose, baron, you will be going home before long, when the war comes to an end. Shall you also be like some of the Japanese I have had the pleasure of knowing? I mean to say that the Japanese are, as a rule, pleasant enough and friendly enough while with us, but after they have gone back to their country we seldom hear from them. But when they happen to revisit this part of the world, they return to us and are as pleasant and friendly as before, as though nothing had happened in the interval.'

–'Ah! I understand. I am afraid I shall be like them. We Japanese are not good correspondents. In that respect I think the English are the best. It seems writing letters is a part of their pleasure. They write so many letters even in the midst of hasty travelling. Our heads somehow seem heavy when it comes to the task of letter-writing. When we go back to Japan, unless we are engaged in some offices where foreign languages are needed, we have no occasion to think or to write in them, and we soon forget the thread of the foreign style of thought and tongue, and, therefore, it is difficult even to find good dicta for writing a simple letter. Remember, moreover, there is nothing so difficult as writing simple letters; especially is it so with us Japanese. Then, again, the paper, ink, and pens which we use for our own writing are totally different from yours, and they are useless for writing Occidental characters. Therefore, when we think of writing a letter to an Occidental friend, we might find the ink-bottle quite dry, nibs quite rotten, and the sheets of writing paper may be wanting, and perhaps we should have to send for them all anew. The spelling of quite common words may not be at our command, and if we just wished to refer to a dictionary, we should perhaps find that it had been mislaid somewhere among the heaps of

268

Japanese books, or perhaps had been taken away altogether by a young student. Such being the case, you can well imagine that the Japanese cannot be very good correspondents if they wished. The fact that they do not write letters does not show that they do not remember old friendships, and therefore, if they happen to revisit the West, they would be, as you say, as friendly and pleasant as though nothing had happened in the interval.'

−'That explains the matter very well,' said she. 'I am sure you will be like one of those, especially as you will have so much to do for your country, perhaps in some busy office in the Government.'

−'You are quite right in the first part of your observation. I have no reputation for being a good correspondent. Perhaps you know that the great Marlborough always felt much difficulty in writing letters. He used to say that he would sooner fight a great battle, and with more ease, than write a letter of fifteen lines to his wife, so you will see I have some consolation, because even amongst the English there are those who are not particularly fond of writing letters. As to the second part of your observation, you are wrong. I have no desire to seek office. I do not care for the hustle and bustle of the world. I prefer to spend my time calmly and quietly in the midst of nature, and therefore, after my return to Japan, you will hear of me no more. If you ever happen to hear of me, it will only be when some grave and exceptional circumstance of my country requires my service, whereby I may be obliged to sacrifice my own inclination. But I must now say "exit."'

So saying, I left the group. On my way back home, I dropped into the coffee-room of an hotel and met there accidentally a rich young Scandinavian artist, whom I had met before, when once staying at that hotel. He was with two ladies, an operatic singer and her mother, both of whom were American by birth. From their appearance, and from what I have since heard, they belonged to a well-to-do family. She had taken to her present profession rather on account of a natural gift for singing than from any necessity. Her mother had come over to Paris for a short time to visit her daughter and was staying at the hotel. Through the Scandinavian we soon came to know each other, and as we took coffee together we had some conversation, which naturally turned on the Japanese stage. In the course of the conversation, I furnished them with a number of details in connection with the subject in answer to their questions:

'On our stage some actors act female parts, as was the case with the European stage from the Greeks down to recent centuries in Modern Europe. With us, however, unlike your ancient stage, grown-up actors, not necessarily youths, act all important female parts, and yet they imitate real females so well, that it is regarded as almost a marvel. They have a peculiar method of making use of certain muscles and bones which make their movements resemble those of women. It requires much training from boyhood, and that is the reason why the female characters of the new school, of which I shall speak presently, are not so realistic as those of the old school. Our best actors are those who can act well both male and female characters, but naturally there are some who are more fitted than others for acting female parts. Shikwan is one of the best actors at this moment. I read recently a letter written by a New York lady, while on a visit to Japan, who is reputed a great patron of the stage. It was addressed to Shikwan, and sent, together with a bouquet. In it she says that it was almost amazing to her to have seen him acting the part of a great warrior and soon after the part of a delicate and noble lady, and that she considered him the first actor in the world. I think there is a great deal of truth in her remarks. Most foreigners who first visit our theatre can hardly be made to believe that the female characters are actually acted by males. The architectural peculiarities of our stage are:—First, the greater part of it is a large, round, movable platform on pivots, and is used to great advantage for "decorative properties" as well as for the acting. Secondly, we have the so-called "flower ways" on both sides of the stalls. They can also be used with great effectiveness for some kinds of acting, though it would be rather difficult to have them in the European style of stage building. It is, however, a very common mistake of most Europeans to think we have no actresses. We have actresses as well as actors, only they form different and separate companies, and it is only seldom and of recent date that they act together. Danjiuro was the greatest actor we have had in recent centuries. Kikugoro and then Sadanji came next They were regarded as "the trio," but all three have died within the last few years. We do not think we shall have the same talent again for many years to come. A Garrick, a Henry Irving, or a Sarah Bernhardt is not a production of every generation. Danjiuro in particular was accounted, even by Occidental visitors, among the few of the greatest actors of the world. Curiously enough there was much resemblance between the personal character and style of acting of Danjiuro and Sir Henry Irving. The forte of Danjiuro was historical representations, and so it was with Irving. Danjiuro acted more in spirit, that is to say, with as little action and rhetoric as possible, but with more suppressed but visible emotion. When he began this style of acting in his younger days, he was not popular at first: people thought he lacked theatrical display, but he soon succeeded in manifesting his great ability. Not only did he work out his own way, but he elevated the public taste. He also much improved the social and moral tone of his profession by the force of his character. In all these respects, I think there was much resemblance between him and Sir Henry Irving. The old stage, however, is hampered by much conventionality which is not entirely suited to modern taste. This has brought forward the new school. Oto Kawakami, the husband of Sada-Yakko, was the pioneer of that school. Sada-Yakko, who is known very well to the Occidentals, and is highly appreciated by them, is no more than a gifted amateur, who joined her husband's company through his influence. In Japan it is called the "student plays," because actors belonging to that school are mostly students. In the early days of that school, plays acted by its actors were little else than mere charades, of the most comical nature, even when the meaning was grave. As time went on, they have become more and more skilful, so that eventually something has been produced worth seeing, more especially because they are not hampered by any old conventionality or tradition. They can produce on the stage any incident which they deem worth showing, and they can introduce any innovation which the old school would not dare to do. Besides, these actors being students themselves, they have one advantage of having more educational intelligence than the greater number of the actors belonging to the old school. There is, therefore, much hope for the future in the new school, and it is making rapid progress, so much so, that its influence is being reflected on the old school.'

During the conversation, I was asked by the gentleman to witness the young singer's performance, in which request the ladies joined. I had no other course than to accept. Time in Dreamland flies fast, and I soon found myself at one of the Operas together with the Scandinavian gentleman; and there, to my surprise, I found the young singer was a prima donna. The act was Maritana; she acted the male part of Don Cæsar. The performance went on splendidly, and Act

272

II. was reached. I happened to know the following declamation by Don Cæsar, and when she sang it I was thrilled, because each word sounded as though uttered by our own heroes of times gone by:

'Ah! per pietà, signor, non raddoppiate
  L'aspro mio duol! Almen mi fosse dato
  Per grazia di morir come un soldato!

Come sul campo il milite
  Pugnando suol morir,
  Concedi a me da libero
  Soldato i di finir!
  Tosto l'acciar fulmineo
  Decida omai di me!
  Dirà ciascuno, il misero
  Da prode morto egli è,
  Dirà ciascuno, il misero
  Da prode morto egli è
  Da prode morto egli è.

Se di mia stirpe l'ultimo,
  Rampollo in me sen'va,
  Degli avi degno il povero
  Don Cesare morrà.
  Se freddo avel marmoreo
  Non si concede a me,
  Mi basta sol che dicano:
  "Da prode morto egli è."'

'Ah! spare, oh spare my ancient name
  From such foul disgrace—one boon,
  It is the last I shall ask thee,

'Tis to die, e'en like a soldier.

Yes! let me like a soldier fall,
Upon some open plain,
This breast expanding for the ball
To blot out ev'ry stain.
Brave manly hearts confer my doom,
That gentler ones may tell,
Howe'er forgot, unknown my tomb,
I like a soldier fell,
Howe'er forgot, unknown my tomb,
I like a soldier fell,
I like a soldier fell.

I only ask of that proud race,
Which ends its blaze in me,
To die the last, and not disgrace
Its ancient chivalry.
Tho' o'er my clay no banner wave,
Nor trumpet requiem swell,
Enough, they murmur o'er my grave,
"He like a soldier fell.'"

The curtain fell: my companion asked me if I would like to see the stage room of the singer. I assented, we passed through the Green Room, and entered her room, where she was sitting on a chair, her mother with her. After an exchange of a few words, she plucked a few blossoms from a branch of orchids in a vase on the table near her, and put them into my button-hole, saying, 'Allow me,' and then, plucking some more, similarly favoured my companion. At that moment the stage-bell rang, and as I thought we were dashing out of the room and down the stairs, I awoke, and saw my young secretary standing before me. He said: 'The dinner-bell has rung; you have slept very long.'

APPENDIX

I

POLITICAL ORGANISM OF JAPAN

This article is intended to explain the salient points of the political organism of the Japanese Empire, a subject on which many people have expressed to me their wishes to be informed. The chief sources of my authority are, of course, the Imperial Constitution and the Imperial House Law promulgated February 11, 1889, but I have also made use of several other important laws and known facts bearing on the subject.

THE EMPEROR

The emperor is sacred and inviolable according to the constitution. His majesty is the sole depository of sovereignty. Legislative power is given to the Imperial Diet, but the theory of our constitution is that the emperor himself exercises that power with the concurrence of the Diet. Other attributes of the emperor, such as the authority for convoking or dissolving the Diet, sanctioning or vetoing laws, promulgating the same, declaring war or making peace, ordering amnesty or pardon, or conferring honours, such as titles of nobility, etc., are much the same as those of the most of the Western monarchical countries. One important feature which is without a parallel in the constitution of almost all other countries (except perhaps some resemblance in the Austrian constitution) is that in

275

Japan the emperor has the power to issue 'Urgency Ordinances' which have the same force as the law when urgency requires such enactments in order to maintain public safety or to avert public calamity, and it happens that the Diet is not sitting, though such ordinances have to be submitted to the Diet and its ex-post-facto consent obtained in the next session, and they lose their force in case such consent is withheld by the Diet. Another important feature is that in Japan, unlike several constitutional countries, all matters relating to the organisation of the army or navy or the determination of the number of the standing army are entirely within the sphere of the Imperial prerogative and beyond interference by the diet though the latter has an indirect voice by reason of its participation in matters of 'supply.'

THE IMPERIAL SUCCESSION

The established usage in respect of the Imperial succession of Japan has always been in the main that of primogeniture on male lines. There had been, however, no hard-and-fast restriction similar to the Salic Law before the promulgation of the Imperial House Law of 1889, and, accordingly, we have had several empresses on the throne of Japan, though there was never an instance of a reigning empress having a consort. The Imperial House Law has prevented for ever any female succeeding to the throne. We can therefore sum up the order of succession to the Japanese throne as that of the male primogeniture, viz., from the father to the eldest son, then to the eldest grandson and so on, in the direct line, in default of which, to the collateral line. The order of all these is similar to that which appertains to European primogeniture. The ceremony of coronation is always to take place at Kioto, the old capital, so also is the Daijo-Sai, the grand festivity, which is celebrated but once in a reign. The full age of the emperor, the crown prince, and the

276

eldest son of the crown prince, who has become direct heir to the throne owing to the early death of the crown prince, is fixed at full eighteen years, whilst with all the other members of the Imperial family it is full twenty years, like ordinary subjects of the emperor. When the emperor is a minor, a regency is to be instituted. When the emperor is incapacitated by grave causes from discharging his functions, the same thing also takes place. The order in which the regency may devolve upon members of the Imperial family is as under:

(1) The crown prince.

(2) The Imperial grandson, being already direct heir-apparent.

(3) Other princes.

(4) The empress.

(5) The empress-dowager.

(6) The grand empress-dowager.

(7) Princesses who have actually no consorts. Precedence amongst the princes is determined by the order in which they stand for succession to the throne, and that of princesses is determined in a similar way.

During the minority of the emperor, a grand guardian (Taifu) is appointed. In case no person for that office be named by the will of the departed emperor, he is to be appointed by the regent after having consulted the Imperial family council and the Privy Council. He cannot be removed unless the matter first be submitted to the consideration of the above-named councils. When a prince or princess is appointed regent, he or she shall not, during the tenure, abdicate in favour of any one except in the case where the crown prince or his eldest son, who had already become direct heir to the throne, has become qualified for the function on account of his attaining full age.

THE GOVERNMENT

The administrative affairs of the empire are discharged by a minister-president of state, and a number of the ministers of state. The ministers of state as they stand at present are: (1) The Interior. (2) The Foreign. (3) Finance. (4) War. (5) Navy. (6) Justice. (7) Communications. (8) Education. (9) Commerce and Agriculture. The chiefs of these ministries, viz., the ministers of state, form the cabinet under the presidency of the minister-president. The system and actual working of the cabinet is similar to those of the advanced Western nations. A cabinet meeting is held usually once a week, and important affairs of state are discussed therein. The cabinet as a body is responsible to the emperor for those affairs, though each minister has great latitude of action in matters which fall exclusively within the sphere of his ministry. There are many matters which do not require personal discussion. These are circulated among the ministers in the form of documents for their signature. Matters discussed or considered in document by the ministers, and which require Imperial sanction are submitted to the emperor by documents, or personally explained to his majesty by the minister-president or other ministers as the case may be; but when very important matters are discussed in the cabinet, it is always in the actual presence of the emperor. There is a minister for the Imperial household, but neither he nor his ministry have anything to do with state affairs, i.e. politics; consequently, the minister of the Imperial household is not a member of the cabinet.

278

There is a Privy Council, which consists of a president, vice-president, and about two dozen councillors, and these form the supreme consultative council of the emperor. It discusses and considers important state affairs when it is commanded by the emperor to present its views on any given matter.

The Ministry of Justice has control of the administrative sections of judicial affairs, but law courts have their distinctive organisation, and the judges are quite independent of administrative interference. They are appointed for life and can be dismissed only for grave causes indicated by law.

Besides the War Ministry, there is a General Staff Office, and in addition to the Naval Ministry there is the Naval General Staff Office. The demarcation of the spheres of their competency is that administrative affairs relating to the army and navy are controlled by the ministries, and those relating to technical and strategic matters, or such like, are controlled by the staff office. Both staff offices have a chief and a vice-chief. They are naturally not members of the cabinet. In time of war a special Imperial headquarters under the direct control of the emperor is constituted.

All officials in Government service have before their appointments to undergo a requisite examination, except when the appointment is for the position of the Ministership of State.

THE DIET

The Imperial Diet consists of two houses: the House of Peers and the House of Representatives. There is no difference of privilege between the two houses, except that the annual budget is to be first submitted to the House of Representatives, and that the latter may be dissolved, while no law exists for the dissolution of the former; further, that the president and vice-president of the Upper House are appointed by the emperor from amongst the members, whilst those of the Lower House are appointed by the emperor out of three candidates for each elected by the House.

The Representatives are elected by direct votes of electors. Until recent years the country was divided into many small electoral districts (nearly three hundred, in fact). Each district elected one representative, and a few elected two representatives, the difference having arisen from the difficulty of demarking the Sphere uniformly, on account of the local peculiarities and the number of the population. The total number of the representatives amounted to just three hundred. A great change was introduced in recent years in the system of election. Each prefecture now forms one large electoral district, except that all the cities, although they are all situated within the prefecture, form separate districts, each independently. Each district elects a certain number of representatives allotted to it by law, based upon the number of the population of such district. (In cases of extremely small cities the allotment is only one representative.) Each elector may vote for only one candidate whatever may be the number of representatives allotted to that district. Men who have polled the largest number of votes are picked out to the allotted number, and they are regarded as elected, but in all cases the elected must have polled one-fifth of the number obtained by dividing the whole number of the registered electors by the number of the representatives allotted to the district. This mode of election is called the 'large-district single-vote-system.' It easily enables the minority of the district to have themselves represented in the Diet. When any vacancy occurs within a year from the election, the one who has polled the largest number next to the elected takes his seat, provided that he had also polled the requisite quorum of votes as above mentioned. The voting is by ballot (anonymous). There are, of course, some disqualifications for being an elector or a candidate, including the disability of titled noblemen for taking part in the matter. The actual number of the representatives is three hundred and seventy-six. The qualifications of the electors are that they shall be male subjects of twenty-five years old or above, paying ten yen (M 20) of direct taxes and having a year's residence in the district. The qualifications of the candidates are that they shall be male subjects thirty years old or above, and their terms are four years.

The composition of the House of Peers is somewhat complicated. The Japanese name for it is 'Kizoku-in.' 'Kizoku' is generally translated as peers, and it certainly means noble or high families, but not in the strict sense of titled people in the West. For the strict equivalent of peers or nobility, in the Western sense, we have another term 'Kwazoku.' Our House of Peers consists of the following members, who must always be males:

(1) Male members of the Imperial family who have attained their full age.

(2) Princes (dukes) and marquises who have attained the age of twenty-five years.

Both these classes (one and two) sit in the House by their inherent right.

(3) Representatives elected by counts, viscounts, and barons from amongst themselves, each grade separately.

The numbers of such representatives is previously determined, always not exceeding one-fifth of the total number of each grade. They must be twenty-five years old, and their terms are seven years.

(4) Life members appointed by the emperor by virtue of distinguished services rendered to the state, or of intellectual distinction. They all of them must be fully thirty years old; nearly all of those who are thus nominated do not belong to the nobility in the strict sense of the term.

(5) Members elected, one for each prefecture, by mutual election of fifteen highest direct-tax payers of each of the respective prefectures. Such tax payers must be thirty years old, and their paying the taxes must be on account of the lands they hold or of industry or commerce. Therefore, one who simply lives on an income derived from state-bonds would hardly be entitled to claim this privilege. The terms of these members are also seven years. The total number in classes four and five may not exceed the total number in classes two and three, viz., members belonging purely to the nobility.

The Diet is to be convoked once a year for an ordinary session, the length of which is three months, and can be prolonged when necessary. Special sessions may be instituted when necessary. All members of both Houses, except those belonging to classes number one and number two of the Upper House, or those who are in the government service, receive two thousand yen (M 4000) a year, whilst presidents and vice-presidents receive five thousand yen and three thousand yen respectively.

ARMY AND NAVY

The recruiting and organisation of the Japanese army are very much like those of the European continental powers, especially those of Germany, from whom we have learned much. Those of the Japanese navy are like those of England, except that our sailors are taken not only from volunteers, but also by obligatory service; in other words, youths who have to serve as soldiers by the universal service system may be taken for sailors, considerations of course being given to their personal inclination. These latter, i.e. obligatory ones, form about half the total number in the navy.

LOCAL ADMINISTRATION

The whole of Japan proper is divided into forty-five prefectures. The prefectures of Tokio, Kioto, and Osaka are called Fu, whilst all others are called Ken. The difference is more a matter of sentiment than anything else, for there is no difference whatever for any practical purposes. The administrative systems of Hokkaido, Okinawa, and Formosa each diverge from those of Japan proper to some extent, though they are gradually being made similar to those of the main islands. I therefore put those three Islands, Hokkaido, Okinawa, and Formosa, outside the scope of the present paper for the sake of convenience. Each prefecture is presided over by a governor appointed by the central Government. It is partly an administrative district of the state and partly a communal district having its communal administration supported by local taxes. For this latter aspect each prefecture has a local assembly, members of which are elected by direct votes of electors of the prefecture. Each prefecture is divided into counties, and the counties (Kreis) into rural and urban village communities (Gemeinde). Larger urban communities are incorporated as cities and are made independent of counties. Counties are prefectures on a small scale. Each of them is presided over by a Gun-cho, whose office is very similar to that of a French sub-prefect. But counties also have their communal sides like prefectures and have representative assemblages. The communal side of counties, however, is not very important, because communal affairs on a large scale are discharged by prefectures, and ordinary communal affairs are mostly discharged by village communities. Cities and village communities are the real 'self-governments' of the people. Each of them has a representative assemblage, and elects its own executive officials. The composition of these officials differs in cities and village communities; that in the cities is, of course, more complicated. Even amongst the cities there is a great difference in the degree of importance, because there are many cities which are extremely small, inasmuch as a town having a population over twenty-five thousand could as a rule be incorporated as a city. The existing ordinances for the constitution of these local governments are very much like those of Prussia—in fact, the ordinances for those of the cities and village communities are in a great measure founded upon those of Prussia. The chief points of difference are that, unlike Prussia, our prefectural governments subordinate direct to the central Government, with no intermediary which represents the latter and superintends the former, and that, unlike Prussia, there is in Japan no 'Gutsbezirk' (signorial community) side by side with ordinary communities.

THE CONCLUSION

Such is the political organism of Japan. My description, however, is only the merest skeleton of it. That such a skeleton should be endowed with the proper spirit requires that the whole nation from the sovereign down to the lowest member of the community should be animated by sincerity and loyalty and supported by a liberal and tolerant régime. That Japan is doing her best in those respects, I can only ask my readers to infer from their own observation of the admitted progress that she has been fortunate enough to accomplish so far.

I may, however, explain some of the more important points bearing on the question. The emperor is extremely popular amongst his people at large. I may say that it is not mere popularity in the ordinary sense of the word, but a popularity which is more of the nature of reverence. This reverence for the emperor on the part of the people is manifested in their extreme loyalty. On the other hand, the emperor has not the least inclination to take advantage of it and abuse it for selfish purposes. His majesty entertains the keenest sense of duty in regard to his position, not as a person privileged to do whatever he may choose, but rather as a person to whom is intrusted the great task of taking care of the people over whom he reigns. Thus there exist between the sovereign and his subjects mutual confidence and love, which cannot fail to prove the greatest blessing to the country in any hour of national emergency.

As to the position of the Diet versus the Government, party landmarks are not so strong in Japan as among most of the Western nations. True it is that in Japan also there are several political parties, but the Government is not 'a party government' as it is in England or America. In that respect the Government of Japan most resembles that of Germany. According to the constitution, the Ministers of State are responsible only to the Emperor, but every practical statesman knows that no government can be satisfactorily carried on without concurrence of the Diet so long as there is such a body, and therefore in Japan, also, every Ministry has to do its best to count on such good relations with the parties as it can secure; but, nevertheless, party feeling does not run so high, and party struggles are not so severe as to make the formation of a Cabinet depend on party issues.

The cause of all this is plain so far as we are concerned. The emperor does not interfere with politics, but when at the hour of supreme necessity he manifests his will, his subjects, one and all, instantaneously obey it, and rally around the throne, forgetting for the time being any differences of personal opinion. It was so at the time of the Sino-Japanese war, and again in the Russo-Japanese war. This state of things is due, amongst others, to the liberal administration of the Imperial régime. The press, speech, and right of meeting are for all practical purposes entirely free. Personal freedom is guaranteed by the constitution. Taxes are levied, but no abuse of authority is known. The people at large have no real grounds of complaint or grievance against the Government as such, and have absolutely none against the Emperor. Moreover, Japan knows no difficulty in matters of religion, and consequently no party based upon religious notions exists to give trouble to Government. If this or that section of the people has any disputes with the Government or between themselves, those are essentially questions of some temporary and passing character. Hence in Japan it is not a difficult matter for the people at large to unite themselves under a common national policy in a time of national emergency.

II

JAPANESE EDUCATION[1]

In this paper I shall sketch something of the systems of education in Japan, especially that of elementary education.

My readers, however, must not think I have anything wonderful to show to them; for, as a matter of fact, I have nothing to take them by surprise. All that I can sum up is, that we are doing those things with the utmost sincerity, as we do other things which are already manifest to the Western public In days gone by, that is to say, during the feudal period, there was one college in the capital town of every feudal lord, in which the children of the retainers of Samurai were educated. There were some hundreds of such lords, some great and some petty. Their ranks and importance differed considerably, and naturally the number of their retainers differed; in consequence the scale and magnitude of such colleges also varied. The most famous of them were those of Mito, Chosiu, Kumamoto, and others belonging to great lords. Above all, there was one such belonging to the Shogunate itself. It may be here noted that institutions where the young Samurai practised the use of swords, or spears, or firearms, or the art of jiujitsu, were established sometimes in connection with, and sometimes independently of, these colleges. There were also many plebeian colleges in different parts of the empire. These were mostly private institutions founded by savants. The founders were generally of plebeian origin; but there were among them many who were originally Samurai, and who betook themselves to such occupation from love of independence, or some other causes. But it must be remembered that, though they did not belong officially to the cadre of Samurai, yet the social respect paid to them was great. In such a private institution, the founder himself was the master, assisted by those of his pupils who were more advanced than others. The master taught the advanced pupils, or gave general lectures for the benefit of all; and the advanced taught and gave lectures to the less advanced. The pupils were generally youths of plebeian gentry, but not exclusively so, because many of the youthful Samurai from all parts of the empire enlisted themselves as pupils,

287

especially when any such institution had become famous on account of the achievements of the master and of the general work of the institution.

The curricula of such colleges, both of the official ones of feudal lords and of private ones, were diverse, but generally comprised elementary as well as higher education. There was, of course, no uniform course of study to restrain the method of teaching; and every inventive faculty was employed in each college, so that many special characteristics were observable. But one thing which is undeniable was, that ethical training formed one of the most important branches everywhere.

The chief feature of the college institutions of those days, especially of private institutions, was enforced privation and hardship. I can never forget the days when I, in common with all others, of course, ate meals only twice a day, and those, too, of the simplest diet. The food often consisted of nothing else than a little rice with a very little salt, or the like. We ourselves were cooks in turn. We swept and washed out, not only our own rooms, but those of the master also. We often used cold water in the depth of severe winters for the purpose of washing, and suchlike. We heated the water in turn for the baths of our fellow pupils. We sometimes sat up whole nights in winter with scarcely any fire to warm us, in order to accustom ourselves to rigid discipline. In those days no idea of sanitation in the modern sense entered the minds of the master or of ourselves; neither did any outward show of appearance trouble us, nay, the more one was regardless of those things, the more was one thought strong in character. It is, no doubt, due to the training of those days that I, personally, for instance, cannot bear the trouble of appearing like a grandee, or a fashionable person. Thus, for example, I, who never used gloves in my boyhood, cannot endure the discomfort of wearing them, even on winter days.

Amongst the lower classes (peasants or shopkeepers) there was generally one or other private person, in village or town, who could teach elementary writing and reading, and who taught the children in his neighbourhood by establishing a sort of private school. This was very commonly done by a priest of the Buddhist or Shinto temple of the place. It seems that at one time this was done almost universally by the priests of Buddhist temples; so much so, that we have the term Tera-ko-ya. Tera means a Buddhist temple, Ko means children, and Ya means a house—Tera-Ko came generally to mean children who go to learn elementary writing and reading, and Tera-ko-ya to mean the place where such children were taught. We have a famous tragedy, one act of which is called The Scene of Terakoya. There is a translation in German of that act by a German scholar. It is a scene which represents a tragic incident taking place in the tenth century A.D., in a private school for children opened by an old retainer of a nobleman. It has nothing to do with a temple; and yet it is called The Scene of Terakoya.

It was, however, only after the inauguration of the Meiji era that education became thorough and universal. In the earliest days of this era there was an officer called Daigaku-Betto (Chancellor of the University), who was a functionary of great dignity. In the course of a few years a special Ministry was instituted for education, with a Minister of State, who, of course, had a chair in the Cabinet; and that system has ever remained the same. The Minister of Education controls the educational affairs of the whole country. At first the sphere of direct control of the central Government was naturally limited to higher education; but, with the abolition of the feudal system and the gradual consolidation of local administration, the sphere has extended step by step, and has culminated in the present system of universal education.

For the system of education, also, we are indebted to Europe and America; for the method of its practical working is, like many other new institutions, borrowed from the Occidental nations. The only difference perceptible, perhaps, lies in the fact that in Japan the moving force of the whole system is manipulated by the central Government to a greater degree than it is in any other country—certainly far more so than it is in England. The question of how far popular education should be interfered with by the state, or rather what difference of advantage exists between the system whereby the state takes upon itself far-reaching responsibility and one whereby a great margin is left to an independent development of private institutions, is a matter which admits many pros and cons. It is not, however, my business to discuss this problem in this place. The fact remains, that with us the state exercises conspicuous influence in the matter. Almost all the educational institutions of Japan are official or public; for they belong either directly to the state or to the local administrations (Prefectural or Communal), and they are all controlled, directly or indirectly, by the Ministry of Education. There are some private institutions also, it is true; but their number is very small when compared with the others, and even those must abide by the general direction of the state. The reason of this is, that private undertakings for elementary education have to be similar to the compulsory education imposed by the state, and such similarity can only be acquired by following the general direction of the state. In those of a higher standard, it is because there are many things in which certain privileges are given to those persons who possess certain educational qualifications. For instance, in obtaining a postponement of actual enrolment for military service, or in becoming a candidate for civil service examinations, such educational qualifications are generally measured by the standard of certain public institutions; so that private institutions of higher standard have to conform themselves to the direction of the state, if they wish to avail themselves of the aforesaid privileges. The chief reason why in Japan the state takes upon itself so much responsibility in education is, apart from the intrinsic merit per se of the system, that the country, under the circumstances of the period, could not afford to wait patiently the natural growth of extensive private enterprises.

Putting aside special and technical educational institutions, as well as those of a private nature, the grades of our educational institutions are: (1) the Universities; (2) High Colleges, which may be regarded as preparatory Almæ Matres for universities; (3) Middle Schools; (4) Higher Primary Schools; (5) Common Primary Schools.

The first two belong to the state itself. The last three belong to local administrations—in fine, there is one or more of the Middle Schools in each Prefecture, supported by the prefectural taxes, the number varying according to the requirement of the locality; and one or more Higher Primary Schools in each county, and one or more Common Primary Schools in each village-community, all supported by local rates. The case of cities is similar to that of a county and its village-communities put together. The system is thoroughly carried out throughout the country; for I can say that there is no community where a Primary School is not provided. In populous towns there are Kindergarten for the benefit of little boys and girls under school age, though the number of such Garten is still only a few hundreds in all.

Elementary education is compulsory for both boys and girls: the school age begins at six. Common Primary Schools are the places where compulsory education is given. The course is four years. Excuses for absence are taken only in certain cases. According to the official report of the school year of 1901-2, the percentage of the boys receiving requisite elementary education was 93.78, and that of the girls 81.80, the average being 88.05.

The present system of our writing, which is more commonly used than another which consists of phonetic letters only, is very cumbersome, because it consists of a mixture of Chinese ideographs and our phonetic letters. It is a great drawback to our education, nay to our national life. Boys and girls, however, have to learn it; and, therefore, the poor children of Japan have to take more pains than those of other countries, which are blessed with the common use of a phonetic alphabet only.

Boys and girls of all classes attend the same schools— children of rich merchants and county gentry side by side with those of coolies or humblest peasants. Our schools are essentially national institutions for all classes on an equal footing. No class distinction is to be found in them. This holds good with higher institutions. There exist, of course, no longer any colleges like those of former days, which belonged to feudal lords, and were more or less exclusively used by the Samurai class. The emperor and empress have established, out of special interest for the education of nobility, a peers' school and a peers' girls' school in Tokio. But even these schools are not exclusively attended by boys and girls of the nobility; for children of the commons who possess a satisfactory social standard are admitted to them. On the other hand, too, children of the nobility do not necessarily join those schools only; for many such children are sent to ordinary schools, from convenience of locality or from some particular inclination of the parents. The zeal for education has been carried to such an extent, that primary education was made universally free, by a recommendation of the Diet. Without questioning the means of the family to which the children belong; although, under some special circumstances, trifling fees, almost nominal, may be imposed by special permission of the proper authorities.

The method of teaching in Primary Schools has developed itself in the following manner. A few years after the abolition of the feudal system, namely in 1872, the first Normal School was established in Tokio; and some seventy young students were collected. An American school teacher was engaged to train these youths for the purpose. They were divided into two classes, those who acquitted themselves with greater credit at the entrance examination having been given a place in the first class. The American teacher taught the first of these two classes exactly in the same manner as he did in America, the students having become as mere children. One or other of the students belonging to the class so taught, taught in turn the other class in a similar manner, though somewhat modified to suit our requirements. In conjunction with this practice, charts and simple text-books were prepared by some officials of the Ministry of Education who were attached to the school. This was soon followed by an establishment of five more Government Normal Schools in different parts of the empire, and a Women's Normal School in Tokio. In the course of a few years each Prefecture came to establish its own Normal School under subsidy of the Government; and the Government Normal Schools were abolished, except those established in Tokio, which were maintained as before, as a model for the local Normal Schools.

In the development of this scheme the graduates of the first Normal School inaugurated in Tokio played an important part, of course. Since then the system has remained the same in the main; but the method of teaching has been gradually improved by our inventions to meet our own requirements, supplemented by new intelligence brought back from the West by officials or students sent abroad for studying such matters.

The mode of making teachers at present is as follows. There is a High Normal School and a High Women's Normal School established in Tokio by the state; and another has been recently established in Hiroshima, also by the state. Their chief object is to train teachers for higher local institutions, viz., teachers of Prefectural Normal Schools, Middle Schools, and suchlike. In each Prefecture one or more Normal Schools are established. The maximum of accommodation of the Prefectural Normal Schools, together with the numbers of the students to be trained therein, is determined by an ordinance of the central Government, and is made obligatory upon the Prefectures. The students who are trained in Normal Schools, both High and Prefectural, are supported by the State or by the Prefecture, as the case may be, on condition that they serve as teachers for a certain number of years. Teachers thus trained in Prefectural Normal Schools become teachers of all elementary schools. Teachers of this kind are not, of course, quite sufficient in number to fill up all the positions in all schools; so that the want, for instance, of assistants of minor importance is filled up by those to whom certificates are given on certain examination for qualification to take up such position. And, moreover, teachers of some special subject, for instance, drawing, or cutting and sewing, are appointed from amongst those who hold special certificates from the proper authorities. I may here add, that a system of additional emolument for long services and pensions on retirement of teachers, to the local funds of which the state contributes a certain quota, was promulgated some fifteen years ago, as an inducement for their devotion.

Rigidity of physical training, in the way of privation and hardship, has become a thing of the past. But in its place physical training of a sportive and gymnastic character, after the Western style, is much practised. To this, in the case of boys, training of a military character (jiujitsu, fencing, and military drill and manœuvre) has been added in the case of higher grades. This begins from Higher Primary Schools, varying according to age. The credit of the introduction of military drill and manœuvres into our schools and colleges is due to the late Viscount Mori, who was at one time Japanese Minister in London. Moreover, school children are often taken out by their teachers for so-called 'distant excursions'; and, in the case of the higher grades, this often takes place during summer vacation for many days or weeks, in the shape of camping out and manœuvring, or of round trips to places of historic interest, something like a pilgrimage. Such trips of Large numbers of students, which are called 'educational excursions,' are personally conducted by the masters.

I do not propose here to describe in detail the curriculum of the Primary Schools, still less those of all institutions of higher grades, as this would only weary my readers. All these curricula are in the main similar to those of the Western nations. There is, however, one branch of which they would like me to say something: it is the teaching of morality. In former days in Japan, moral teaching meant more than half of education. Even under the altered circumstances of recent time, this notion is still kept very vividly. Especial stress in this respect, however, is laid in Primary Schools. One thing noticeable is, that with us the morality taught in the public schools is entirely secular.

Some vague notion of heaven or of a supreme being or gods, in a vague sense, might occur here and there in the course of it; but morality never has any colour of a religious, still less of a denominational character. The main principle of morality is laid down in an Imperial injunction commonly called the 'Imperial Educational Rescript,' which is reverenced by teacher and student alike; but, besides this, there are several text-books, based upon the principles laid down in the Rescript, and written in a style to suit the requirements of the grades, indeed, of each class, on a progressive method. The entity of the Rescript and the text-books form an embodiment of practical ethics illustrated by practical examples. They teach how to be honest, how to be straightforward, how to be loyal, how to be patriotic, to honour one's parents, to be truthful to friends, and suchlike. On this point, however, I must refer my readers to my article entitled 'Moral Teaching of Japan,' in which I have given a detailed account of the subject.[2]

Nevertheless, I may add a few words. In Japan all virtues are mainly viewed as a point of duty of those upon whom the conduct of those virtues is incumbent. Thus to be loyal to the emperor is the duty of a subject; to be patriotic is the duty of a citizen to his country; truthfulness is the duty of a friend; and reverence is the duty of a child to its parents; and so on. In teaching morality to children, the sense of duty is constantly kept in view. Then again, in Oriental ethics the term 'name' has an important bearing. It may often be translated as 'fame'; but it has in reality a wider and more pious signification. We have a proverb: 'Tigers leave skins behind when dead, and men leave (or should leave) names.' Here the term 'name' may certainly be translated as 'fame'; but we often say that 'we must not disgrace the name,' meaning that we must not disgrace ourselves or our family by committing any unworthy action. In Japan, to acquire fame and not disgrace one's

296

family name are concurrent thoughts. Fame does not mean a satisfaction of vanity. The trend of thought is something like this 'Do not commit any bad act, for it will disgrace your name, which is the greatest shame to one's self and to one's family. If your name shines out, so much the better, as it is a sure sign that you have behaved well or have done something good, something worthy of yourself, your family, or your ancestors; but to seek notoriety out of mere vanity is despicable, for it is not good conduct and does not deserve a good name,' This notion of 'name' permeates very widely in our idea of morality, which fact will explain many cases wherein a Japanese prefers death to life. Perhaps the word 'honour' may convey the nearer meaning of the word 'name'; in fact, the Western word 'honour' is generally translated in Japanese by a combination of the words name and fame, as 'Meiyo.' This notion of 'name' is impressed in one way or other upon the minds of our youths from childhood, that is to say, from their days of elementary education; and it exercises a great influence in after life.

[1] The Independent Review, August 1905.

[2] See The Risen Sun.

III

ANGLO-FRENCH DIPLOMACY IN JAPAN FORTY YEARS AGO[1]

It is now some forty years ago since there took place in Japan some very interesting episodes of English and French diplomacy, which are little known to the Western public.

It was during the last days of the Shogunate and before the restoration of the Imperial régime. The Western powers with whom Japan had treaty relations were still few in number at that time. The principal of them were: The United States of America, England and France. Holland, though secondary, as she is, had some semblance of equality with the others from the fact that she was a nation which had had commercial relations with us for a longer time than they. Russia and Germany were already in treaty relations with us also, but in the practical sphere of diplomacy they had not played much part. It was England and France who displayed the greatest activity in that sphere. They were both represented by very interesting characters: England by Sir Harry Parkes and France by Léon Roches. It is needless to comment on what an interesting character Sir Harry Parkes was, as doubtless his biography is well known to my readers. I will give here, however, a concise outline of his life.

At the early age of fourteen years he was attached to an English consulate in China. He soon acquired the Chinese tongue, and his extraordinary activity and ability gave him good chances of advancing his position. At the time of the Anglo-French expedition to Peking he was attached to the English army, and many adventurous and romantic incidents are told about him in connection with it. After that expedition he was made English Consul-General at Shanghai, and soon afterwards transferred to Japan as minister, in succession to Sir Rudford Alcock. Sir Harry may be regarded as an adventurer.

Léon Roches was of a similar character; he began his career in Algeria in a most adventurous and romantic manner. He was subsequently made French agent in Tunis and thence was transferred to Japan, as minister, by Napoleon III. It was through his influence that France succeeded in drawing the Shogun's government into her confidence. Military instructors were sent from France, the Yokosuka dockyard was constructed with French materials, a young brother of the Shogun was sent a little later on to Paris, where he stayed for many years as the favourite of the court of Napoleon. In other words, French influence was paramount in Yedo, the present Tokio, the site of the Shogun's government.

Parkes arrived in Japan at that juncture. In the Crimean war, England and France, needless to say, were allies; so also were they in the Chinese war. At home the Courts of St. James' and that of the Tuileries were on intimate terms. Besides, in Japan, their interests, broadly speaking, were identical, and, therefore, their policy did not diverge very much, as far as their national interests were concerned, and yet their views concerning the domestic politics of Japan presented a marked difference. It was the time when, as every one knows, Japan was divided into two camps of public opinion. On one side the Shogunate partisans and on the other the Imperialists, amongst whom Chosiu was the most prominent. France sided with the Shogunates, whilst England gradually gave her sympathy to the Imperialists. Several reasons seem to have existed in connection therewith. At home, though Napoleon was apparently still at the height of his power, he seems to have felt the necessity of making some pompous display of power abroad, in order to appease the growing discontent among the people. Léon Roches was just the sort of man who would have done things which would suit Napoleon's secret designs, and therefore, when the conflict between the

299

Shogunate and the Imperialists reached an acute state, it is said that France offered to help the Shogunate with her money and even with her military forces. On the other hand England, or rather Harry Parkes, thought that the Imperial cause was more just, and, therefore, deserved more sympathy.

It is now pretty well known to Western readers that, though in the administrative authorities the Shogunate appeared potent, in the question of the legitimacy of the title, that is to say, the sovereignty, the Imperial court was viewed as the only lawful head by the Japanese in general, nay, it was so in the point of fact. But in those days, foreigners used to say and to think that the emperor was only the spiritual head and the Shogun was the temporal chief of Japan, and they were unable to see what turning movements were approaching, the result of which would be the restoration of the Imperial authority and the consolidation of the country under one single head in the person of the emperor, as the sovereign de facto as well as de jure. It was only natural for onlookers to fail to penetrate such matters, and Léon Roches, sagacious as he was, was unable to differ from others. With Harry Parkes the case was different. He had grown up in the Far East: he was well acquainted with the Chinese ideographs; he understood Oriental thought contained in books and documents, written with those ideographs. Besides, several of his countrymen already in Japan had kept keen observation of the true situation and had intercourse with several Imperialist patriots, and their counsel could not fail to be valuable to Sir Harry. He was soon able to realise the relative positions occupied in the organic composition of Japan by the Imperial court and the Shogunate respectively. Thus the English policy, that is Parkes, came to differ from that of France, that is Léon Roches. Roches's sympathy continued to be on the side of the Shogunate, even after the latter had suffered defeats,

300

which may be shown by the fact that when Admiral Enomoto left the Bay of Yedo with his fleets after the submission of the Shogun and went to Hakodate, several French military instructors went with him. It is true they left the troops of Enomoto before the latter was brought to submission, but they would not have gone with him at all if the French representative had ceased to sympathise with the Shogunate's cause. Roches's influence had been gradually eclipsed by that of Parkes. It is imaginable, however, that should the advisers of the Shogunate have accepted Roches's offer as to money and forces, the course of the history of Japan might have presented some difference, although the ultimate end would have been just the same. Nevertheless, thanks to the loyalty and patriotism, before which there is no difference of sentiment and opinion amongst the Japanese, no countenance had been given to the policy of Roches by the Shogunate, which preferred its own downfall rather than an acceptance of foreign assistance.

As to Parkes, although his sympathies were elsewhere than with the Shogunate from the beginning, officially speaking he was a minister accredited to the court of the Shogunate. Nevertheless, he had sufficient foresight how to protect English interests, and, moreover, several other causes made him incline towards the Imperial court.

A year or two before, Ito and Inouyé returned from England to Chosiu. They were thoroughly changed from fierce anti-foreign partisans to pro-foreign propagandists. On account of this visit to and return from England, they became acquainted with several Englishmen who were then in Japan, such as Lowder, Glover, and Satow. When they, together with Takasugi and Yamagata and others, revolted against the then government of Chosiu, which temporarily had gained the power and favoured more conciliatory policy with the Shogunate, and established a new one in defiance of the Shogunate, Takasugi held an opinion that the time would soon come when the question of Chosiu versus the Shogunate would become one of Japan versus Western nations, and that it would be better for him to prepare himself for the future eventuality, leaving domestic affairs in the hands of his friends. He communicated this idea to his intimate friends, Ito and Inouyé, who agreed with him. He asked Ito to accompany him. Together they left their homeland of Chosiu and went to Nagasaki with the full intention of going to Europe, which would be the second voyage for Ito and the first for Takasugi, though the latter had once been abroad as far as Shanghai a few years before.

This was just the time when Parkes was appointed English minister and expected to arrive at Japan from Shanghai before long. At Nagasaki, Takasugi and Ito met with Glover and Lowder. They were told by them that Parkes was a person of interesting character, and that by effecting communication with him some great work might be done. Besides, they were told, it was not time for them to leave their home for Europe. Time was important, and it would be far more interesting if they were, for instance, to take up a plan for opening Shimonoseki to foreign trade. They agreed and returned to Chosiu. In no time the government of the Shogun despatched the second expedition to Chosiu, and war commenced, the result of which was a total repulse of the Shogunate troops.

Here I must say something about Satsuma. Kagoshima, the capital of Satsuma, had been bombarded by the English fleet a few years before. When peace was made, some kind of friendship began to be felt between the English and Satsuma men. Several young and promising Samurai of Satsuma repeatedly visited Nagasaki, and in one way or another they were also acquainted with the Englishmen whom Ito knew. Before the war with the Shogunate, Ito went to Nagasaki several times, chiefly for purchasing war materials, but it may be presumed that a good deal of diplomatic conversation took place between him and the Englishmen as well as Satsuma men. From these circumstances, and also from the circumstances which brought Sakamoto of Tosa into close contact with Ito and his friends, an understanding soon began to grow between Satsuma and Chosiu, which ultimately resulted in their secret alliance. In the course of a few years the tide of events turned greatly in favour of the Imperialists, and the Shogunate at last came to an end.

Soon after the battle of Fushimi no time was lost in intimating at the initiation of Ito the restoration of the Imperial Government to foreign representatives, who were at the time staying at Osaka. It may be presumed that an early acceptance of this situation was largely due to an understanding existing previously between the English representative and the Chosiu and Satsuma, through such men as Ito, Inouyé of Chosiu and Godai and Komatsu of Satsuma who were also frequenters of Nagasaki. Soon after that event the first audience was given at the Imperial Palace of Kioto to English and French ministers. At that time there were still many anti-foreign fanatics: on the way taken by Parkes from his quarters in a temple to the Imperial Palace, he was attacked by a fanatic. Several of his mounted English escort were injured. Goto and Nakai, whose names are well known in Japan, were escorting Parkes. They did their utmost in defending him, and killed the assassin on the spot, in consequence of which Nakai received severe injuries on his forehead. Parkes returned to his quarters; it was a critical moment for the Imperial cause. Ito was at the Palace: it was his duty to introduce the ministers to the emperor. Roches arrived at the Palace, but not Parkes. Presently a note addressed to the French minister came from Parkes, and also the tidings of the occurrence. Ito put the note into his pocket for a moment and told Roches to have his audience first, because it was no use to wait for Parkes. The audience ended and the note was handed to Roches, but it was too late for him to say anything. As to Parkes, Ito and others found no great difficulty in pacifying him, especially because the sincerity of the Government was demonstrated by the action of Goto and Nakai. Parkes had an audience of the emperor next day; and thus the foreign relations between the Imperial court and those of the Treaty Powers were formally established.

Thus we see that France once backed a wrong horse, but it was not in any way due to her fault. We have soon entirely forgiven and forgotten, nay more, good friendship soon began to be felt between the two nations. Military instructors, as well as jurists, were invited from France. The army was organised and distributed after the French system. The Code Napoleon was studied and translated into Japanese. The French language was studied in the schools. Even a special school was instituted by the Government for studying the French language and law. Of recent years, I am sorry to notice things have not gone so satisfactorily. Some sorts of coldness of feeling have entered between the two countries, compared with the Anglo-Saxon races. It is natural enough that there should exist more sympathy between Japan and England and America, because the latter two have a far more extensive intercourse with us—the greatest number of foreign residents in Japan being first English, next American. And yet I do not see why French and Japanese friendship should not be restored to the warmth of former days, or indeed be made warmer than in those days. Let us hope France does not repeat too often her errors of backing wrong horses—for on our part we have no thought of remembering long other people's errors which may be committed against us.

[1] L'Européen, July 15, 1905.

IV

SKETCHES OF SOME CHIEF FIGURES OF ACTUAL JAPAN

ITO, YAMAGATA, INOUYÉ, MATSUKATA, KATSURA, OKUMA, SAIONJI

It is impossible to give a comprehensive account of the lives of these personages, because to do so would be to write a history of Japan of the last half century. I will, however, give you the chief points.

Marquis Ito is considered by common consent of the Japanese as the greatest statesman of Japan at this moment; there is scarcely a single political institution of modern Japan in which he has not shared the initiation. Many people in the West call him the 'Maker of New Japan,' and it is not far from fact. In other words, I may say that the greatest service which he has rendered to Japan is her Europeanisation, for it has been done more by his efforts than by those of any other. It is, however, a remarkable fact that he was in his youth one of the most ardent participators of the anti-foreign party. Not quite fifty years ago, when but a young man of seventeen or eighteen, Japan was in a state of internal commotion; the country was divided into two camps of opinion, one pro-foreign, and the other anti-foreign. The Prince of Chosiu belonged to the latter. There were many young men in Chosiu who were ardent in the anti-foreign propaganda, and young Ito was one of them. It was they who occasionally tried to attack foreigners, and on one occasion actually set fire to the buildings just completed to be used as foreign legations. Most of these young men were pupils of Yoshida Shoin, who was known as a pioneer of the new Imperial régime which resulted in the unification of Japan under one single sovereign, and therefore is sometimes compared with Mazzini of Italy. Shoin held anti-foreign sentiments and imbued the men of his day with his views. But it must not be understood that Shoin was an anti-foreign à outrance, because we can see from his writings that his views were not opposed to foreign intercourse altogether, but he did not like the manner in which the Europeans forced their way into the Far East in those days. In one of his essays he states 'let us first consolidate the empire and then let us send our ambassador, say, for example, to San Francisco, and there conclude a treaty.'

His primary object was to restore the Imperial authority to its ancient condition, and thus consolidate the empire. However it may be, the fact remains that Chosiu was the foremost of the feudal clans who adopted the anti-foreign action. Even at that time, however, there were some even in Chosiu who had the foresight to make some 'live machines,' as they called the young men of talent who were to meet future necessities when the empire might ultimately be opened to the West, and some of the young men referred to above also saw the necessity of making of themselves such machines. In consequence of this, five young men of Chosiu sailed to England contrary to the then existing prohibition of the Shogun government Two of these five were the present Marquis Ito and Count Inouyé. They got on board an English ship at Yokohama, with some difficulty and risk, of course. At Shanghai they separated. Ito and Inouyé went on board one sailing vessel and the other three on board another. They knew little English then. One of the words they knew was navigation. On board the English ship Ito and Inouyé told the captain of the vessel that they wished to learn navigation, and he set them to work as common sailors. They all reached London after several months' voyage round the Cape of Good Hope. I may here mention that Yoshida Shoin, when Commodore Perry came to the coast of Uraga, had tried to get on board one of his ships and be taken to America in order that he might personally see the Western countries, but was refused, and in consequence he suffered imprisonment on account of his venturesome attempt. It is, however, mentioned in Perry's Expedition, commenting on Shoin's attempt very favourably, that 'a nation which produces such a youth had a great future before it.' Of course, Yoshida's name was not then known to Americans, and they, therefore, knew nothing of his character. Regarding this incident, we may say that the five youths who left Japan in the above manner were in a measure fulfilling the cherished desire of Shoin.

Ito and Inouyé soon perceived what kind of people the Western nations were and what kind of civilisation they possessed. In the meantime the internal commotion of Japan accelerated to a very acute degree. The troops of Chosiu bombarded several European merchantmen in the strait of Shimonoseki from their fortifications, and soon afterwards some troops were sent from Chosiu to Kioto, where much political complication prevailed at the time, between the partisans of the Shogunate and Chosiu. When the news of the bombardment of Shimonoseki reached England, Ito and Inouyé thought that anti-foreign policy would be futile, and that it would be better to devote the national energy more to the internal consolidation of the empire. To this end they determined to go back to Japan in order to persuade their Prince and government to their newly acquired views, and on leaving the other three behind in England, they told them to finish their education so that they might realise their hope of becoming 'live machines.'

The history of what they did when they reached Japan is recorded in the contemporary diplomatic documents of England and some other countries, and also in some English books on Japan, so I need not dwell upon it here. I may, however, state that they ultimately reached Chosiu with much difficulty, having been first conveyed to an island near Chosiu by an English man-of-war. Just at that time the troops of Chosiu, which had been stationed in the neighbourhood of Kioto for some months, fought against the troops under the Shogunate and were defeated. In the meantime, the combined fleets of England, France, the United States, and Holland, made their entry into the straits of Shimonoseki. Before the youthful Ito and Inouyé had succeeded in persuading their Prince and compatriots to adopt pro-foreign policy, Shimonoseki was bombarded. Peace was concluded, which was greatly due to the endeavours of Ito and Inouyé and their bosom friend Takasugi. Soon after the Shogun government decided on an invasion of Chosiu, and surrounded it on all sides with the troops of the Shogunate under its immediate command, and also those of the feudal lords who were partisans of the Shogunate. The government of Chosiu underwent a crisis, and a more moderate party, which did not approve the daring policy of the previous government, came into power. Many members and supporters of the previous government were ordered to put an end to their lives, and submission was made to the Shogunate. Inouyé had been attacked by assassins shortly before, and lay in a dying condition resulting from several wounds which he had received.

Takasugi, who was on the point of being arrested, fled to Chikuzen. Ito remained in Shimonoseki, where his services were indispensable to the government of the town on account of the constant calls of foreign vessels, but he was daily in danger of assassination.

In the meantime there arose some difference amongst the partisans of the Shogunate, by reason of one section thinking that the terms imposed upon Chosiu for its submission were too lenient, and therefore would be injurious to the prestige of the Shogunate, and they insisted on recommencing war operations.

It was a critical time for Chosiu. It was then that Takasugi returned from Chikuzen and determined to revolt openly against the government of Chosiu. At that moment Kawasé[1] had a group of voluntary soldiers under his command. Ito also had a certain number of like troops stationed in the neighbourhood of Shimonoseki, and these three with their troops uniting in one common cause, took possession of Shimonoseki in open defiance of the government. Almost simultaneously Yamagata and others, who had each a similar troop of soldiers under their command, openly revolted against the government. The leaders soon effected a junction and quickly defeated the partisans of the government, and thus Chosiu was made once more an open foe of the Shogunate. At that time Inouyé recovered from his wounds, and he also, putting himself at the head of a large band of volunteer troops, took part in the civil strife within the clan which has just been mentioned. A little after this the forces of the Shogunate once more surrounded Chosiu, but they were all defeated by the spirited troops of Chosiu. The Shogunate now found its position very precarious. Before the war it had thought itself all-powerful, and had been of the opinion that Chosiu would simply be frightened at the sight of its troops, or if any battle were to be fought, one coup de main would be enough to crush the whole of Chosiu. But as events turned out, it was quite the contrary. There was much hesitation on the part of the Shogunate whether to push on the war or to make peace. It was powerless to continue fighting, but at the same time thought they would lose prestige by asking for peace. Affairs were then allowed to drift, which brewed discontent among its own partisans. In the meantime many powerful feudal clans, which the Shogunate regarded as friends and supporters, began to sympathise with Chosiu on account of its singleness of purpose and fidelity to chivalry. Among others, Satsuma went so far as to conclude a secret understanding with Chosiu against the Shogunate. In the course of a few years the Shogunate came to an end, after the battle of Fushimi, which was fought between the Imperialists and the partisans of the Shogunate. In this engagement Chosiu and Satsuma took the most important parts on the Imperial side. War still continued in the eastern and northern parts of Japan for some time, the Imperialists being always triumphant. Thus the Imperial régime of our days was inaugurated.

During this state of transition, Ito, Inouyé, and Yamagata played their parts in different capacities, the latter more as a soldier and the two former as politicians and diplomatists, I may here add a few words. Takasugi died a little before the battle of Fushimi, without seeing the consummation of his cherished ideal, being not quite thirty years of age. Yoshida Shoin was the same age as his distinguished disciple when he was put to death some years before. Young men did wonderful things in those days. At the very beginning of the new government Ito was governor of Hiogo (Kobe), which was then with Yokohama the centre of foreign relations. It was then that he formulated and presented to the Imperial Government his plan for the future policy of the empire, the chief object of which was the unification of all systems, namely military, educational, economical, and suchlike. His views were regarded as being too radical at the time, but created some sensation and gave rise to the term 'Hiogo opinion.' Ito has continued practically ever since to occupy one or another, or even several high positions simultaneously in the Government. He made several trips to Europe and America. It was in 1871 that he went to America chiefly to investigate the banking systems of America, because it was thought that the economical system adopted by America after its civil war might be utilised by Japan. Later on, in the same year, he visited America and Europe as one of the ambassadors headed by Iwakura. On their return to Japan the Korean question was at a climax. Most of the statesmen who had remained at home were for war, while those who had returned from Europe were for peace. As the result of this difference of opinion the formation of the cabinet was modified. The great Saigo and some others resigned, while Ito was appointed a cabinet minister with the portefeuille of public works. It was the first great trial which the new Government had to undergo, but it managed to tide over the difficulties. Okubo was now the backbone of the new Government, and Ito his chief collaborator. The administration of the Japanese Government was now carried on more and more on the lines of Western enlightenment. In 1875 a Japanese gunboat was fired at off the Korean coast. Early next year an embassy, with the late Count Kuroda as chief and Count Inouyé as second, was sent to Korea to settle the matter. It was then that I accepted for the first time governmental service, and went to Korea as a member of the staff. We concluded a treaty of peace with Korea and made her open the country to foreign trade: we preferred peace to war.

In 1877 the civil war of Satsuma broke out, in which the great Saigo was made by the rebels their chief. During the struggle Okubo and Ito were the strong supports of the Government, whilst the command of the Imperial troops at the front was chiefly in the hands of Yamagata. I may perhaps mention that during the first half of the war I contributed my services to the Government in a pure civil capacity, and during the latter half of the war was attached to Yamagata's staff. The war lasted nearly nine months, with the result that the rebellion was suppressed and the new régime of the progressive administration was placed on a firmer basis.

In 1878 Okubo, who was then Minister of the Interior, was assassinated, and Ito succeeded to his place, not only as Minister of the Interior, but in his capacity of being the moving factor of the Government.

In 1882 Ito was despatched to Europe to study the constitutional systems of the various governments, with a view to preparing a constitution for Japan; he returned home the next year. In 1884 another difficulty arose with regard to Korea and China. Early in 1885 Count Inouyé was despatched to Korea, where he concluded a new treaty, and soon after Ito was despatched to China, where he concluded the well-known Tientsin treaty, which had a very important bearing upon Korea. In the latter part of that year a great reform was made in the administrative system, and Ito was appointed Minister President of the State. In 1888 Privy Council was instituted, and Ito was appointed its President and his former office was taken by Count Kuroda. The first and most important task the council had before it was the elaboration of the Imperial Constitution. The materials which it had to work upon was chiefly those which Ito had brought back from Europe, and which he had been maturing ever since his return. Early next year the Imperial Constitution and the Imperial House Law, together with several other laws in connection with the constitutional régime then in contemplation, were promulgated, with all solemnity and to the great joy of the whole nation. In 1890 the first session of the new Diet instituted by the Constitution met in Tokio, and Ito was appointed the first President of the House of Peers.

Since then he has held the post of Minister President of the State several times. It was during his premiership that the Sino-Japanese war took place ten years ago. Ito's present post is President of the Privy Council. It may be said here that even when he is out of the cabinet, his influence is felt and his services are rendered to the state. There are a few persons who are called 'elder statesmen,' At present they are Ito, Inouyé, Yamagata, Oyama, and Matsukata. Elder statesmanship is not an institution recognised by a written law. It is a unique position, more of a personal nature, and therefore it cannot be called a council or assembly, but the members are collectively or individually taken into the emperor's confidence. The privilege to this honour may only be looked for by those whose meritorious services to the state stand out above others, and the fact of their occupying such a position is contentedly acquiesced in by the general public. Ito is the principal of these elder statesmen. Another of Ito's great services, was his constant endeavour during many years to keep harmony, in other words, prevent the oft-threatened conflict between men of different clans, especially those of Sutsuma and Chosiu, though few people are aware of that fact.

Such, as I have given it, is a brief sketch of Marquis Ito's life, which necessarily brings in some of the general history of the time. Particulars it would be impossible to give, owing to the fact that that period of our history being so eventful, they are far too numerous.

From what I have narrated above, glimpses of Yamagata and Inouyé may be gathered. I would, however, add a little more.

Yamagata is also a Chosiu man, and was at one time also a pupil of Yoshida Shoin. He is more of a soldier, though he ranks also very high as a statesman. He fought the battle of Shimonoseki at the head of a band of voluntary soldiers of Chosiu, when bombarded by the combined fleets of the four powers. He took a very important part in the civil war in Chosiu, and in the war which took place when Chosiu was surrounded by the Shogun troops. After the battle of Fushimi, when the Imperialists made the expedition to the northern and eastern part of Japan, he commanded the troops of Chosiu in the province of Echigo. After that war he visited Europe, and on his return initiated the adoption of the European system of universal service. At first, of course, there was much difficulty in the matter, but his energy and sagacity won the point Since that time he has almost always occupied some position connected with the army, with the exception of occasional intervals when he fulfilled some civil offices. He has been Minister of War, Chief of the General Staff, and suchlike. Roughly speaking, we may say that the completion of the organisation of the Japanese army is due to him. At the time of the civil war of Satsuma he held the chief direction of the campaign, though the title of Commander-in-Chief was intrusted to a prince of the Imperial family. In that war it was proved that the new troops formed on the system of universal service were more efficient with regard to discipline and cohesive power than the Samurai force of one of the strongest feudal clans. In the Sino-Japanese war he commanded an army in the Liaotung Peninsula, though he had in the middle of the war to return home on account of illness by a pressing order of the emperor.

At present he is once more the Chief of the General Staff. His predecessor was Marquis Oyama, but as the latter's presence as Commander-in-Chief in Manchuria became necessary, Yamagata took his place. I may also add that Yamagata was Prime Minister several times, besides holding from time to time other ministerial portfolios.

Count Inouyé is also a Chosiu man, but he was not a pupil of Shoin, as he was born in Yamaguchi and not in Hagi, where Shoin lived. He was in his early age attached to the court of the Prince of Chosiu, as a sort of companion to the heir of the Prince. When, however, the political atmosphere became heated, he was one of the youths who formed the bands of the anti-foreign party, and as such became a bosom friend of Takasugi and Ito. He was one of those who set fire to the new buildings for the legation. We have already seen how he visited England with Ito and others, and in what circumstances he went home. Their experience after returning to Chosiu was of the most exciting and varied character. It is often most thrilling to recount the incidents connected therewith. But of course I cannot describe them in the space of this article. I may, however, say that the political part of the affairs in connection with Chosiu which resulted in turning the attitude of Chosiu against the Shogun and at last effecting an alliance with Satsuma, with the results of the overthrow of the Shogunate, are greatly due to Takasugi, Ito, and Inouyé, who were eventually supported by Kido, the great Chosiu statesman. The decision which brought about the decisive battle of Fushimi, though the Imperialists were inferior in number to the Shogunate troops, was chiefly due to the determined counsel which Inouyé offered at the Imperial court on behalf of Chosiu.

He held many high posts in the Government, but not so many as Ito or Yamagata, which was perhaps due to his

315

character being more impetuous than the others. It was Ito who initiated the abolition of the feudal system, which idea was taken up first by Kido and then by Okubo, both of whom were the principal statesmen in the new Imperial régime; and it was Inouyé who, when the system was finally abolished a few years afterwards, carried out the measure and wound up the most complicated and difficult affairs of all the governments of feudal lords, who numbered several hundreds, thereby consolidating the new régime. Inouyé was then the acting Minister of Finance, and the Minister of Finance of those days had a far wider sphere of action than at the present time, as there had not been instituted as yet the Ministry of the Interior. He still exercises great influence in the political and economical affairs of the empire, as one may see from the fact that he is one of the few elder statesmen.

The life of Matsukata is not so striking as those of the preceding figures, but he is also one of Japan's able statesmen. He is a Satsuma man. He took up civil service from the early stage of the new Imperial régime, and gradually advanced his position from a local governor to the rank of cabinet minister. Distinguishing himself as a financier, he was Minister of Finance for a long time, and it was he who succeeded in adopting the gold-standard system in Japan. He also occupied premiership several times, and has also been Minister of the Interior. He is now a privy councillor and president of the Red Cross Society of Japan, and as elder statesman is still rendering valuable services to the state.

I may here interpose some words about the present premier, Count Katsura, who is a Chosiu man. He was a boy soldier at the time of the civil war in Chosiu. When the Imperialists were sent to the north and east of Japan to suppress the combinations of the feudal lords in those parts who had arisen against the new Imperial régime, he, though under age, was placed at the head of a detachment of the Chosiu troops which escorted an Imperial envoy to persuade some of the lords to submit to the Imperial summons. The lords, however, did not obey the summons; on the contrary, they assumed an offensive attitude to the Imperial messenger and harassed his escort. Katsura and his men, as well as men of some other clans who were among the escort, had a very hard time, having been obliged to fight their way out. At last reinforcements arrived, and the fighting was turned in their favour. During that time Katsura distinguished himself and was an object of admiration. After a few years he was made a military attaché to our legation in Berlin, where he devoted his energy to the study of military science and organisation. He stayed there during many years, and therefore was absent during the Satsuma war. On his return he devoted his services to the organisation of the army, chiefly under Marquis Yamagata in the ministry of war, in which he was made vice-minister in course of time. He was, before the outbreak of the Sino-Japanese war, chief of the garrison at Nagoya, and in that war had the command of a division in Liaotung, where he distinguished himself as a practical and strategical general. He was at one time Governor-General of Formosa, at another Minister of War, and on the resignation of the Ito cabinet in 1901 he was appointed Minister President of State, which office he now holds.

I will now give an account of Count Okuma. He is a Hizen man: he talks well and is possessed of a good memory. He is, no doubt, one of the ablest Japanese in our day. His life has not been so striking as that of Ito, Inouyé, or Yamagata in the pre-restoration period, because the clan to which he belonged was a peaceful one in those days, and did not offer any opportunities for adventurous youth. A little before the restoration he was a student at Nagasaki, where he studied English to some extent. There is no doubt, however, that he was considered clever among his fellow-clansmen. It is to be remembered that the clans that did the greatest work for the restoration, and produced most of the able men, were Chosiu and Satsuma and then Tosa. Therefore we often say Satcho, which is a term made by a combination of Satsuma and Chosiu, and sometimes Satchoto, which is a term standing for Satsuma—Chosiu—Tosa when Tosa is added to them. But we sometimes include Hizen, which is the province to which Okuma belonged, and say Satchotohi. It came about in this way. Saga in the province of Hizen was also one of the great feudal clans. Soon after the restoration the Imperialist party, of which the Satchoto were the important element, enlisted on their side the support of Saga, which was only too glad to identify its cause with that of the Imperialists. Besides, the Prince of Saga was an able man and was not likely to let the chances slip. Hence Saga soon became a force in the Imperial politics of Japan, and able men coming therefrom found their way to the central political arena of Japan. It was thus that Count Okuma was brought on to the political stage. His natural ability soon made him conspicuous among politicians, and he rose to high positions. The Prince of Saga had had a predilection for European civilisation even before then, and European ideas had already been introduced in the clan previously. Thus, for instance, an iron factory, though not successful, was established in the province. Such surroundings, as well as his stay at Nagasaki, had made young Okuma familiar with European ideas. He was a great gain to men like Ito and Inouyé. They soon formed a sort of combination among young statesmen of their own type, and thus they began the work of introducing European ideas in Japan. The first railway between Tokio and Yokohama, for instance, was constructed chiefly through the efforts of Ito and Okuma, despite many prejudicial objections which still existed.

Okuma is a man of great energy, and also a man who can stir up youth to do that which he wishes to be done, thus qualifying himself as a good party leader. He is also a good financier, and has done much for the state for many years, side by side with Ito, though for consummate ability and profound and constructive statesmanship greater credit is, by common consent, given to Ito. In 1881 serious differences of political opinions arose in the cabinet, in consequence of which Okuma resigned. He then organised a political party called 'progressionists in opposition to the Government on one hand, and on the other hand to the Liberal party which had been organised by Count Itagaki two years previously. Since then he has been out of office for many years, but has kept his party together in a creditable manner. In 1888 he was appointed Minister for Foreign Affairs in the Kuroda cabinet. In the next year, on account of the revision of the treaties, an attempt was made against his life, and he lost one of his legs by the explosion of a bomb thrown at his carriage. He resigned office; his party remained and still remains faithful to him, though he has never been a member of the Diet.

Since then he has once more occupied the position of Minister for Foreign Affairs and also that of Premier, but the tenure of his office on both occasions was short, and his official career not particularly brilliant. He does not enjoy much popularity among other statesmen, and his influence in the Government circle is not great. This was, perhaps, the chief cause of his failure in recent years. He exercises, however, great influence among the people at large, and his personal ability is undoubted. His patriotism is also not to be questioned, because on any occasion of emergency he gives up his personal prejudices and supports the Government. It was so during the Sino-Japanese war, and also since the beginning of the Russo-Japanese war. His memory is almost wonderful, and his perception is very quick. Although he has never left Japan, he knows Europe almost better than many who have made it their special study. He can also remember figures very well. Regarded in the light of sonorous tone and weighty argument, he is not a great orator, but he is a very fluent speaker and an excellent conversationalist.

I will now give you a sketch of the life of Marquis Saionji, the leader of the Constitutional party, which is the greatest political organisation in and out of the Diet. His name also appears in the Western papers from time to time. He succeeded Marquis Ito in the leadership of that party when the latter had accepted the Presidency of Privy Council, and was obliged to give up the leadership of the party which owes its creation to him. Marquis Saionji was a companion in his boyhood to the present emperor. At the time of the restoration, when but fifteen years of age, he was despatched to the northern provinces of Japan, at the head of an Imperial army, to subjugate those provinces. He was afterwards a resident in Paris for many years, and, therefore, he must be remembered by many Parisians. He was for some years our Minister in Berlin, and was also Minister of Education, Minister for Foreign Affairs, and President of Privy Council at different times. He was Minister President of State ad interim at one time. Though a scion of a high court noble, his sentiments contain a strong democratic element, side by side with refinement and nobleness of aristocracy.

In the above sketches I have employed the titles of nobility while speaking of those celebrities, but it may be observed that they were, except Saionji, originally men of comparatively insignificant origin, and their titles are the gift of the emperor in recognition of the services rendered to their Imperial master and their beloved country.

320

[1] The present Viscount Kawasé, who was Japanese Minister in London.

V

AN OLD SPEECH BY THE MARQUIS ITO

In a recent number of the Japan Times I came across the following account of a speech made by the Marquis Ito in Washington, some thirty-four years ago, when he was there on a mission. The speech gives a very good outline of the great change which had then already been effected in Japan and the broad forecast which was aimed at by her for her future. One who reads that speech would at once perceive what ennobling aspirations Japan had then on the lines of occidental civilisation, and how far she has succeeded in that aspiration, as has been shown by the war between her and Russia. I therefore incorporate the accounts of it, borrowed verbatim from the Japan Times, which may also be regarded in a measure as a supplement to the preceding article.—K.S.

MARQUIS ITO IN WASHINGTON

THIRTY-FOUR YEARS AGO

Marquis Ito recently received from Mr. Hioki, Secretary of our legation at Washington, a package containing interesting reminders of his sojourn in the American capital thirty-four years ago, when he spent a few months there for the study of the financial system of the Republic. In his work of investigation he received most valuable assistance from Mr. H.J. Saville, the Chief Clerk of the Treasury, and it was from this gentleman that these interesting relics of the distinguished statesman's visit were originally obtained by Mr. Hioki. Mr. Saville is still living in Washington, and preserves a most vivid recollection of the Marquis's visit. The documents relate to a farewell dinner given by Marquis Ito at Welcker's, Fifteenth Street, on April 28, 1871. Among the guests on the occasion, we find the names of President Grant, Vice-President Schuyler, Speaker Blaine, Secretary Fish, and other members of the cabinet, and a number of senators and congressmen. Among the Japanese present, besides the host, were the late Count Mutsu, the late Viscount Mori (then our Minister at Washington), the late Baron Nakashima, and Mr. Genichiro Fukuchi. On that occasion the Marquis delivered a speech in English, which, apart from the interest derived from the personality of the speaker, deserves attention on account of the light it throws upon the liberal aspirations of the makers of New Japan— aspirations which have since been so successfully realised. We reproduce below the speech exactly as it stands in the copy before us:—

'Taking advantage of the opportunity afforded me by the assembling here of so many of the gentlemen who have assisted me to accomplish the object of my coming, I desire to extend to them my sincere thanks for the many courtesies received at their hands, and to assure them that I return fully satisfied with the result of my mission, and with an abiding faith that all they have taught me will bear good fruit in due season.

'It seems to me that an examination of the past as well as the present condition of the world will show that civilisation has not reached its highest development, but that progress in that as in other things is possible in the future. As an evidence of this I would instance the fact that this nation, which less than one hundred years ago was unknown, now ranks second to none in civilisation and in importance. This fact tends strongly to encourage the oriental nations to efforts towards a higher civilisation than they now possess.

'The inquiry naturally is: What is the reason the oriental peoples have not reached the same degree of civilisation as the European? Are the material resources of the oriental countries insufficient? Is the native force of the people deficient? No: these questions we put aside, and we find the explanation mainly in the character of the government. You ask whence came this peculiar character? I can only answer, I think from education. It seems to me that all the highest order in modern civilisation derives its strength from the development of the intellect, and the improvement of the scientific knowledge and accomplishments of men. It is further strengthened by development of the inherent principles of natural law, the encouragement in the people of a high ideal of right and wrong, and the strong political organisation made possible by such a foundation; so that we may conclude that the highest degree of civilisation belongs to that nation which has most developed a high order of general education and broad principles of political liberty.

'I doubt if the question of strength materially influences the destiny of nations. As an illustration of this we know that the civilisation of Egypt, India, Greece, and Rome has not been lost, but has been merely transferred from those countries to the West, as the star of the empire travels. The loss of civilisation in these nations sprang not from the fact that they were physically weak, but from the more subtle one that within themselves they contain an inherent weakness.

323

'A more modern instance is the late Franco-Prussian war. None of us doubt the strength of the French nation, the skill of its generals and ability of its soldiers, and yet how have our hearts been wrung with sympathy for poor France when brought in contact with the more superior force of Prussia—superior not only in material strength, but in skilful soldiers, in able generals, and in wise counsellors. So I say strength has very little to do with the development of civilisation, strength is merely relative; civilisation is the quality which is never lost, and never can be conquered.

'I find very erroneous ideas prevail in America as well as in Europe in relation to my country. The Empire of Japan consists of numerous islands in the Oriental Sea, along the coast of the Asian continent. I think the recorded existence of the nation extends over something more than two thousand five hundred years, during which time its intercourse with foreign nations has been exceedingly limited. In the seventeenth century intercourse began with the Portuguese, Spanish, and some other European nations, but the decline of these led to its decay. Our people have not been ambitious. They have been satisfied when they have reached that competency which gives support, and as a result they have not sought foreign intercourse.

'Seventeen years ago the American Government sent an envoy to our country, with instructions to advise us to open our ports to foreign intercourse, and this advice so kindly given was acted on. Since that time our intercourse with foreign nations has been growing, until at present Japan bids fair to be as well known as America.

'With the commencement of this intercourse, the Japanese people began to realise that they had not reached the highest stage of civilisation, and they began the

324

investigation of what constituted European and American civilisation. Beginning by the introduction of some of the most useful of the foreign arts, sciences, and mechanical inventions into their country, they have so far progressed as to have at this time reached the necessity for sending missions abroad to obtain a knowledge of the foreign systems of finances, and we have come to America to study your financial system as well as to obtain additional knowledge in other branches of civilised government, which will be of benefit to us in our efforts to reach that high estate which you have already attained. And this we hold as strong evidence of the progress of Japan in civilised ideas. I wish I could express to you how great that advancement has been.

'But to return to the history of my country. About seven hundred years ago the power of the commanding general became so great that he was enabled to usurp the authority of the emperor proper; and from that time, descending through father and son, this power became stronger, until at last the government of Japan had virtually fallen into their hands; and instead of the Government being spoken of as the Mikado's government, it came to be known as the government of the Tycoon, who was in reality the powerful ruler of the people.

'But no one family enjoyed the power of the Tycoonety in peace. During the existence of what is known as the Tycoon's government six of the principal ducal families of the empire contended for the position of Tycoon, and each in his turn came into possession of the reins of government.

'Out of the quarrels of these ducal families grew a system somewhat resembling the feudal system of Europe. The constant fighting of these antagonistic elements made this possible. About three hundred years ago the Tokugawa family came into possession of the power and dignity of the Tycoon. From this time the feudal system founded in the necessities and strengthened by the wars of the many as aspirants for power came to be a fixed institution, and the reign of the Tokugawa family proving to be a peaceful one, its hold on the country became thoroughly well established.

'Before the usurpation of the Tycoon the form of government was absolutely monarchical, with no independent princes or powers.

'As a result of the Tycoon's rule, not alone the Tycoon's position became hereditary, but also all the highest governmental positions—generals, ministers, and princes, the latter being originally merely governors. With the establishment of intercourse with foreign countries, and the consequent development of the progressive people of Japan, they began to realise their unsatisfactory form of government under which they were living. They became dissatisfied with the rule of an authority which did not encourage ability, and whose strength lay in hereditary claims to power. This sentiment growing stronger and stronger, they at last resolved to abolish the power and office of the Tycoon and return the real power to the hands of the emperor. This resolution on their part has given rise to the stories of revolution in Japan, the revolution being in reality only the efforts of the better people to form a stable and reliable Government with the proper and respected power at its head, assisted in its control of affairs by ability, integrity, and faithfulness wherever found.

'This came to be an accomplished fact four years ago, and to-day, as a result, we have the former vassal and servant of the prince sitting in the high seats by his side, and counselling with him in the affairs of the nation.

'But the Japanese people do not mean to stop here. There is now a growing sentiment in Japan which strongly favours constitutional monarchy, a growing feeling against hereditary power, hereditary rank, and hereditary possessions. It may be that the bright hopes of some of my people will not be realised at once, but if the past is taken as an index of what is to come, I am encouraged to say that the progress of the future will find Japan, in a very few years, in the front rank of advanced and civilised nations, with a Government as liberal in form and generous to its citizens as that of any monarchy under the sun.

'In Japan, as in other parts of the world, there must necessarily be differences of opinion. We have among our people radical and rapid progressists; conservatives, always making haste slowly, always studying the situation, always moving with great caution and circumspection, often unwisely wasting their opportunities for advancement by too great caution or timid fear; others timid because of the fear that they will lose their property or position by any change; others, the selfish Utopian, who builds an impossible castle, hoping that the foundation stones may be precious jewels, resting in his land only; and, lastly, there are yet a few who are opposed to foreign intercourse, and who believe that its strength lies in closed ports and selfish sufficiency unto themselves.

'To the outsider in Japan all these differences may appear as elements of weakness, when in fact they are elements of strength; and, perhaps, in no country can this be so well appreciated as America, where the strength and success of the Government depends so much on the agitation of questions by the people. The time is coming when Japan will stand among the first in its civilisation and progress. The question with us is: "How can we most rapidly reach this high state of development?" To my mind the best

327

answer is by educating the people and developing the country.

'We are grateful to realise that the American people understand our efforts, and more especially that the distinguished company of gentlemen here assembled understand them. The prevailing sentiment in America, it seems to me, is in favour of the brotherhood of nations; and feeling this when we left Japan, we felt that we were coming among a people who would encourage and assist us in every way possible. We have not been deceived. Every assistance has been rendered us; every facility for study afforded us, and we will return to our country freighted with knowledge, and, as we hope, equal to the test, which we confess is a great one, of putting in motion such reforms and improvements as shall place us upon a footing equal to the best of nations.

'In the years to come it is to be hoped that the intercourse between Japan and America, the sister nations on each side of the great Pacific Ocean, may be founded upon that strong feeling of brotherly love which so unite distant peoples, that through storm and sunshine they will ever be true friends and earnest assistants—co-workers in the great cause of humanity and the development of the world in its moral, social, intellectual, and material aspects.

'In conclusion, I desire to extend to all of the gentlemen here present, and to thousands who are unavoidably absent, my sincere thanks for the great courtesy and kindness which I have received at their hands; and if it shall ever be my pleasure to meet any of you in my country, it will afford me the greatest happiness imaginable to extend to you the warm hand of fellowship, and to give you such a reception as will prove how entirely and truly I appreciate all you have done for me.'

VI

THE COMMERCIAL MORALITY OF THE JAPANESE[1]

In accordance with your request that I should write an answer to Mr. Joseph H Longford on the commercial morality' of the Japanese, which has appeared in the Contemporary Review, I venture to write these lines for your perusal. I do so rather hesitatingly, as I have no desire to enter upon a dispute with that distinguished writer.

There is, it seems to me, a great deal of truth in what Mr. Longford says; but, at the same time, it is, I think, painted blacker on the side of the Japanese and brighter on the side of the foreigners out there than the facts warrant.

To begin with, it is true that in Japan we had the classification of the people into four, viz. soldiers, farmers, artisans, and traders, and thus traders stood the last. From this fact ordinary critics make a hasty conclusion that Japanese traders—in which term big merchants are included—occupied in every respect a position which was inferior even to that of common peasants; but this is not fair. In social matters they often occupied very good positions; in fact, there were many to whom special considerations similar to Samurai were accorded. The above classification has much deeper meaning than a mere social caprice, and it is derived from a theory of political economy of the classical China.

According to that theory, agriculture is considered the foundation of a nation, and commerce is a mere act of transportation of things already made, and, therefore, comparatively of little value. That such a theory should have existed in China is a matter of no surprise, for even in the Europe of a little more than one hundred years ago there flourished physiocracy, the doctrine of which was almost identical with that of the Chinese. The Japanese classification of the former days was considerably due to the influence of that theory, and therefore the relative positions of the Samurai, farmers, artisans, and traders were more of theoretical notion than a social fact. This is a distinction very important to be kept in view when one discusses things Japanese.

That the Samurai as a class despised dealings in matters of profit is an undoubted fact, but a trader's position was not so degraded as Mr. Longford represents. He says:—

'Just as the training and social precedence of his ancestors for hundreds of years and of himself have made the Japanese soldier a model without flaw of loyalty, devotion, and courage, ready to sacrifice at any time life or property for his sovereign and his country, so have oppression and social degradation combined to make the merchant a no less striking model of dishonesty and timidity, unwilling and unable to make the smallest monetary sacrifice for his own or his country's fair fame.'

Surely this is sweeping assertion. If we take individual cases into account, striking characters in the ranks of merchants are abundant in records and in memory. Even in the movement which resulted in the restoration of the present Imperial régime, countless men whose origin belonged to mercantile circles may lay their claim of participation to it. True, they were men who generally cast

330

off their original occupation and enrolled themselves in the ranks of patriots, so that they may be considered as exceptions. But even as a class in the ordinary sense of merchants they scarcely deserve that kind of condemnation. Osaka in former days had some resemblance to free cities of the West, and every one well acquainted with things Japanese knows what a well-developed mercantile system it possessed. So also the so-called Omi merchants. Even with regard to merchants and tradesmen of all parts of the country there was little room for them to be so dishonest as the writer describes. Under the feudal system commercial occupations were almost hereditary. They had almost no freedom of removal from their accustomed abode. Their customers were the children or grandchildren of those who were customers of their fathers or grandfathers. If a merchant under such circumstances made dishonesty his customary trade, and expected prosperity, he would surely be totally disappointed, and would suffer a deserving penalty. Besides, in those days social sanction, from the very nature of the conditions under which they found themselves situated, was most severe. Yes! Merchants and traders of those days were honest, far beyond one can imagine. If any dishonesty or any shortcomings in respect to commercial probity have become observable, it is necessary evil produced by the changed circumstances of the time, chiefly on account of foreign intercourse.

Mr. Longford speaks of the early Japanese traders who flocked to the newly opened ports as being 'without exception adventurers with neither name nor money to lose, with keen wits and the determination to exploit to the utmost.' This is, in a measure, undoubtedly true, and accounts for the lamentable condition which for a long time existed in the trades at the open ports. But this is not the only cause. On the parts of foreign merchants who came out there to trade, there was much to be criticised; I mean

331

to say, they were also mostly adventurers in a measure; they were also inconsiderate, even arrogant. A Western merchant who, leaving China, was passing through Japan, violated intentionally time-honoured etiquette against one of the most powerful 'Daimio,' saying, 'I know how to manage these Orientals,' and was murdered in consequence. It is a good illustration of the kind of conduct of the Europeans of those days towards us; hence no sympathy existed between them and our traders—the dealings were viewed, naturally, very differently from those which they were wont to carry on with their native customers of several generations' standing. Business is business, so the common saying goes, but even in business mutual respect and friendly feeling go a long way. How can a model trade be expected to be created under such circumstances?

Then, again, in Japan commercial goods were, and are still, to a great extent made by hand on small scales. No big industrial factories existed where one could order a large number of articles identical in every respect as one could do in Europe. Foreign traders, not taking these conditions into their serious consideration, often gave similar orders as they were used to do in Europe, and when articles delivered to them were found to be not perfectly identical, they often took advantage of that fact, and gave much trouble to the native contractors, who did not expect to meet with so much severity. There existed also very bad customs among foreign traders; the essence of those customs was known by the name of 'Haiken,' or 'Kankan.' These terms, literally meaning 'to see,' were used to veil the facts of detaining goods at their storehouses, often for an unreasonable length of time; in the meantime ascertaining the commercial conditions of their home, and returning the goods when they found the transaction was not likely to be beneficial to them. Native traders had serious grounds of complaint against those customs. As a matter of fact, at one time the matter was brought to a very acute state, and the native traders began to try to get rid of them by combination, but with little success. I imagine Mr. Longford will remember the incidents which occurred in connection with that matter in Yokohama years ago. I can also state on good authority that there were even some cases wherein foreign traders themselves practised, toward their compatriot at home, some actions which appear not to have been in unison with Western honesty, and taking advantage of our unfortunate reputation attributed the fault to the Japanese when matters were discovered. The notorious case wherein a large foreign firm dealing in silk, who took off the labels of native manufacturers and changed them into a single kind which he liked, was boycotted by them when the matter came to broad daylight, may also be recollected by him. Another thing which foreign traders were wont to do was that they often ordered things direct from small manufacturers at a cost far less than their real value. Japanese merchants often said that they could not compete with foreign traders, inasmuch as foreign merchants often got things at less expense than they themselves could. This is surely an extraordinary phenomenon. But the fact was that those foreign traders often succeeded in making that kind of contract either by giving some tempting inducement at the beginning or canvassing several manufacturers one after another, always showing the last most advantageous offer, and bringing down the price by bargaining in a skilful and cunning manner. Under such circumstances it was not surprising if those contracts were often unfulfilled, simply on account of the inability of fulfilment by the contractors. There was also another circumstance which caused commotion and disorder in all commercial dealing in Japan. It is to be remembered that the new order under the new system of government, especially the abolition of the feudal system, widely changed the accustomed occupations of the Japanese at large. Chances for making wealth and for entering upon various enterprises almost entirely changed their hand. Besides, four hundred thousand families (2,000,000 capita) of Samurai, who gave up their hereditary allowances, now had to make their earnings chiefly by becoming traders or sometimes agriculturists, occupations to which they were entirely unaccustomed. They naturally experienced failure after failure. It was then that a new term, 'Trades of Samurai,' meaning thereby an undertaking which is precarious or even doomed to failure, came into existence. In one sense it was sad to think about, but the fact was so. Under such circumstances one can well imagine that dishonesty, or rather failure of fulfilment of promise, although against one's conscience, it maybe presumed, was often experienced even among our own community. This also might have had some indirect effects upon foreign trade.

Critics say that commercial probity in China is better than in Japan. It may be true; I shall not dispute. The Chinese are excellent traders, and besides, as every one knows, no such social revolution, as was the case with us Japanese, has ever taken place. That accounts for the difference between Chinese and Japanese traders in the first place, but that is not all. The Chinese are, individually speaking, very docile; they would not think of quarrelling with foreign traders, under whatever humiliating circumstances they might find themselves placed, so long as they could make some profit. But this is very different with us Japanese. Take, for instance, the case of a 'Rikisha' man; if he were a Japanese, and suppose a foreign rider whipped him, as they often do, because he did not run quick enough, the probability is, he would ask to be excused carrying the rider any further, or turn round to the rider and ask for an explanation. He would do so no matter whether or not he would get his fare; but if it were a Chinaman, the probability is that he would calmly suffer the treatment, and proceed just at the rate he could run, his thoughts being concentrated on obtaining as good a fee as he could get, and would be looked upon as an honest man in consequence. This state of things exists in the matter of trade at large. Chinese tradesmen would suffer without anger, any arrogance or unreasonableness of foreign traders, and exert such wonderful patience in order ultimately to attain their objects, whilst Japanese merchants would sooner break the contract than suffer such treatment with such patience. The consequence is that Japanese merchants are viewed in rather a bad light.

The effects of the Great Change, both political and social, have been subsiding already for some time, and the order of things at large has also begun to settle down. The condition of our mercantile circle is, in consequence, much changed; so also the attitude and characters of foreign traders have begun to alter considerably. I am, therefore, most sanguine that all complaints of foreigners against our commercial probity will soon become a thing of the past.

I am sorry to speak about foreigners in this manner, but I am sure impartial observers will admit that what I say is not far from fact. At all events, their conditions were not so bright as Mr. Longford pleases to represent them to have been. Unfair criticisms are not calculated to promote the friendly feeling of nations, and my statements, which I believe no other than those of true fact, are hereby made more for promoting in future the goodwill which has already begun to exist between us and the Western traders of late years.[2]

[1] The Magazine of Commerce, August 1905.

[2] See the note at the end of the volume.

SUPPLEMENT

There appeared an interesting letter, written by the Manager of the Publication Department of the Times, in the columns of that paper, October 7, 1905. As it has important bearing on the preceding subject, I take the liberty of subjoining it in full.—K.S.

THE CHARACTER OF THE JAPANESE PEOPLE

TO THE EDITOR OF THE "TIMES"

Sir,—In last Monday's issue of the Times there was a long letter from the Right Rev. William Awdry, Bishop of South Tokio, Japan, in which he says that 'in general a Japanese would value the promise of an Englishman more than the bond of a Japanese'; and that the Japanese are deficient in a certain group of qualities, including honesty in trade. It seems to me that it would be unfair for the Times to allow such a charge against Japanese integrity, endorsed by a bishop, to go unchallenged, when the Times has, in its own office, records that prove a promise made by a Japanese to be at least as trustworthy as a promise made by an Englishman. During the past eight years the Times has sold, in almost every country in the world, sets of the Encyclopædia Britannica on the instalment plan, giving credit for periods of two, three, and four years. The regularity with which such payments are made is certainly a fair test of the average honesty of any nation, and a much more severe test in the case of Japan than in the case of England, because it is more difficult there than here to enforce payment by legal proceedings. Ninety-five per cent. of the encyclopædias sold in Japan were sold to

Japanese, not to foreign residents, and the statements I am about to make refer exclusively to purchases made by the Japanese themselves. In Japan, as elsewhere, each purchaser, when he signs his 'order-form,' promises to pay, on certain dates, certain sums of money. In Japan the monthly payment was 10 yen, equal to about a sovereign, while in this country the amount was a guinea. In Great Britain less than half the payments arrived on the day promised. In Japan less than 1 per cent, of the payments were even one day late, and more than one-half of the payments were made the day before they were due, because the Japanese did not like to run the risk of any accidental delay that might make them even one day late. The cost of collecting these instalment payments in Japan is less than half as much as in England, simply because the Japanese are so punctilious that clerical labour and postage are not expended in reminding them that their payments are overdue. They seem to look upon every debt as a debt of honour, which must not be forgotten for even a day. There is certainly no such delicacy of feeling in this country about commercial transactions.

I find it difficult to believe that the Bishop of South Tokio is right when he says that the Japanese do not trust one another; and I know that he is wrong if he in himself believes, as he implies, that the Japanese are not 'honest in trade.' But I quite admit that Englishmen who have long resided in Japan did not believe that it would be prudent for the Times to adopt in Japan the instalment system of selling books, previously unknown there. When the representative of the Times arrived in Japan to sell the Encyclopædia, he naturally asked English residents there what they thought of the project. With one exception the answer was: 'You cannot sell the Encyclopædia Britannica here because almost every English and American resident has already obtained a copy from England, and, of course, the Japanese

337

will not buy—fortunately for you, because if they did they would not pay.' The only English resident who did not say this said: 'Of course you can sell any number of Encyclopædias to the Japanese, but you will never be able to collect the payments when they have once got the books. No Japanese will pay for the Encyclopædia when he finds he can get it without payment.' In the face of this advice, the instalment plan of sale was adopted, with the results above described. I many add that the Japanese bought five times as many Encyclopædias as were sold in France and Germany combined, fifty times as many as in Russia, more than in any other country except India, Australia, and the United States.

When I see a bishop of the Church of England, who has lived in Japan since 1898, write with so little appreciation of the Japanese, I wonder whether some of our countrymen are not as blind as the Russian statesmen who, in the early days of the war, described the Japanese as 'yellow monkeys,' and as blind as the Ambassador of the Tsar who made the statement in Tokio, before the war, that the mobilisation of one army corps in Russia would frighten the Japanese into immediate submission. No one in the Times office, at any rate, can doubt that the standard of integrity among the Japanese is so high that when young men, who have bought the Encyclopædia, abandoned their employment to go to the front, their families promptly paid the instalments due, under circumstances of the utmost difficulty.—I am, sir, your obedient servant,

The Manager of Your Publication Department.

Printing-house Square, E.C., October 5.

338

VII

JAPAN AND FOREIGN CAPITAL[1]

Japan, far from becoming antagonistic to the occidental nations, as it was prognosticated by some of the Continental journalists, has given another proof of her readiness for the identification of her economic interests with those of the occidental people.

Hitherto in Japan there has been no law which regulated the mortgaging of a railway, or a mining enterprise, or a factory, together with its working system, as a corporation, that is to say, mortgaging the whole system of a railway, a mining enterprise, or a factory as an economic whole, comprising not only each particular material object but also all the organic components of its working system as the subject matter of mortgage. A radical change has now been effected in the matter.

According to the Japanese laws there are two methods for a commercial company in contracting a debt. One is the ordinary borrowing of money from a creditor, and the other is borrowing in the shape of debentures by public subscription. Now in ordinary borrowing of money the liability may be secured by mortgage, but the debentures could not be secured by mortgage, although of course the liability extends to the whole property of the company.

The first effect of the new change is the provision which enables companies to guarantee debentures by mortgage, and the second effect is the provisions which relate to the creations of economic corporations of railways, mining works, or factories for the special purpose of instituting mortgages of their economic entity.

To make the matter easier to comprehend, I will first explain it with regard to railways.

The permission of the Government originally given to the company is in the nature of a licence or concession which is to be viewed more in the light of a personal matter of the original company, and therefore it could not be a subject matter of a public auction, and therefore according to the old law, if a railway company becomes bankrupt, all the material property, either movable or immovable, would go to new hands, but the licence itself cannot but become extinct with the dissolution of the original company, viz. the original grantee.

This being so, if a railway company fails to fulfil its liability for debenture and goes into bankruptcy, the ultimate result would be that the railway system would be broken up, and the creditors would get their satisfaction only from the sale of each piece of the material property sold by public auction. Even in the case of ordinary debt, whereby all the material property can be mortgaged, the result would be practically the same.

All these inconveniences have now been removed by a series of new laws passed by the last session of the Imperial diet and promulgated on March 13, 1905, by the Imperial Government. The articles of the laws are very numerous and minute, so that it would be unnecessary to dwell upon them here in detail, but the more important parts may be summarised as follows:

(a) The economic entity of a railway company may be constituted a special economic corporation for the purpose of mortgage.[2]

(b) In default of payment of the mortgage liability, the whole, i.e. the corporation, may be subjected to auction. This provides the means for transferring, together with the material properties, the original permission of the Government, namely, the licence, to the purchaser, viz. a new company.

(c) A company, which in reality may be taken as a syndicate, may be formed for advancing money by means of debentures. Such company may acquire legal recognition and may represent the creditors of debentures. It forms a particular kind of commercial company, and is called 'trust company.'

(d) At the option of the creditors, means of compulsory control of the railway in the interest of creditors are also provided for in the laws.

(e) Special provisions are made to meet the cases where the syndicate and investors are of foreign nationality: namely, the means of recognising foreign syndicates by the Japanese Government, and also the means of affording convenience for foreign investors.

(f) Further provisions are made for facilitating the registration of constituting the said corporation, and the registration of the mortgage thereof, for these affairs, as far as railways are concerned, are now entrusted, by the new laws, to the Minister of Communications, to whose control the railways belong, and not to the local courts of law, as is the case with all other kinds of mortgages.

This change of our laws gives very great facility to foreign investors who may be willing to lend money on railway securities.

The case of mining enterprises were similar because they are also based on licences. For them also much the same changes have been effected by the new laws, so that their economic entity may now be mortgaged in the interests of either an ordinary creditor or investors in debentures.

The cases of ordinary factories differ in origin from those of the railways or mines, they not being based on a concession or licence like railway or mining enterprises. But for them also the new laws have made provisions for the means of constituting corporations for the purpose of guaranteeing debenture by mortgage. Provisions have also been made for guaranteeing debenture by mortgaging ships, any definite property either immovable or movable, or any legal claims which are secured by written instruments.

[1] The Outlook.

[2] The law also permits the companies constituting such a corporation of a part of the whole for a similar object. But as its general purport does not materially differ, I omit its account in order to avoid confusion.—The Author.

VIII

THE LANGUAGES OF CHINA AND JAPAN

People often ask me if there is any affinity between the Chinese language and ours. I can at once say there is no affinity whatever, but this requires much explanation before I can clearly show it.

The written language of China, viz. ideographs, is the same all over the extensive sphere of China proper, but its pronunciation is different almost in every province. The spoken language of the Chinese is, roughly speaking, the same as the written language, as is the case in the Western nations. Therefore, the Chinese residing in different provinces do not understand each other colloquially, except those educated in the Mandarine Chinese, which is in fact the pronunciation used in Peking amongst the Mandarins and studied by all Mandarins in provinces as well as those in Peking.

The first difference between Chinese and Japanese is that the former is monosyllabic, whilst the latter is polysyllabic. The second difference, which is a natural consequence of the first, is that in Chinese there is no declension of nouns or conjugation of verbs, whilst in Japanese there are conjugations of verbs and a method of the formation of the cases of nouns which is in purport similar to declensions. The third difference is the position or order of words in sentences. The fourth difference is the difference of pronunciation of the Chinese ideographs, viz. characters, even when they are used in our writing in their original shapes.

I will now explain in detail all these points in the succeeding pages.

To begin with, Chinese is monosyllabic, as I said. Each word, which always has one signification, be it a noun or a verb, has only one sound. Thus a harbour in Chinese is kong, whilst it is minato in Japanese; and a man in Chinese is jen, whilst it is hito in Japanese. It is the same with verbs.

The sound of each word of Chinese never changes, whatever position it may stand in relation to other words in the same sentence, that is to say, there is no declension and no conjugation. Each word is represented by a distinct ideograph, and, from what I have just said, it follows that the form of the ideographs also never changes, in the same way as the sounds do not change.

In Chinese different shades of meaning as to the actions and agents are expressed by the position of the words, by addition of some other words. In simple sentences, therefore, it resembles English very much; thus, for instance, when a Chinese says: 'John likes Paul,' it is plain, like English, that he who likes Paul is John, and he who is liked is Paul. When a Chinese wishes to express the same idea in the passive voice, he would say, 'Paul by John is liked,' which is the same as 'Paul is liked by John,' Neither has Chinese any preposition like English or French, nor any post-position like Japanese, to designate the cases, except a few which resemble prepositions meaning 'from,' 'to,' and 'by,' but even these are very sparingly employed and by no means with any regularity. When a verb is used as a substantive the form is still identical; thus one identical ideograph, 'like,' may represent a verb 'to like' or a substantive 'liking.' Of course there are many terms designating one thing or one action consisting of more than one sound; such are, however, combinations of two or three distinct words, like the English word 'firearms' or 'seesaw,' and therefore none of them could properly be called one distinct polysyllabic word.

In Japanese, unlike Greek, Latin, or German, there is no proper declension in nouns. In this respect it is more like English or French, but it has a method of forming the cases, so that in this respect it differs from Chinese. Our cases are

344

formed by putting after them the so-called ga—no—ni—wo—thus:

Hana ga saku	-	Flowers blossom
Hana no Kage	-	The shade of flowers
Hana ni chikazuku	-	Approach the flowers
Hana wo Miyo	-	See the flowers (imperative).

Ga is generally omitted in writing. It is more like the Greek Ge, which is often suffixed to the nominative substantives. Ni is equal to the English to and the French à; but such ideas as the English by or in, or the French en or par, are generally expressed by it. There is another particle wa for the nominative, its position is the same.

Made (until, jusqu'à) and yori or kara (from, de) are also put after the substantives. In fact, all equivalents to English or French prepositions are put after the substantive, and therefore they are more appropriate to be called the postpositions.

In Chinese the idea of time is generally very vague, it is mostly left to the conjecture of the hearers or readers, as the case may be, from the context of the whole sentence. But when it is necessary to express it, it is also done by addition of some words, such as 'already' or 'once.' Thus a Chinese would say, 'John once like Paul,' meaning 'John once liked Paul,' or 'John already come,' meaning 'John has already come.' But this is very different in our language. We have regular declensions of verbs in both the active voice and the passive voice and their form is accordingly changed. Thus, for instance:

Kitaru   -   come

Kitaran   -   shall come

Kitarishi -   has come

Kitare   -   come (imperative).

I shall here develop my dissertation a little further, and make some comparison between our language and some of the European languages.

In Japanese there is no gender in nouns, for grammatical purposes, although some words from their very nature signify male or female; thus, for instance, otoko = man, onna = woman, ondori = cock, and mendori = hen. To us it sounds very odd that the Germans give feminine gender to the sun and masculine to the moon, whilst the French do vice versa, or that both the French and German give masculine gender to 'regiment' or 'battalion,' but feminine gender to 'company.' In this respect the English method of dividing into masculine, feminine, and neutral, allowing only on rare occasions, for poetical purpose, personification of inanimate objects, sounds more rational and comprehensible to our ears. It follows, therefore, that our nouns do not modify their forms on account of the gender, and that it is more like English in this respect.

We have, moreover, no number in the nouns. Whereas in European languages nouns which have no number are exceptions and very few, all the nouns in Japanese are without number without any exception. When we wish to express any particular numerical idea, we make use of a numerical adjective in a similar manner as the English would say 'a sheep,' 'ten sheep,' or 'numerous sheep.' Here again we can see that our nouns never change their form on account of the number. It is true, we also put after the nouns ra, tachi, or domo to signify plural, but it is rare, and the style becomes rather clumsy unless it is done very carefully.

Furthermore, there is no gender or number in our verbs. All conjugations are the same whatever gender or number they may relate to. It goes without saying that in Chinese also there is neither gender nor number in its nouns and verbs. It also goes without saying that in Japanese as well as Chinese there is, like English, no gender or number in adjectives. I may also add here that, like Latin, there are no articles either in Chinese or Japanese.

As to the adverbs in Chinese, they are as a rule identical with adjectives, the difference between them being only perceived by the context, although there is a certain form which always gives adverbial signification, and which is done by putting another word after an adjective (there are three or four words which are used for the purpose of thus forming adverbial terms). In Japanese adverbs are formed by suffixing ni and to, like the English ly and French ment. As shizukani (slowly) yuku (goes), and shizushizu to (slowly and slowly) yuku (goes). To may be written toshite according to euphony.

The use of conjunctions in Japanese and Chinese is much similar to that of the Western languages, except that in both Chinese and Japanese it is very commonly understood. Thus where the Europeans say, 'East and West' or 'black and white,' we both, Chinese and Japanese, would simply say, 'West East' or 'white black,' unless we have some particular reasons in giving emphasis to the distinction.

In Chinese the pronouns also have no gender, so also in Japanese. When we particularly wish to designate gender, we say, 'that man' or 'this woman,' which in reality is no longer a pronoun. As to the number of pronouns, it is formed by adding another word after it; but in Chinese this is by no means uniformly done, for in most cases where the meaning is plain enough, the same person as that of the singular number is also used for the plural. It is so especially with regard to the third person, but even in the first person this occurs sometimes, as for instance when two opposing objects, one of which is on one's own side, are collectively spoken of. There is something similar in English as far as the third person is concerned, but the Chinese carry it even into the first person. Thus in English may be written, 'When the enemy attacked us we have repulsed him,' but a Chinese would go further and write,

'When the enemy attacked me, I have repulsed him,' without meaning that he, the writer himself, did it alone, or did it at all, but that the army on his side did it.

In Japanese the number of the pronouns is far more precise than it is in Chinese. One thing which may be novel to the Western readers is that in Chinese there are many different I's and you's, and still more in Japanese. They all signify, when used, a certain difference in degree of politeness. It is one of the difficult points in our colloquial language. I may here note that in the West it is almost impossible to carry on a conversation for a few minutes without making use of so many I's, he's, and you's, but, like Latin, pronouns are used very sparingly in Chinese, still less in Japanese. In Latin the form of the verbs suggests very easily the person which is the substantive understood. In Chinese the context suggests it, while in Japanese the construction of sentences based upon conjugation does it.

Relative pronouns, who, which, qui, que, or dont, do not exist both in Chinese and Japanese. This is one of the great difficulties when we translate Western books. We must write the phrase governed by the relative pronouns as a distinct one or else must employ a clumsy method in rendering the whole sentence.

From what I have stated above, it would appear that Chinese is very simple as far as the analysis of the words is concerned, for they have no declension and conjugation. The difficulty of the students of Chinese does not lie in remembering different forms of declensions and conjugations, but first in remembering so many ideographs, one by one, and secondly to make head and tail of the agglomeration of ideographs, for one can never tell from their form which is a noun and which is a verb, or which is an objective or which is a possessive case. Definite

349

meaning of Chinese sentences could only be appreciated by those who have accustomed themselves by long experience. But even such people often differ in their interpretation of some phrases, by giving different attributive to one or other particular ideograph in a sentence, not only in its meaning but in its position as regards the part of speech. This often occurs in interpretation of classical books. All this, however, does not signify that Chinese is a poor language, because its literal standard is really very highly developed.

The Japanese language is also simple enough as far as the analysis of words is concerned. Nouns never change their forms under any circumstances, except that their cases are made by the use of ga, no, ni, or wo, which is only an addition. Verbs are conjugated, but it is done simply to denote time and voice, and for no other reason. In a word, we may say that Japanese grammar is very easy. The real difficulty of Japanese is in the proper construction of phrases, for it is by it that many shades of meaning are suggested. True it is that this is more or less so with all languages. Difference of the degree of politeness or gracefulness is manipulated by difference of construction everywhere, but the variety of this difference is more complicated in Japanese than in any other language, and it can only be acquired by long practice and observation. This is why all foreigners who study Japanese think it is so easy at the commencement and so difficult after they have made a little progress. Nevertheless, colloquial Japanese is on the whole easy, because one can learn it easily so long as he is not sensitive of nicety or grace. There is in open ports even a new Japanese spoken between foreigners and natives, in which no ga—no—ni—wo is used, or no conjugation of verbs employed, and yet it is perfectly intelligible.

Now as to the difference of the order of words between Japanese and Chinese. Where in English one says, 'I cannot

350

go,' in Chinese one would say, 'I not can go,' whilst in Japanese it would be, 'I go can not.' This order of Japanese has a slight resemblance to German, but the difference lies in that, whilst in German it is chiefly so in subordinate sentences, it is in Japanese uniformly so under any circumstances. In Chinese a verb which governs an object directly or indirectly always precedes the object; thus, like English, a Chinese would say, 'Girls eat cakes,' or 'he goes to Paris,' but in Japanese the verb succeeds; thus a Japanese would say, 'Girls cakes eat,' or 'he Paris to goes.' In this respect of order there is some resemblance between Latin and Japanese.

From all that I have said it is plain that there is no affinity between Chinese and Japanese so far as construction is concerned, but I may go further. There is no resemblance whatever suggestive of same origin between any Chinese and Japanese word, except those whose introduction into Japan at later ages is clearly known.

In speaking of the Japanese language in the foregoing pages, I have made no difference between the colloquial and the written one, but in fact there is much difference between them which requires some notice here. Even in the West written phrases can be, and are often, much shortened than spoken ones; but in Japan this difference is carried almost to the extreme, so much so, that they assume almost entirely different shape, the phrases of the spoken language being unsparingly curtailed in those of the written one. Of course, there are some old books which were written like the colloquial, and of late years much movement is made for an assimilation of the written and spoken languages, making the written one approach the spoken one. But as the matter stands at present the difference is still very great.

I am afraid my explanation is becoming too minute and consequently tedious, but I presume I must complete it. In the writings, too, there are in Japan two systems, one of which consists of our own phonetic letters, and the other consists of a mixture of our phonetic letters and Chinese ideographs. Unfortunately, the latter system is in common use. It is done in the following manner. The order of the words is not changed, but nouns and verbs, for instance, are written in the original ideographs with the significance of the cases or conjugations, which are written in the phonetic letters succeeding these ideographs. Let me take an example in the English word 'telegraphed' or 'telegraphing,' and let us write 'telegraph' in the original Greek letters, writing 'ed' or 'ing,' which is the part of the pure English, in the ordinary English letters. This will give you an idea of our using Chinese ideographs in our sentences. But our method is still more complicated. Besides the above examples we read very often the ideographs thus used, not according to their pronunciation but according to so-called 'kun' of the word, which is in reality a translation. In English books the term 'viz.' is used and is read as 'namely.' Here 'namely' is not pronunciation but translation. This is an example similar to our 'kun' of a word. When to read by pronunciation and when to read by 'kun' entirely depends upon the construction of the phrases, but one thing is certain, and it is that in Japan one has to know both the pronunciation and 'kun' of Chinese ideographs.

The Japanese pronunciation of Chinese ideographs is not the same as any kind of the modern Chinese pronunciation, and therefore even one simple word expressed by an ideograph is unintelligible between a Chinese and a Japanese, though they understand when it is written. In China the pronunciation of ideographs underwent much change; besides it has varied according to localities. In Japan the pronunciation of those Chinese ideographs, which is comparatively ancient, has been preserved on account of our possessing phonetic letters, by the use of which the preservation has been effected. But then there are two kinds of pronunciation of those ideographs, on account of its introduction into Japan at different periods from the different localities. This is an additional difficulty we have in reading Chinese characters used in Japan, though the usual customs where to use one or where the other are usually plain to educated people.

Japanese phonetics consist of fifty letters.[1] Five of them are vowels, being equal to a, e, i, o, u, and each of the rest represents the sound of two Roman characters, i.e. a consonant and a vowel; thus, for instance, the sound of ka or ke is represented by a single letter without spelling.

I said above that the modern Chinese pronunciation is different from the ancient one. It goes without saying that the style of phraseology is much changed, even in a greater measure than the modern English writing is different from that of the Elizabethan epoch. The Chinese, which has been studied in Japan indeed very commonly, is the ancient one, i.e. classical Chinese, and we are familiar with classical Chinese even more than the Chinese themselves. As a system of writing, that of the pure Japanese, which consists of phonetic letters, is in its quality far superior to the other one, which is in our common use, nay, even superior to the proper Chinese system itself. Our phonetic system, however, has not made sufficient progress on account of the introduction of the Chinese system, to which we had paid too high value and devoted too much attention, the result being the mixture of Chinese ideographs in our phonetic system, that is to say, the other system just mentioned. Even in the West there is some similarity to this. Take, for instance, some modern English books. One would scarcely find a few lines in which a large number of words which are Latin or sometimes Greek in origin is not contained. Are there not even now names for new inventions coined from Greek or at least from Latin? And is not all this due to the fact that such words sound more scholastic or else more concise or accurate? If it were not so, why does one call a horseless carriage 'automobile' instead of 'self-moving carriage'? Fortunately for the Western nations, however, there is no difficulty in transcribing Greek or Latin words in their modern letters, inasmuch as those letters are similar to, in fact evolved from, the Greek and Latin letters, and therefore, when once a Greek or Latin word is employed, it is easy to get naturalised, as it were. But, unfortunately for us, the Chinese method is ideographs, and our own is phonetic, and one cannot be directly transcribed from the other, except that either it be translated or merely phonetically represented, which in truth presents much ambiguity. For this reason the original ideographs themselves have come to be interposed between the phonetic letters as I have illustrated above, and the ideographs so interposed have never become thoroughly 'naturalised,' from the very nature of the case. Thus one would see that as far as the mechanical side is concerned, the deep study of Chinese has given much drawback to Japan. On the mental side, however, I may say that it has helped us in enriching our thoughts for many centuries, inasmuch as there is rich treasure for ethical teaching in the classical Chinese, although this is not the place for me to dwell on that topic.

I may add a few words. Philological researches of different Asiatic languages are still very incomplete, but I understand from what is stated by experts that there is some resemblance between our language and those of Korea, Manchuria, and indeed Mongolian tribes: first, in that all those languages are monosyllabic like ours; second, in the order of words in forming sentences. Moreover, it is said that there were already discovered several words which are much similar to ours. No satisfactory statement could be made as yet, but it would be a matter of no common interest if further researches be made. It goes without saying that there is much similarity, so it is said, between ours and the language of the Inoes, who are rapidly disappearing from the surface of the earth, despite our taking care of them. They once occupied the greater part of Japan and were a brave race. It is no wonder that there is that similarity in the tongues, though it is a matter of question whether they left their words behind them or we gave them those words. For example, Kami, which in the colloquial Japanese means god, superior, or upper part of anything, is Kamui in Ino, the meaning being the same. This word, then, must surely belong to the same origin. There are also many names of rivers and mountains in Japan which, beyond doubt, are of Ino origin.

[1] These phonetic letters were invented in Japan between the seventh and eighth centuries A.D., during which time they gradually became improved. As to their form they are a simplification of some simple Chinese ideographs, and as to the principle of their formation, it is based upon, the Sanscrit.

IX

ONCE MORE ON JAPAN AND FRANCE[1]

The French and the Japanese have some sort of resemblance in their character, and therefore they are not wholly antagonistic to each other by nature. France once committed a great error, it is true, together with another country, in backing Russia against Japan after the Sino-Japanese war, but Japan has forgiven her for it, and has even forgotten it long since. It therefore mainly depends on France if the friendly relationship subsisting between her and Japan shall be maintained.

There are two things which we have to examine in this connection: first, the question of Indo-China; second, the effect of the Franco-Russian alliance upon Far Eastern affairs.

Much has been talked about Japan's having designs upon Indo-China. It is, in truth, nothing more than a resuscitation in part of the old bogey of the Yellow Peril. According to that bogey, Japan is to pick quarrels with every civilised nation, and is ultimately to swallow up the whole world. Nothing can be more absurd than that; but at times it has been made use of by the Russians and Russophiles with a certain amount of success. To me it appears almost amazing that so great a psychological incongruity should exist simultaneously in the minds of some of the Occidentals, in that, while they exhibit almost unreasonable contempt of the Orientals on the one hand, they give credit for almost superhuman potentiality to the same people on the other. Whatever this may be, the question of Indo-China resolves itself into this:

The yellow peril alarmists began to talk about Japan as being intent upon seizing Indo-China. The Colonial party of France has utilised this theme for the promotion of its own object, and the Russophiles have utilised it for inciting the public to hate and detest Japan in favour of Russia. Surely an act of gross injustice and cowardice! For, as a matter of fact, on the part of Japan there is no such intention whatever. Indo-China is very different from

Korea and Manchuria in respect of its relative position to Japan. There is nothing worth mentioning politically, strategically, historically, or economically in the mutual relations between Japan and Indo-China. All this I have shown in the utmost detail in an article which I have contributed and published in a well-known French review. Sensible French people have now begun to see the truth of it, so that they have almost ceased to pay serious attention to the false alarms of the yellow peril agitators. Indeed, the France of to-day appears to be very different from the France of this time last year. The lapse of one year has been sufficient to disclose many falsehoods by which the public was once taken in. It has also disclosed the relative merit of Russia and Japan in many things. Which government—the Russian or the Japanese—is the more enlightened? Which troops—the Russian or the Japanese—are more humane and orderly? Which people—Russia or Japan—is more compact as a nation? Which of them—Russia or Japan—has better ethics and morality? In which of them—Russia or Japan—are laws better administered and more loyally adhered to? In which of them—Russia or Japan—are philanthropical works, such as the Red Cross Society, better organised and more honestly carried out? Above all, in which of them—Russia or Japan—does the justice of its cause in the present war lie? All these things have now become very widely known to the public, hence the difference of their attitude. I do not think France ever will be foolish enough to stretch forward her fists against Japan on account of the yellow peril bogey concerning Indo-China. I am rather in hope that the day will come when those Russophiles will repent the mistake they made when they abused Japan contrary to the dictates of justice and equity.

The second question, namely, the effect of the Franco-Russian alliance upon Far Eastern affairs, is rather a delicate one to discuss. On the whole, however, I can say this:

Considering the delicate position in which she is placed, France has managed things well to the extent that we have not much to complain of (except one important matter, which I will elucidate presently). True it is that she has made many unfair accusations against us with regard to the commencement of the war and also with regard to the yellow peril bogey, but then the same, if not a harsher thing, has also been done or said in some other quarters where we might have expected more impartiality. Her general conduct as a neutral has not been very satisfactory. But then we remember that in some other quarters also very bitter pills were given us to swallow, altogether beyond our reasonable anticipation. We put up with all this unfairness, because we are quite confident that sooner or later the time will come when the world will clearly see how undeserving we are of such calumny.

The important exception I made above is the question of French neutrality concerning the treatment of the Baltic Fleet. In this respect Japan has grave reasons to complain of what France has been doing. As the whole world knows, the Russian Fleet has been obtaining abundant facilities from France all the way along from European waters to those of the Far East. It was abusing French hospitality in Madagascar for a very long period. Japan repeated her protest, or at least called French attention from time to time. When France pleaded her innocence at Madagascar on the pretext that the fleet was outside the territorial waters of France, Japan, relying on incontestable proof to the contrary, remonstrated. France was very tardy in executing what she said she would do, but Japan showed much patience, almost beyond common endurance. The same thing began to be repeated in the waters of Indo-

China, the very door of the seat of the war. However moderate and good-natured Japan may be, this was more than she could endure. This was the real cause of the strain of an event which has been recently threatening the continuance of friendly relations between France and Japan.

According to some French papers, the view is held that France has not infringed her duty as a neutral, but Japan does not coincide. The French contention is that, according to the French law of neutrality, there is no time limit for affording asylum to a belligerent ship, and therefore, whatever length of time Russian ships may spend in French waters, France is under no obligation to tell them to quit the place (so long as they are not accompanied by prizes), and also they may be supplied with victuals and even coals. Japan contends that this is not a just interpretation of the laws of nations. Japan's view may be formulated as follows:

1. The twenty-four hours rule may not be a condition universally accepted, but justice and equity demand that in its spirit it should be followed by all nations. It has already been adopted by many nations, including Russia herself; as a matter of fact, the world has come to view it as though it were already a rule universally accepted, and it behoves every civilised nation to promote its adoption, or at least a practice similar to it in spirit, for the sake of consolidating international morality, viz. justice and equity. At the time when Russian ships, after the sea-battle of August 10th last year, sought asylum in the waters of Kiao-Chow and Saigon, both the German and French authorities respectively hastened to dismantle them, because the ships would not leave the place indicated at the prescribed time; this was done in exact accordance with the spirit of international law, and in reality it amounted almost to the

same thing as observing the twenty-four hours rule. Why should France now say that no time limit can be made in the case of the Baltic Fleet, which requires all the more vigilance than would the case of a few solitary ships?

2. The so-called French law of neutrality is not in fact a law in the strict sense of the term. It is a sort of an instruction issued in the beginning of the present war by the French Minister of Marine, although based upon a similar document issued at the time of the Spanish-American war. It is immaterial whether or not it is a law in the strict sense, but we cannot deem it has a just rule if it were to be interpreted as has been done by some of the French papers. True it is that in that document no time is mentioned, but does it mean that France has to or must allow all belligerent ships to stay in her waters whatever length of time they like? Certainly not, I should think. If it is so, why should France adhere to that sort of interpretation even when its adherence is obviously contrary to justice and equity?

3. Even if we admit for a moment that the French rule as interpreted by those papers be applicable to the cases of some solitary ships seeking asylum; it is certainly not applicable to cases like that which we now have in view, because no such case as that of the Baltic Fleet has ever been within the contemplation of those who framed such a rule. As a matter of fact, however, it would be inapplicable even to the cases of a few solitary ships if it were to be interpreted in the way that was done by those journals.

4. Even admitting for a moment that the interpretation of those French journals is correct as far as the strict letter of the rule is concerned, it does not give them the right to say that their doings are internationally correct. It must be known that in the laws of nations the spirit of international morality, namely, justice and equity, has greater weight

than municipal laws, lex loci. If this were not so, how was it that England had to apologise to Russia a long time ago for an act—personal seizure of an ambassador—which had been done in a civil matter perfectly in accordance with her law? Therefore the mere fact that France has her own law of neutrality (in fact no law in a strict sense) is no defence for her doings unless its justice and equity can be maintained in the eyes of the law of nations. I may further add that the above is the raison d'être why prize courts of different countries make it their theory, unlike ordinary civil or criminal courts, that they administer prima facie the law of nations and not lex loci. It is another raison d'être why matters relating to neutrality, prizes, and cognate matters are generally dealt with in the shape of instructions (in other words, interpretations of the law of nations), and not in the shape of a law of the land in the strict sense. Japan, therefore, cannot submit to the ruling of those French instructions as interpreted by those journals, inasmuch as she does not think it internationally just and equitable.

5. And, moreover, that part of the French instruction which those journals so habitually quote is not the only part which has an important bearing on the question. In the instruction it is also mentioned that no belligerent may use a French port for purposes of war (dans un but de guerre); and also that belligerents sojourning in such ports may not make use of them as the base of operations of any kind against the enemy. Japan's insistence is that France should adhere to that spirit. My wonder is why those French papers which try to uphold one part of the instruction should totally ignore other parts of the same instruction.

6. The theory of asylum in the case of the ships is not so rigid as the case of an army. I admit it. Japan does not demand that it should be made on the seas as rigid as it is

on land. But it must never be allowed to go beyond the limit which justice and equity allow. I take the theory of asylum on the seas to be this: No neutral is justified in helping either of the combatants, but the nature of the seas is such that the neutral may give a certain grace of time to combatant vessels which seek shelter in its neutral waters, before it proceeds to dismantle,—(no immediate internment as in the case of the land force),—and it may also give them certain victuals—even a certain amount of coals—as it would also be contrary to humanity if they were to hang about, or to cause starvation of the men on board in mid-voyage on account of the mere lack of coal or food. Beyond this, the spirit of the law of nations is that a neutral ought to allow nothing. Can any one boldly assert that the theory of asylum can be applied with fairness to a case like that of the Baltic Fleet, which is far from seeking asylum, but is deliberately endeavouring to administer coups to its adversary and proceeding to the very seat of war. If he can do so, where is the justice and equity of the so-called law of nations, which the Occidentals boast of, not without just title, and claim that it forms one of the essential parts of Christian morality?

7. As to the talk about the three-mile limit of the territorial waters, there is already much divergency of opinion even amongst the jurists. To put it forth as a defence in a case like that of the Baltic Fleet affairs seems to me too puerile. The matter, however, becomes all the more grave when even that limit is not observed, and it has been constantly ignored by the Baltic Fleet.

Such are the views which we Japanese have taken in the matter. Some French journals (erroneously basing their assertions on the views I have personally expressed) say that Japan has taken up English views of international law in opposition to the Continental views, so that France ought

362

not to yield to Japan's protest. This contention is not correct. We do not hold these views because they are English ones: we do so because they are in our opinion the only views which are internationally just and equitable. We are now fighting against a foe so formidable, as the whole world knows, that to us it is a matter of life and death. We have sufficient patience and fortitude, but we cannot run the risk of sacrificing our very existence without some protest when we think that we are not being treated with justice and equity.

I am glad to add that the views we hold seem to have come at last to be shared by the more responsible part of the French amongst the governmental circle, as well as by the general public. The newspapers which are still sticking to their old contention are very few in number, and they seem to have some particular reasons of their own. I can never think a nation like France could consciously and wilfully offend against justice and equity, and the only thing we anxiously hope for is that the declaration of the French Government may be honestly and effectually followed up. Whatever may be one's intention, the drift of events often creates unlooked-for incidents, and that too often against one's will, when it is too late to avoid the consequences. Let all parties concerned be careful in this matter of vital importance.

[1] The Deutsche Revue, June 1905.

X

JAPAN AND EUROPE[1]

You ask my opinion on the future of the Yellow Peril cry. From an ethical point of view it is an unjust and unreasonable accusation. From a practical point of view it is idle and useless talk.

I have spoken and written on these particular points so often that I do not feel inclined to reiterate any more. I will, however, consider the matter from a different point of view and solicit any answer which may be advanced against my conviction. I do not do this from any thought of vanity; I should be very sorry if it were ever taken in that sense. I would simply ask those who agitate and cry the Yellow Peril, the means they would suggest for the adopting of their propaganda, if their words are not to be empty ones.

Suppose any country wanted to subjugate Japan, and should want to send an army to fight on the soil of Japan, what number of men do they think would suffice? No general in the whole world would, I am sure, be bold enough to undertake the task with under one million men. I have reason to believe even that number would not suffice, but for a moment let it be that number. What country in the world can send that number over the broad ocean? Germany, France, England, or America? Russia seems to have the greatest chance, being nearer to Japan. But her experience is already known.

Suppose the idea of a land campaign be abandoned, and only a fleet be sent to intimidate Japan by sea battles, or by harassing her commerce. There would certainly be a better chance for any of the Occidental fleets than for the armies, in coping with the forces of Japan. Above all, I frankly admit that England would be the most formidable foe in that respect. But excepting England, is there any other country that can say with certainty that it can easily crush the Japanese navy? Is it Germany? is it France? or is it—America?

But supposing our navy were crushed; what next? It would, of course, be a very ugly thing for us, but it would not mean the subjection of Japan. Our sea-coast towns may be bombarded, our commerce may be harassed, but Japan will still subsist within her soil, for she can live without depending on any other country for food. And, besides, disturbance of commerce would not be a loss only to her.

Moreover, any country which should embark on such an enterprise would have need to think it over twice (or, indeed, three or four times) before undertaking it, and to calculate the probable benefit it could get therefrom, and the probable expenses it would incur; not to speak of the result of any possible failure. It may be presumed that Japan would not tamely be intimidated by any action undertaken by any country which is not based on justice and equity, and which, therefore, is not open to reason.

Further, is there any country which would willingly embark on such an enterprise single-handed? I think not. The reason is too obvious for me to elucidate.

Putting aside altogether any question of justice and equity, if such an enterprise is to be embarked upon at all, it would have to be by common action of all the Western Powers, somewhat similar to that when the combined forces of Europe rose against France some hundred years ago.

But let me ask if such a thing is possible under the present circumstances? The claims of Japan to the kind consideration of humanity have already become so widely spread that she could no longer be trampled upon easily. Man is, after all, a rational being. Do the writers of the

365

articles on the Yellow Peril (articles which even now repeatedly make their appearance) not know the fact that even in France there is a large number of people who have recently purchased Japanese bonds, not to speak of Germany, where those bonds have been openly floated by banks of high standing? Even if all the governments of the West should be willing to agree to such an enterprise, I do not think the people at large would move with them.

Japan is modest enough, Japan is honest enough. Why does she deserve a general ostracism? She might become, it is possible, a Power of the world. She might become, it is possible, more civilised on the lines of occidental civilisation, after which she strives so earnestly. Are these to be blamed as her sins?

To me the Yellow Peril cry, which is so often revived in some quarters of the Continent, is either a sort of what we call 'guchi,' that is to say, useless repetition of complaint of some unreasonable disappointment, or a perpetuation of wicked instigation and selfish intention. In either case, it is not at all a laudable action; indeed, I may say it is wasteful calumny for no material good will come of it inasmuch as its object can never be achieved from the very condition of the world. The people who entertain that idea would be doing far better service to their country, to the progress of civilisation, to the general cause of humanity, if only they put aside such a silly notion, and busy themselves in teaching their fellow country-folks to accustom themselves to the changed circumstances of the time. It would be a far more manly and noble act if they revised their old notions, which in a measure may be called prejudice.

As to ourselves, the Japanese, we shall only be glad if we can enjoy a peaceful and harmonious life in the happy family of the world, as we are determined to do, in spite of all the obstacles which may be laid before us.

[1] Written for the Potentia Organisation, July 1905.

XI

THE INDO-CHINA QUESTION[1]

INTERVIEW WITH THE BARON SUYEMATSU

The eminent statesman, Baron Suyematsu, kindly dictated in English to one of our editors answers relating to certain questions with regard to the relation between Japan and Europe, especially France and Germany.

With the disclosure of the alleged Kodama report in view, how far may one give credit to the alleged Japanese plan of invasion of Indo-China?

I know all that has been written in France on the subject. All those rumours appear to me to have come originally from Russia, and to have been put into circulation in order to excite French opinion against Japan, in other words, it is nothing else than a mere repetition of the Yellow Peril cry.

Japan does not covet Indo-China. I have shown elsewhere that the French colonies in the Far East have no perceptible influence upon the situation of Japan, either from a political or an economical point of view. Japan has sufficient to do at home, she does not want to plunge into external adventures, such as meddling with Indo-China or picking a quarrel with a country like France. You may be sure that it would be more politic for France to cultivate amicable relations with Japan than irritate her by such accusations. Even if those accusations honestly represent the true sentiment of the French, the Japanese would only take them for malicious manœuvres directed to aid Russia, and they could not produce any good impression on the minds of the Japanese.

Is there any reason to believe that the so-called Kodama report was forged in Russia rather than in France?

I have demonstrated elsewhere that the document which was recently made public and attributed to Kodama containing some military indications on the plan of an invasion of Indo-China is a perfect forgery. I have exposed elsewhere several technical errors therein which would never appear in an authentic official document. But whether it is authentic or not, I do not attach any importance to the matter, from a political point of view at least. It is the duty of all the military and naval authorities to keep themselves ready for any emergency. For example, France ought to keep herself always prepared for any possible difficulties which may arise on her frontiers in the east, and in the south, and on the western coasts; the same with Germany, with Austria, with Italy, even with the United States.

It appears to me that, if the general staff-office of France or of Germany, or the military or naval authorities of any country whatever, were to remain without the least knowledge as to what measure should be taken in case of a danger, they would be neglecting their duty to their country. I can then say that all the Japanese officers, both in the army and in the navy ought to study constantly the measures which Japan should take in any emergency. I believe it is the same in every country in Europe. This, however, does not belong to the sphere of practical politics. It is the duty of statesmen and politicians to maintain a friendly relationship with all other countries as far as possible; and, consequently, to keep absolute control over their armies and navies. The army and navy ought to serve as instruments and machines in their hands, and not they, the civilians, become the instruments of the army and navy. You may be quite assured that in Japan the army and navy are the machines of the statesmen, and that the statesmen are not their machines.

Can the fabrication of the so-called Kodama report be demonstrated by a precise fact?

I shall not say whence the document emanated. I believe it was composed by some one who does not lack a certain knowledge of Japan, but who has drawn false deductions from his knowledge of similar matters of other countries. Here is the best example. The document speaks of the native contingents of Formosa. Now there exist no such forces in Formosa. The garrisons of Formosa are sent there from Japan. On the other hand, in the colonies belonging to other countries there are generally troops formed of native contingents. It is notably so in French colonies. The author of the document in question, reasoning from these facts, thought that it ought to be the same with Formosa.

Has Japan any fear of another alteration of the Treaty of Shimonoseki being imposed upon her?

The combined action of Russia, Germany and France, for imposing on Japan an alteration of the Treaty of Shimonoseki appears to us to have been a great error on their parts. I can positively say that there are many eminent persons in Germany and in France who regret that action. Even in Russia, in certain quarters, a belief seems to be entertained that, but for the fault then committed, the present misfortunes would not have happened. As to ourselves, we are not hypnotised by the errors then committed by those three powers. We intend to remain friends of France, of Germany, and even of Russia, in spite of the injustice we have suffered, provided, of course, those powers wish to keep friendship.

We do not overlook the possibility of another combination which those powers may have an idea of forming against us, and it behoves us to be watchful. Nevertheless, to tell you my candid opinion, it is scarcely possible that a similar intervention should be renewed. I do not think France would push her docility so far as to follow Germany a second time. It would be necessary that Germany should set the example, aided by Russia and France, to come out to the Far East, especially because the Russian fleets have ceased to exist. I admit that the German fleet is strong, but I do not believe it is powerful enough for one to say with certainty that it can easily crush Japan. At all events, what pretext has Germany to enter into war in the Far East? Among other things also she would have to count on the opinion and sentiments of two countries at least, I mean England and the United States. I do not, therefore, consider a new combination possible. Japan cannot be intimidated by mere barking.

If, however, Europe should choose to take such a course, we should gravely reflect. I do not believe your country for example would ever undertake an expedition against Japan.

You have disapproved a small expedition to Tonkin and we are a little more serious than the Tonkinese. France might no doubt, if her honour demanded it, judge it worth the pain to engage in a war with Japan, but under no other circumstance do I believe her disposed to take such a part.

Japan will always continue to advance on the lines of occidental civilisation. I do not see the reason which will prevent Japan from acting in concert with France or Germany, provided of course these powers do not enter upon an action which may appear to her altogether unjust or iniquitous, in which case she may not be able to march with them hand-in-hand.

Would Japan be offended by France introducing civilisation into Indo-China?

We are not at all opposed to your introducing Western civilisation into your colonies. On the contrary we shall be quite contented, but in introducing your civilisation into your colonies you have to be prepared that it signifies an amelioration of the condition of the natives. If it were so, why should we make the least objection? But in the hypothesis that the introduction of civilisation has in view neither amelioration of the condition of the natives nor progress of commerce and industry, we might then conceive a sort of suspicion. Supposing that you augment the garrisons, the fortifications, the naval forces, one would see in it nothing but an expansion of your military power and not an introduction of civilisation in the sense understood in France. Even in that case we would not raise objections, unless it were done with a view to menace us; but here I shall offer you a suggestion. Is it really worth your while to develop there incessantly your military and naval forces in order to oppose Japan? Would not the

371

enterprise be rather costly? Would it not be infinitely better to employ your energy in cultivating a good understanding between your country and ours instead of rivalling each other by crossing armaments?

[1] L'Européen, August 5, 1905.

XII

THE AUSTRALIAN QUESTION[1]

AN INTERVIEW

Baron Suyematsu gave a Daily News representative his opinion of the 'Spectre of Japan' as conceived by many Europeans. The Japanese Baron, a burly, cheerful man, laughed heartily as he dealt with the alarmist fears of the 'Yellow Peril.'

Our talk began over Mr. Bruce Smith's notice of motion in the Australian Parliament.

'Yes, I have seen the proposal,' said Baron Suyematsu, 'and I am very glad an Australian representative has taken up the question. He proposes to amend the Immigration Restriction Act so as to permit Japanese to enter the Commonwealth. The reason given is that Japan has placed herself in the front rank of nations, has granted religious freedom, has established consulates, and become the honoured ally of Great Britain. I understand that Australian papers are saying there is no chance of the motion being carried. I care not whether the motion is carried or not this

372

time. Of one thing I am certain—it will be carried eventually.

'What reason has Australia for shutting out the Japanese?'

'The dread of cheaper labour and of the "Yellow Peril," as it is called. Whatever there be in that, it certainly does not apply to the Japanese. This is already being realised in Australia, as Mr. Bruce Smith's motion shows. The Japanese are making it clear that they have to be regarded by Europeans in a different light from the rest of Asiatics. Europeans consider themselves superior to all other races. I do not blame them for thinking that, for of modern civilisations theirs is certainly the best. But with the exception of the British people, Europeans have not yet realised that modern Japan is built up on European methods. She has no more to do with the so-called "Yellow Peril" than America has. She takes her place by the side of the other powers, with very much the same civilisation as theirs. England having been the first to recognise the new Japan, I am certain her colonies will soon follow. That is why I feel it is only a question of time before Australia excludes Japan from its Restriction Act.'

A MISTAKEN IDEA

'Yet Australia has been talking freely enough about the Japanese menace.'

'I know. It is quite a mistaken idea of the Australians that if Japan triumphs in the present war she would be a menace to Australia. They say that if we win we shall be masters of the East and the paramount power in Eastern waters. What, they ask, is to become of Australia, if we take it into our heads to make a descent upon their shores?'

373

Baron Suyematsu again laughed boisterously, as one who can afford to make merry at an extravagant idea.

'The whole thing is so utterly preposterous,' he went on, 'that it would not be worth considering were it not typical of what is being said all over Europe. Our fight for national existence against Russia has been misconstrued everywhere. We seem to have filled the Western world with all sorts of vague fears, France is saying that we shall soon deprive her of Indo-China. Germany declares we have designs on Kiao-chau. The Dutch say that Java is no longer safe from our machinations. Never was such nonsense talked of a country which, after all, is but fighting to preserve its national existence.'

'And you say Japan has no intention of arming the Asiatics against the Europeans?'

'The whole idea is absurd. Japan wishes to become one with the European nations. I might even say she aspires to become a member of the European family. It is a mistake to think that Japan is going to form a Pan-Asiatic Association. Japan is the only country in the East that can rise on European lines. Her example could not be followed by other Asiatic countries. We are said to be the successors of the Tartars, at one time the disturbers of the world's peace. Nothing of the kind. Russia would be more fittingly the successor of the Tartars. The Tartar races have been merged in the Russian Empire.

'I am sure,' added Baron Suyematsu, in a final word, 'that Europe will soon find its fears about the "spectre of Japan" are all ill-founded. England, I am glad to believe, never had those fears, and before long I hope to see her colonies in the same frame of mind. I hope the Commonwealth Parliament will lead the way.'

XIII

THE ANGLO-JAPANESE ALLIANCE AND AMERICA[1]

AN INTERVIEW

'Our people,' said Baron Suyematsu, 'like the British people, favour the renewal of the Anglo-Japanese alliance. They also favour its extension. The nature of such extension demands careful thought, of course. I will not go into details, but I will say that a more effectual alliance is desirable from the standpoints of both England and Japan, and I also think from the standpoint of America. Japan's interest is too obvious to require mention; but England's interest, in my opinion, is equally real. Russia and England are in contact throughout Asia and friction is constant. England needs strengthening against Russia and also against other powers active in the Orient.

MONROE DOCTRINE OF THE PAST

'America's relation to this problem is more difficult. Monroeism is thought to stand in the way. I appreciate the delicacy of venturing to discuss the policy of a nation other than my own, but I feel that Americans are too sensible to resent an honest expression of opinion. Monroeism is not part of the constitution, but the dictum of a statesman. This dictum was made when our planet was very large, before the development of steam and electricity. The nations were isolated and insulated by distance and non-communication.

'At that time American theory and practice relative to foreign affairs were in harmony. America was actually self-contained, but to-day the world is a tiny ball and America's flag and America's interests are on every sea. America is sovereign in Hawaii and the Philippines, and yet the American people cling to the idea of leaving distant matters alone. Nevertheless the state department is widely and intelligently active.

AMERICAN INTEREST WORLD-WIDE

'Theoretically you do not participate, actually your participation bears upon international events everywhere. Witness Secretary Hay's initiative respecting the Jews, as well as despatch after despatch aimed at Russian aggression in Manchuria. The world's interests are becoming woven into a solid fabric. Great nations cannot escape the responsibility this involves. American theory and practice, in my judgment, will go on diverging until the notion of non-participation will be merely an antiquated abstraction.

'Therefore I refuse to regard as hopeless the idea of an American-Anglo-Japanese alliance, guaranteeing the peaceful development of the vast resources of the Far East. Such an alliance exists essentially now—an alliance springing from cognate ideas, wishes, purposes and principles. This is the best possible foundation for that formal compact which the evolution of industry and commerce seems to me unmistakably to foreshadow.'

[1] An extract from the Chicago Daily News.

NOTE TO DIALOGUE V.

Since the bulk of the present work went to press, I came across the following communication printed in the Outlook. I take the liberty of subjoining it herewith, without any vain intention of flaunting the virtues of my countrymen.—K.S.

JAPANESE CHARACTER

To the Editor of the OUTLOOK

SIR,—I have received during the last few weeks letters bearing such eloquent testimony to the nobility of Japanese character that I am sending you some extracts in the hope of your publishing them. The letters are from a friend of mine, who with her husband has lived in Yokohama for many years, and can therefore speak with considerable authority. The first extract is about the soldiers themselves—

Mine you know is a busy life, and I found work among the military hospitals and also among the brave wives of the soldiers so fascinating that from the New Year till early June I let all social duties slip, so much so that I had a nervous breakdown in June, and since then have had to go very slow.

We had a splendid time at our seaside cottage at Negishi this afternoon, any amount of our dear brown soldiers round us. There are five hundred quartered in that fishing village just now; they were resting, bathing, boating, washing their clothes or cooking their chow, but never a rude word or an uncouth action; no rowdyism, but all as civil, quiet, good-tempered, and alert as possible; they are a marvel; and my children go in and out among them and love them, like I do! I could kill white idiots when I hear them speak of those fine fellows as 'an inferior race.' Ye gods! 'inferior' with never a camp follower to their name, and rapine unknown even after the fiercest fight! What European race can show a record like that? I wish I could be home for six months and tell what the soldiers and their wives are—what miracles of cheerful patience and manly dignity the wounded men are as they lie hacked and maimed, sometimes till almost all semblance of manhood is gone, yet never a murmur does any one hear from their lips—no, not if they are armless, legless, and even blind. And you would not dare condole with them! They say and believe they 'are greatly honoured.' When they embrace Christianity, they shame the brightest Christian among us, and I come away from visiting the hospitals feeling so small, so humble, yet at peace with all the world. We have very, very much to learn from this great people.

This second extract, about a soldier's wife, may come home to your readers even more:—

I allow two families a small sum of money every week. One case is that of a young woman, under twenty years of age, who has a child and an aged parent to keep, and her husband went to the war a few weeks ago, leaving her penniless and on the verge of having another baby. A few days ago, when I went to take her weekly money, she refused to take it, saying she had got a little work to do and could now manage without any help, as there were so many in much greater need of help than herself; and she would not take the money, though she was earning even less than I was allowing her. That is what I call a real heroine.

How many at work amongst our poor last winter could give such evidence to character as that?—I am, sir, yours, etc.

ENGLISHWOMAN.

NOTE TO DIALOGUE VIII.

Before the preceding pages had been printed two events worth mentioning here took place. One is the lamented death of Sir Henry Irving. The other is the public discussion which took place under the auspices of the London Shakespeare League, on the best method of presenting Shakespeare's plays on the modern stage. On the latter subject perhaps I may add a word. While in Japan the tendency is to introduce women-players into the company of male players, and improvement of scenery is much sought after on European lines, both of which are due to the occidental influence, it is curious to notice that exactly reverse movements, namely the dispensing with the female players and the returning back to the primitive simplicity of stage properties, are advocated in England by competent persons with regard to the representation of Shakespeare. I extract below among others a passage of the speech of Mr. Bernard Shaw on the occasion of the discussion referred to above:—

When Mr. Gilbert said that he would like to see the women's parts played by boys, he was not uttering a jest. In some of the performances at Westminster School, he had seen boys in women's parts much more effective than any professional actress. If women players had been proposed to Shakespeare, he would not only have been scandalised, but he would have pointed out that it was impossible to get the force from women that was obtained from boy actors.

NOTE TO THE ARTICLE ON 'COMMERCIAL MORALITY'

In the October number of the Anglo-Japanese Gazette (London) is published a criticism by Mr. Curtis, editor and proprietor of the Kobe Herald, on 'the ridiculously sweeping assertions,' as he calls it, made by Mr. Longford in his article. I subjoin herewith a passage which relates to Mr. Longford's assertion that a 'cordon' is drawn by the Japanese round the trading centres of Yokohama and Kobe, and that foreign merchants are suffering under the 'thraldom':—

Well, let me say that no sane, fair-minded man who knows anything whatever of his subject would ever dream of accusing the whole Japanese people of a lack of commercial morality. All this talk about a cordon being drawn round the treaty ports is rubbish. No such barrier exists, save perhaps in the imagination of a few who cannot shake off the prejudices and disabilities of the past. The idea sounds absurd to me, knowing, as I do know, that all the go-ahead firms have been doing their utmost for some time past to open up connections in the principal cities. Mr. Longford seems to think that business is conducted in Japan to-day just as it was twenty years ago. He apparently does not know that some foreign houses have trusted clerks or travellers all over the country; that some foreign business men run up to Osaka and Tokio daily; and that business journeys to Maidzuru—the great, fortified naval base on the Sea of Japan—Nagoya Sasebo, Hiroshima, and other important centres, are matters of everyday experience now.

In the same number of the same journal is also published an important article from the pen of Sir Tollemache Sinclair, Bart., concerning Bishop Awdry's letter published in the Times. Sir Tollemache strongly repudiates the accuracy of the bishop's charge of dishonesty and immorality against the Japanese, which Sir Tollemache calls the bishop's 'utterly erroneous accusations,' basing his contention upon an elaborate comparison of the statistical facts of Japan and many other nations relating to several important subjects having bearing on the question. Among other things, he writes:—

This clerical censor, who endeavours to find a mote in his Japanese brother's eye, but does not see the beam in his English brother's eye, cut the ground from under his own feet on the subject of the imaginary dishonesty of Japanese traders, for he tells us that a house was built for him by Japanese tradesmen admirably without any contract, and at a moderate expense; and I should like to know, if any Englishman did the same thing in England, whether he would not be unmercifully fleeced. Bishop Awdry says he is a friend of the Japanese, but they will probably say to him, after reading his letter, 'Save us from our friends, as to our enemies we will take care of them ourselves.'

And he winds up the article with these words:—

What excuse has he to offer for the gross and discreditable and unfounded insults which he has heaped on the heads of those under whose protection, and in the enjoyment of whose hospitality, he resides.... In short, it may justly be said of the letter written by this superfluous bishop, 'what is true is not new, and what is new is not true.'

www.ingramcontent.com/pod-product-compliance
Lightning Source LLC
Chambersburg PA
CBHW072345290526
45794CB00001B/13